ఴఴ

WHICH CRAFT?

Esoteric Journeys Through Poetry & Song

Volume 1
Vocal Arts:
The Hermeneutic Dimension

Volume 2
Winterreise:
Reflections on a Winter Journey

Volume 3
Which Craft:
W. A. Mozart and The Magic Flute

Volume 4
The Esoteric Wagner:
An Introduction to Der Ring des Nibelungen

Volume 5
The Journey in Parmenides' Poem

Volume 6
Noetic Excursions

Also

PI NARATI, An Opera
Libretto – Michael Besack; Music – Joyce Whitelaw

WHICH CRAFT?

W.A. MOZART
AND
THE MAGIC FLUTE

❖

Esoteric Journeys through Poetry & Song

Volume 3

❖ ❖ ❖

Michael Besack

Library of Congress Cataloging-in-Publication Data

Besack Michael.
    Which Craft? : W.A. Mozart and The Magic Flute /
Michael Besack.
        p. cm. -- (Esoteric journeys through poetry & song; v. 3)
        Includes bibliographical references (p.) and Index.
        ISBN 1-58790-013-0
        1. Mozart, Wolfgang Amadeus, 1756-1791 Zauberflète
        2. Mozart, Wolfgang Amadeus, 1756-1791 -- Freemasonry
        3. Mozart, Wolfgang Amadeus, 1756-1791 -- Symbolism
        4. Freemasonry -- Symbolism. I. Title. II. Series

ML410.M9.B36 2002
782.1--dc21   2001048902

Manufactured in the U.S.A.
REGENT PRESS
Berkeley, California
www.regentpress.net
regentpress@mindspring.com

CONTENTS

1. The Modern Egyptian Priesthood.............................. 1
2. Mozart and the Enlightenment............................... 51
3. Ritual Action... 99
4. Toward Egyptian Masonry...................................125
5. The Magic Flute and its Symbolic Structure 163

    The King.. 166

    Darkness and Light....................................172

    The Genealogies of Darkness & Light............. 179

        The Two Armed Men...............................188

        The Trials by Fire & Water...................... 192

    The Three Temples....................................195

        The Temple of Nature............................ 195

        The Temple of Reason........................... 196

        The Temple of Wisdom.......................... 197

    The Four Worlds....................................... 199

        The Cosmic Layer................................. 211

            The Queen of the Night............. 211

            Sarastro...................................... 218

        The Creative and Formative Layers....... 230

            Tamino & Pamina....................230

The World of Action.................................... 248

    Papageno & Papagena.................... 248

    Monostatos.................................... 260

Illustrations.. 263

Notes.. 265

Bibliography... 277

Index... 287

1

THE MODERN EGYPTIAN
PRIESTHOOD

Mozart has been the subject of numerous studies and his image has evolved in rather unpredictable ways. From early stories of his alleged poisoning by Salieri to more recent assessments of his deceitful character, the legend has grown and taken many turns toward the controversial. The musical genius, portrayed in the past as an enlightened champion of truth and virtue, must now be approached on different terms. The real Mozart is found in his odd operatic creations. There is Don Giovanni, of course, but also the devious puppeteer from *Cosi fan tutte*— Don Alfonso— who incarnates Mozart's evasive spirit and develops into a quiet version of Goethe's Mephistopheles: the demon who uses falsehood to arrive at truth.

The Magic Flute is Mozart's last opera and must be given a special place among his works for the stage. It was composed at a time when the established European order was disintegrating as rapidly as Mozart himself. By the end of 1790 the composer's finances had completely deteriorated and his health was so poor that he passed out from exhaustion, for minutes at a time, as he worked on ***The Magic Flute***.[1] In the same general period, the French Revolution was picking up steam. Its most violent manifestations were just around the corner. Austria's last reform-minded ruler, Emperor Joseph II, died in February of 1790 and the final years of his reign produced a complete reversal of his progressive initiatives. The Masonic elite responsible for his early policies was forced to tone down its universalist message. The majority of Austrian Lodges were either closed or amalgamated under tightly controlled jurisdictions. There was a sense of imminent danger— of a growing outside threat that had to be urgently contained.

Freemasons were viewed as powerful conspirators with substantial means at their disposal. The international character of Freemasonry and its more or less disguised approval of revolutionary causes resulted in a lot of soul searching among aristocratic early backers. Visible correlations between global Lodge activities and the revolutions in both the United States and France had eroded royal goodwill toward Masonic causes.

Count Johann Anton Pergen, the Viennese minister of police, referred specifically to Mozart's Lodge— the most important in Vienna— in the following memorandum addressed to the emperor:

"The mania to establish such secret and deceptive organizations has never been greater than in our own time. We know for a fact that many of these secret societies, which are known under various names, are not, as they claim, dedicated solely to rational enlightenment and practical humanity. Rather their intention is nothing less than to undermine the power and prestige of the monarchs, encourage liberation movements, and sway the people's opinion by means of a secret ruling elite. The loss of the English colonies in America was the first operation of this secret ruling elite; from there they sought to spread their influence further, and it is beyond doubt that the fall of the French monarchy was the work of such a secret society. And France was not the only scene of anarchy, as proved by the emissaries sent into all countries and the incendiary literature they distribute. The French Masonic Lodges, especially, seek to produce similar attitudes among their brothers in other lands. A noteworthy example is a publication from the Lodge in Bordeaux, which states: The wise principles of the new French constitution correspond so closely to the Masonic principles of freedom, equality, justice, tolerance, philosophy, charity, and social order that their success seems assured. Indeed, from this point on every good French citizen is worthy of being a Mason— because he is free." [2]

The publication in question, mailed from Bordeaux, was addressed to Mozart's Lodge and one can easily imagine the suspicions it generated. To the ruling classes of eighteenth-century Europe, revolutionaries were like a plague of rats suddenly unleashed in the midst of their orderly existence. Repression was inevitable and during these grim times the Viennese flocked to performances of *The Magic Flute* because they were fascinated by its outlook on the human condition. The general public had no clear idea of what Mozart and his Viennese Masonic brethren were up to; but they sensed that the Pied Piper had arrived:

> And into the town that begged for some magic,
> No witches arrived, nothing evil or tragic.
> Instead in the square stood a figure of wonder,
> He piped a sweet tune that caused rats to dance,
> To pick up their tails, to scamper, to prance. [3]

The rodents— of which Monostatos is a perfect prototype— can be induced to dance. Identifying them with the forces of evil helps in basic ways, but does not explain their sudden emergence. Like the plagues of Greek antiquity, said to have been brought on by transgressing kings, darkness always materializes when light starts to fail. The plague-spreading rats and the mysterious piper come in a single package.

If we follow Monostatos' development, we will note that he first appears on the side of the solar priesthood headed by Sarastro. His presence in the Temple is a sign of contamination. As the archetypal Moor, he is the ritual opponent of the forces dedicated to a restoration of the Temple. In the second act, Monostatos switches his allegiance to the Queen of the Night. For the Wagnerians among us, he is very reminiscent of Alberich, the antihero of **Das Rheingold**. The same Alberich who forswears love and dedicates himself to the single-minded pursuit of power, obtainable through gold.

To Tamino's love-driven hero, Monostatos opposes the frustrated, sullen suitor: the social outcast who will stop at nothing to avenge his rejection. The traits that make him an unlikely object of love, are precisely those that transform him into an efficient and highly appreciated manager of slaves.

People have been puzzled by **The Magic Flute**'s paradoxical characterization of Masonic values; such as Sarastro's acceptance of Monostatos, his ownership of slaves and his patronizing attitude toward women. Sarastro's toleration of the Moor, for instance, goes against our modern sense of what is appropriate and we assign such dramatic lapses to vague notions of what was culturally acceptable in Mozart's time. But that may be too simple. Deviousness was one of Mozart's dominant traits and David Schroeder (**Mozart in Revolt**) suggests that it penetrated most of his theatrical compositions:

"Musical deception plays a major role in virtually all of Mozart's operas after 1779, and here Mozart found himself in very good company among his contemporaries, particularly those in the field of literature[...] The eighteenth-century is often mistakenly labelled the 'Age of Reason' [...] and would more suitably be called the 'Age of Disguise' [...] The fascination with masks, disguises, masquerades and deception in literature in many respects reflected behavior in social settings. Masquerades became the rage across Europe in the eighteenth-century, associated with pre-Lent Carnivals in some countries and held year-round in others[...] The lasciviousness and deceptiveness of masquerades and Carnival attracted Mozart enormously throughout his short adult life; here he was in his true element."[4]

The Magic Flute was written at a time when Mozart had fully mastered the art of deception. In its capacity for uneasy enchantment his last opera should perhaps be compared to Plato's *Cratylus*, which deals directly with double meaning in the context of language. The fact that both works are still considered less than credible, in spite of their authors' reputation for genius, creates an interesting problem.

The *Cratylus* probes the tricky subject of names and their meaning. Are names independently meaningful, or are they just labels? Does the phonetic mask hide a permanent, magic identity, or should that identity be equated solely with the mask? In the *Cratylus* common language is viewed as a disguise behind which alternate realities are hidden. When Cratylus declares that the name '*Hermogenes*' (Born-of-Hermes) cannot be applied to Hermogenes, the son of Hipponicus, with whom he is having a conversation, one senses that the reference to Hermes is key. Part of our being is 'what is seen' (the mask— the son of Hipponicus); the other is 'born-of-Hermes' and remains hidden to the uninitiated.

The language of what lays behind the mask is hieroglyphic in nature. It points to an inner landscape that cannot be fathomed in the absence of formal knowledge. A Mason first learns how to spell and in his approach to meaning he must follow the risky road opened by Plato. The language game is dedicated to the creation of signifiers. That is why an encounter with a swan (French *Cygne*), in a medieval tale, is to be interpreted as a sign (French *Signe*). Phonetics with overloaded meaning provide the desired esoteric reference. The ordinary is thus elevated to higher levels of meaning for those who can read between the lines. Such encounters on ritual journeys point to riddles that must be solved. An aspect of the Craft that appealed immensely to Mozart, as Maynard Solomon points out:

"Freemasonry was not a separate sphere that Mozart occasionally entered as a man seeking a formalized respite from his daily life and activities, or as a professional musician seeking patronage, or a borrower seeking sources of cash. It engaged deeper levels of Mozart's personality, even going beyond simple beliefs in humanitarian ideals. Freemasonry gratified his play impulse through its initiatory practices, tests, and ordeals; it touched his religious yearnings through its fusion of contemporary enlightened teachings with ancient traditions." [5]

That Mozart felt compelled to organize his own secret society at just about the time **The Magic Flute** was written simply reinforces these observations. The composer belonged to the Rite of Strict Observance and like Goethe, Wieland and Herder, was a member of the first specifically German order, built around the Templar Legend elaborated by Baron von Hund. [6]

Where Mozart could have gone from there is anybody's guess. What is certain, however, is that he wrote a plan, in draft form, for a society to be called *Die Grotte* (the Cave), which, based on what his wife Constanze wrote to the publisher Härtel, many years after the composer's death, had something to do with secret Masonic orders. The letter, dated 27 November 1800, accompanied Mozart's essay on the subject, and in it Constanze mentions that court clarinetist Anton Standler would know more about the society. Stadler had completed Mozart's unfinished fragment, but was reluctant to come forward because 'secret orders and societies were so much hated'. [7] Mozart's essay subsequently disappeared.

The composer's declining health is often cited to explain the frequent bouts of paranoia that supposedly assailed him during the latter part of 1791. These were about alleged attempts to poison him and can be understood in the light of his esoteric pursuits. There comes a time when one's inner reality grows powerful enough to dispatch its own demons. As he worked on the **Requiem**, Mozart was transposing the Hiramic legend to his own ritual end.

A revolutionary innovator cannot die of natural causes. His creations are too disturbing for that. They invariably exact a retribution and inspire criminal behavior. In his allegory of the cave, in the **Republic** (VII.514), Plato gives a clue as to why the awakening agent is in such danger. Plato's cave-dweller has never seen the light and "if someone dragged him away from there by force, up the rough, steep path, and didn't let him go until he had dragged him into the sunlight, wouldn't he be pained and irritated at being treated that way?" [8]

The cave, where darkness reigns, is also where Hiram's murderers hide. In Masonic ritual it first appears in the 9th Degree (*Maitre Elu des Neuf*), which introduces the Grades of Revenge (9th, 10th and 11th).[9] The allegory of Mozart's 'Grotto' and its portrayal by Ignaz Alberti in the frontispiece of the first edition of the libretto of **The Magic Flute** suggest an intentional reference. The 'revenge' in question is naturally for the murder of Hiram, the architect of Solomon's Temple, portrayed lying on the floor in Alberti's drawing.

"It is intriguing to speculate on why Mozart wanted to start his own secret society," writes Maynard Solomon. "Perhaps, after all, he did have unvoiced reservations about imperial control of Freemasonry [...], perhaps he did not feel a close kinship with the large number of Rosicrucians and Asiatic Brethren who had registered as members of 'New Crowned Hope' after the *Freimaurerpatent*. Surely 'The Grotto' was intended to be something more than a social club, for if it were only that Stadler need not have been overly concerned about political reprisals.[...] What seems clearest is that Mozart's hankering for secret

*1. Ignaz Alberti's frontispiece to the first edition
of the libretto (1791)*

societies, which is traceable to his early childhood, when he presided over his 'Kingdom of Back', was not wholly satisfied by Freemasonry in its late Habsburg form." [10]

Mozart's biographers have long tried to find a plausible fit for his Masonic inclinations. Proponents of the rationalist thesis point out that Ignaz von Born— Mozart's mentor— was not a mystagogue. Schlichtegroll, who wrote Born's obituary, asserts that "though ailing and frequently tormented by appalling pain" von Born was nevertheless able to "reshape science, destroy the altars of superstition and kindle the light of truth and wisdom and fan it into a brightly burning flame." [11]

The same general line is followed by Philippe Autexier, who claims that "according to contemporary sources such as the *Journal für Freymaurer,* published by 'Zur wahren Eintracht' [where Mozart was made a Master Mason in 1785], the significance of the ceremonies and their symbols was in no way mystical. The aim was rather to produce an experience which all the members of the Craft could share, creating an exceptional relationship between them." [12]

Unfortunately for these positive assessments, a number of genuine mysteries remain. They have to do with the background and interests of Mozart's Masonic handlers. Ignaz von Born, for one, was raised by the Jesuits. He spent six years in a Jesuit school in Vienna, before joining the order as a novice in 1760. That, in and of itself, is quite a pedigree for someone supposedly leading the charge against monastic orders.

There is no doubt that von Born satirized monks and nuns in his *Mönchsnaturkunde* of 1783, where they are shown classified in tables, using the pictorial methods of zoology; but in the end, his fight against local religious despotism and superstition was very much in line with Jesuit core values. The Jesuits were educators and powerbrokers who had no use for the predatory practices of other religious orders. They were rationalists and clever politicians, with a solid sense of organization, and their occasional flights into mysticism had nothing to do with superstition.

"Opposition to the Jesuits was a central issue for many of the Masonic subgroupings; the Rosicrucians had arisen as 'almost

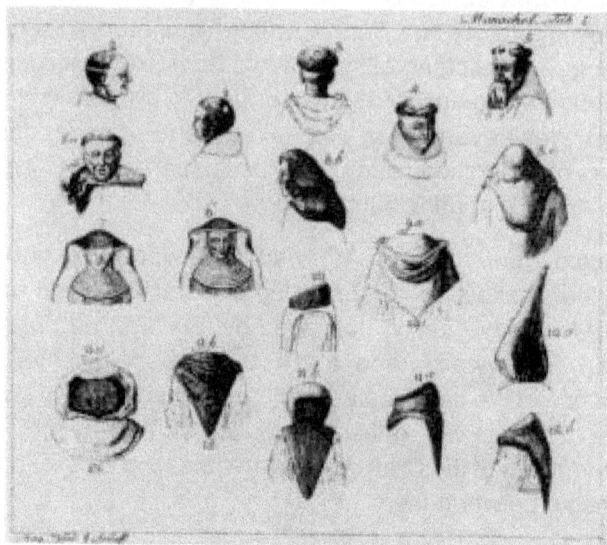

2. *Illustration from Ignaz von Born's **Monachologie***

a mirror image of the Jesuit Order'; and Adam Weishaupt had conceived of the Order of the Illuminati as an anti-Jesuit organization modeled upon Jesuitical methods and organizational forms." [13]

René Terrasson points out that it was Ignaz von Born who instigated Joseph II's reactionary reforms, which triggered the eventual demise of Austrian Freemasonry.[14] Terrasson posits that von Born's intent was to limit the influence of rapidly spreading occult tendencies within Freemasonry. Still, that does not explain why von Born left Masonry altogether, right after the amalgamation of the Austrian Lodges. His declining health may have been one reason; but his complete disappearance from the Masonic scene remains very puzzling.

The Jesuit connection may have had something to do with it. One of the most baffling events of the late 18th century— almost equal in esoteric significance to the medieval suppression of the Knights Templar— was the sudden expropriation of the Jesuits all across Europe. The process started in the early 1760s and culminated in 1773, when the Society was abruptly shut down.

"[Clement XIV] by his own personal decision abolished the Society of Jesus. By an officially published document, he disbanded the 23,000 Jesuits altogether, and he put their Father General and his advisers into papal dungeons, even as he imposed exile and slow death on thousands of Jesuits who were stranded without help or support in dangerous parts of the world. Pope Clement did not explain his decision to the Jesuits or anyone else. 'The reasons [for this decision] We keep locked up in Our Own heart', he wrote." [15]

The opposition to the Jesuits came from rather unexpected quarters. Their attackers belonged to the royal Bourbon family (all Catholics) who reigned in Spain, Portugal, France, Naples and Sicily. In 1773— as the Society of Jesus was being dissolved—Mozart was seventeen years old and looking at 'Egyptian' themes for the first time. It is impossible to know what he was thinking, as he wrote the incidental music and choruses for Tobias Gebler's ***Thamos, König in Ägypten***, but the Egyptian journey was definitely under way.

Gebler was a friend of Lessing and the Berlin bookseller and *Aufklärer* Friedrich Nicolai. During the 1760s and 1770s he was the main point of contact between Vienna and the Northern German Enlightenment.[16] In time he would become a prominent Freemason, joining *'Zur gekrönten Hoffnung'* in 1784.[17]

Gebler was a senior Austrian government official involved in the development of the educational system.[18] That he would have had contacts with the Jesuits, who had a quasi monopoly on education during that time, does not require great powers of deduction. ***Thamos*** was based on Abbé Jean Terrasson's ***Sethos***, a Masonic source book about Egypt. ***Sethos*** was later derided for its fanciful presentation of the Egyptian mysteries, but it must be remembered that Terrasson had translated Diodorus Siculus and that he was a professor of Greek and Latin philosophy at the Collège de France.[19] His knowledge of ancient Greek and Roman sources dealing with Egypt would be difficult to challenge.

But to come back to the Jesuits, it appears that the dissolution of their order followed a most unlikely script. The Papacy they were supposed to defend wanted them shutdown; Catholic royalty— with Spain leading the charge— was clamoring for their destruction, and Freemasons were everywhere advising the Bourbon clan.

"In those days, the most powerful statesmen necessarily belonged to the Lodge. It is certain that the chief advisers to the Bourbon princes were ardent members of the Lodge. The Marquis de Pombal, royal adviser in Portugal; The Count de Arenda, occupying the same position in Spain; Minister de Tillot and the Duc de Choiseul in France; Prince von Kaunitz and Gerard van Swieten at the Habsburg court of Maria Theresa of Austria.[...] Each one of those men held a position of trust and confidentiality in government, and each one avowedly desired the death of the Society." [20]

Staying on the Austrian track, we quickly discover that Gerard van Swieten (1700-1772), who had moved to Vienna in 1745— from Holland— to become the empress Maria Theresa's personal physician, "was also charged with revising the educational system in Austria in order to provide appropriately trained public servants to replace the inept and dishonest appointees who typically served at court." [21] He would also serve as Prefect of the Court Library.

Gerard's son, Gottfried, inherited some of his fathers' functions and was entrusted with important diplomatic missions. The most important assignment of his career was to the court of Frederick the Great of Prussia, from the fall of 1770 until 1777.[22] Berlin was a high center of Freemasonry and one would have expected Protestant Prussia to be inimical to the Jesuits— as Gottfried van Swieten most certainly was— but we will see later that this was not the case.

Most of the Josephinian reforms were managed and spearheaded by a group in which Gottfried van Swieten played a key role:

"While the reform of the educational system was underway, Joseph II named van Swieten as head of the Censorship Commission in 1781, following in his father's footsteps in this as in many of his other duties. [...] Gottfried's effectiveness was shaped by an extraordinarily liberal political climate which Joseph strove to achieve in the first several years of his sole rulership [...] Joseph's Tolerance declaration of 1781, for instance, allowed the 'Augsburg' and 'Helvetic' (Lutheran and Calvinist) and Greek Orthodox Christians freedom of private worship; and in the following year his declaration of 'Tolerance for the Jews', spearheaded by the efforts of Joseph von Sonnenfels, broadened civil liberties as well as exercise of religious activities for the Jewish citizens of Austrian lands. [...] Sonnenfels was Master of the Masonic Lodge *Zur wahren Eintracht*; two members of this Lodge, the bookseller Aloys Blumauer and Joseph von Retzer, evaluated the *belles-lettres*."[23]

Ignaz von Born was the Worshipful Master of *Zur wahren Eintracht* and it was there that Mozart was made a Master Mason on 13 January 1785.[24] The global zeal for educational reform— an area traditionally controlled by the Jesuits— points to battles related to the Jesuits' demise as an official organization.

That the Jesuits saw it coming would be an understatement. Some people even theorize that the Society orchestrated its own temporary demise, preferring to reemerge under the more universal banner of Freemasonry. Biographical sketches indicate that von Born left the Jesuits in either 1761 or 1762.[25] By then the handwriting was already on the wall:

"Pombal in Portugal started the roll of destruction. Between 1759 and 1761, all Jesuits in Portugal and its overseas dominions were arrested, transported by royal navy ships, and deposited on the shores of the papal estates in Italy. All Jesuit property— houses, churches, colleges, was confiscated. [...] Barely six years later, in one single night between April 2 and April 3 of 1767, all houses, colleges, residences, churches belonging to the Jesuits throughout Spain and the Spanish dominions in America were invaded by royal Spanish troops. About 6,000 Jesuits were arrested, packed like herrings into the holds Spanish men of war, and transported to the papal estates in Italy, where they were unceremoniously dumped on the shores, whether alive, dying, or already dead.[...] When a papal conclave of cardinals assembled in 1769 to elect a new Pope, the 'family' of Bourbons made it clear that they would accept as Pope only someone who would guarantee to liquidate the Jesuits. Cardinal Lorenzo Ganganelli gave his assurances on this point to the ambassadors from the Royal Courts of their Majesties. He was elected as Pope Clement XIV." [26]

The story then goes on to say that since the Jesuits had sworn obedience to the Pope, they had to accept his decision to disband the Society. Generations of commentators have pointed out that the Society was no stranger to adverse conditions. Part of the adaptation process was to operate under new, less discernible disguises.

One of these disguises may well have been Freemasonry.

Contrary to the poorly informed speculations of Gérard Gefen in his recent ***Légendes maçonniques autour de Mozart*** [1994], there is ample evidence to suggest that the *Illuminati*, at least, thought that their order was the only one not taken over by the Jesuits— and even that remains to be seen. Mirabeau, Bode, Mauvillon and Bonneville all wrote pamphlets attacking the Jesuits. Mauvillon is quoted as saying that all branches of German Masonry, except for the *Illuminati*, 'are just emanations of the formidable Jesuitic corpus'.[27] Bonneville's publication in 1788 of his ***Les jésuites chassés de la maçonnerie et leur poignard brisé par les maçons*** carries on along the same lines. Bode, in a memoir published at Weimar in 1781, even accuses the Jesuits of 'inventing' Freemasonry as an instrument to fight English Protestants. An assumption examined by Albert Mackey in his comprehensive ***History of Freemasonry*** (1881). Mackey acknowledges that the Jesuits worked on behalf of the Stuart cause and the restoration of James II to the throne of England:

"We are bound, therefore, if on the ground of an anachronism alone, to repudiate any theory that connects the Jesuits with Freemasonry during the life of James II, although we may be ready to admit their political conspiracy in the interests of that dethroned monarch. During the life of his son, and putative successor, the titular James III, Speculative Masonry was established in England and passed over into France. The Lodge established in Paris in 1725 was, I have no doubt, an organization of the adherents of the Stuart family. It is probable that most of the members were Catholics and under the influence of the Jesuits." [28]

How far back these intrigues go is not as important as their practical outcome. Bode thought that, in the Higher Degrees, the 18th and the 30th carried the Jesuit imprint. These are the Degrees singled out by commentators who look at ***The Magic Flute*** through Masonic lenses. It is not clear that the *Illuminati* were as free from Jesuit influences as Mauvillon wanted to believe.

Behind the self-sacrificing policies of the Jesuits lurk hidden principles that regular historians are unlikely to uncover. They are based on the predominance of priestly rule over any other kind of secular power. A smart organization will make sure that it is represented on all sides of the ideological spectrum. There is no advantage to be gained from holding on to a dogmatic position when new realities are inevitable. For a new force to emerge, the old one has to vanish.

It may appear that there is no road from the Catholicism supported by the Jesuits to the universalist approach promoted by Freemasonry; but that is not the case. At a ritual level continuity can be maintained. Historical assessments of Christianity suggest that Masonry was an essential component of Catholicism since its earliest days. The House of Peter, the Roman Papacy, which the Jesuits were charged to protect and defend, was built on Solomonic foundations and locked with clearly identifiable Masonic keys:

"In medieval exegesis, these keys governed not only all references to the building of the church in the New Testament but also its Old Testament prefigurations: Christ was the foundation of the church prefigured in Solomon's Temple (I **Kings** 5ff.), in the house which Wisdom built for herself (**Prov.** 9), and in the cosmological foundation images of the Psalms (**Ps**. 79:69; 86:1; 101:26; 103:5 etc.) The exegetical consequences of this situation were astonishing. Even an instance such as **Eph**. 2:20, where the church of the saints is said to be built on 'the foundation of the apostles and the prophets', was pressed into the christological mold [...] The apparent warrant was provided by the designation of Christ as *summus angularis lapis* in the same verse; based on **Isa**. 28:16 and **Ps**. 117:22, the image of the cornerstone had been appropriated as a messianic prediction in the earliest Christian tradition already (**Rom**. 9:33; **Mark** 12:10; **Acts** 4:11; I **Peter**

2:4-7). Still the verse in Ephesians, together with other texts such as *Rev*. 21:14 where the twelve apostles are called the foundations of the new Jerusalem, did suggest the language of the apostles as secondary foundations after Christ. In this connection, medieval exegetes sometimes could speak of Peter as the 'second' foundation of the church because among the apostolic *fundamenta* he was closest to the cornerstone." [29]

Militant orders, like the Jesuits and the Knights Templar, were pressed into service to protect this edifice. Their focus was never on earthly human objectives, where notions of individual well-being, security and possession dominate. Nor was their action geared toward survival, as historians have shown. Their objective was to sustain an obscure ritual hierarchy with distant Egyptian roots.

That notion was of particular interest to Bernard of Clairvaux, who gave the Knights Templar their charter. He was just as instrumental in defining the role of the Papacy at the time of Innocent III.

"In his study of Innocent's rhetoric, Imkamp found the 'head' metaphor by which Innocent frequently expressed the papal plenitude of power, was 'strongly marked by christological terminology and probably also content' [...] The phenomenon is indeed striking. It is related to the new papal self-consciousness which expressed itself in the title, 'Vicarius Christi'. The title, 'Vicar of Christ', opens a list of papal epithets in Innocent's inaugural oration: "*Profecto vicarius Jesu Christi, successor Petri, Christus Domini, Deus Pharaonis, inter Deum et hominem constitutus*'. The term, '*Deus Pharaonis*', was borrowed from *Exodus* 7:1 and appeared among the string of images for the papal office which Bernard of Clairvaux had incorporated in his treatise, *De Consideratione*." [30]

This view of the pope as *Deus Pharaonis*— or God-King— with a no less magical army of Knights of the Temple at his disposal, is critical to our understanding of **The Magic Flute** and its Egyptian priesthood. The Jesuits were drilled in these principles and Mackey arrives at the same conclusion by a very different route:

"The Jesuits appear to have taken the priests of Egypt for their model. Like them, they sought to be the conservators and the interpreters of religion. The vows which they took attached them to their Order with bonds as indissoluble as those that united the Egyptian priests in the sacred college of Memphis. Those who sought admission into their company were compelled to pass through trials of their fortitude and fidelity. Their ambition was as indomitable as their cunning was astute. They strove to be the confessors and the counsellors of kings, and to control the education of youth, that by these means they might become of importance in the state, and direct the policy of every government where they were admitted." [31]

Ignaz von Born, whose first name, incidentally, matches that of the founder of the Society, was raised in this environment. His interest in the Egyptian mysteries was completely in line with that of his schoolmasters. On the road between the Middle-Ages and Mozart's time one finds a number of key instances where 'Egypt' emerges among Jesuits to buttress theological arguments.

At the beginning of the seventeenth century two Jesuit priests, Nicolas Caussin and the better known Athanasius Kircher, published works dealing with Egypt and tried to use their interpretations of its symbols to justify conservative positions with respect to the Reform movement.

"Caussin's book consists of a Latin translation of Horapollo and relevant extracts from Clement, together with a commentary on them. But what is particularly interesting in it is the introduction. This is not only because he gives a clear definition of the distinctions between Symbol, Enigma, Parable, Apologue or Fable, and Hieroglyph, but also because he makes a firm and conscious defence of the study of Egyptian hieroglyphic. Luther had been suspicious of allegory: the Lutherans too. Hieroglyphics and allegory were closely related. Caussin's defence of them— he was a Jesuit priest— is intimately bound up with the Counter-Reformation." [32]

In Kircher's case, the motivation was very much the same. He approached Egyptology through his work on Coptic manuscripts that had recently become available. In the process he produced erroneous interpretations that made him an easy target for subsequent scholars. But some of Kircher's symbolism has survived. It has even found its way into his critics' wallets.

"Among Kircher's correspondents and most enthusiastic readers was a Scot, Sir Robert Moray, one of the earliest recorded brethren in Freemasonry. In a letter to one of his own correspondents, Moray urgently recommended a particular book of Kircher's, on Egyptian hieroglyphs. One of Kircher's other texts, the **Ars magna sciendi** (The Great Art of Knowledge), depicts in its frontispiece an eye contained in a triangle, illuminated by the effulgent rays of the Deity. This device, of course, was later to find its way into Freemasonry and, from there, on to the dollar bill of the United States." [33]

If Kircher was free to engage in debates on Masonic symbolism, why not Ignaz von Born? The Jesuit does not automatically exclude the Freemason. By Mozart's time, the cause of the counter-Reformation was lost for all practical purposes. There were still rivalries on the European stage, but the most active opposition to the Jesuits came on account of their dealings in the New World, where they still acted as major power brokers. Their problems were caused by a volatile situation in South America, where they were preceded by the Franciscans:

"Franciscan missionaries had already tried to evangelize the 'savages' and herd them into communities. But their efforts were overshadowed by struggles between rival Spanish and Portuguese imperialist forces and by the worst kinds of colonial excesses." [34]

The extent of the problem was first noted by Francisco de Vitoria (1483-1546), the father of European international law.[35] Vitoria argued that the *Indios* were the lawful proprietors of their lands and that neither Pope nor Emperor had the right to seize these lands by force on the grounds that their proprietors were not Christians.

"Vitoria [...] early in 1539 took the subject *'De Indis'* as his theme for a special lecture, justifying his choice with the reflection that the murder, expropriation and exploitation of so many innocent people made it a matter not only for jurists but also for theologians to investigate.[...] Vitoria's lectures on the New World certainly caused an unprecedented commotion and he was condemned on all sides for doing damage to the papacy, the emperor and to Spain. The letter Charles V wrote in his own hand to his religious superior comes close to being a warrant for his house-imprisonment.[...] But his candor and his concern for universal justice lived on in some eminent disciples. Sixty theologians from Vitoria's school at Salamanca sat at the Council of Trent, at which Melchor Cano, who succeeded Vitoria in his chair, played a leading role. Cano, like many Spanish theologians of the emperor's party, was a bitter enemy of the Jesuits, whom he described as forerunners of Antichrist." [36]

The Jesuits were more practical than the Dominicans— more Machiavellian, no doubt— and their experimental communities eventually grew between 1610 and 1767 into what came to be known as the Guaraní Republic: a Jesuit state located in a region that now extends across two Brasilian provinces (Paraná and Rio Grande Do Sul) and Northern Argentina (Misiones and Corrientes).[37] The Guaraní population was composed exclusively of native Indians and Jesuits.

For those who wonder impatiently about the relevance of the Guaraní Republic to **The Magic Flute**, we will point out that it was the greatest utopian experiment of its day and that it was closely followed by European philosophers and writers. It can even be suggested that Act I of **The Magic Flute** is cast as an extension of this idyllic 'elsewhere', with Papageno, the innocent but slightly devious bird-catcher, incarnating the spirit of the New World:

"The beliefs and mythology of the Guaraní may have predisposed them to accept the notion of an only God and an afterlife. They believed in Paï-Sumé, in the concept of a land free of evil, of a 'civilizing hero' [...] What tied them most closely to the fathers' teaching was Christian ritual, with its pomp, gold, incense, and, above all, music, which they loved. A whole literary genre grew up around this theme of the Jesuit Orpheus charming the Indian serpent. From Muratori to Chateaubriand, there has been much ink spilled around this magic flute [...] but Roger Lacombe has asked the very pertinent question, 'who played the Pre-Columbian flute better, the European Jesuit or the Indian?'." [38]

Jean Lacouture insists that music was a passion for these Indians. He also mentions that Domenico Zipoli, a Jesuit and a rival of Vivaldi, composed a number of cantatas especially for the Guaraní and that many missionaries owed their prestige to their talents as flautists or violonists. [39]

The fall of the Guaraní Republic under the combined assault of Spanish and Portuguese forces was at the root of the Jesuits' demise. They were eventually forced to betray the people entrusted to their care, but created enough military resistance to be perceived as the enemy.

"It took nearly eighteen years, from 1750 to 1768, for the Jesuits' enemies, Portuguese or Anglo-Portuguese and then Spanish, to annihilate the Guaraní Republic. It did not come about without political and then military resistance from the Indians, who were of course exhorted, preached to, and led by their men in black.[...] The Portuguese, surrounded and trapped by Indian guerillas, were forced to sign a truce with the Guaraní, who insisted that the text be in both Portuguese and their own language. We can imagine Pombal's fury as he accused his Spanish allies of allowing him to be led into a trap so as to humiliate him. Madrid reacted by sending reinforcements and agreeing to a combined operation." [40]

With what we know of Mozart's well-informed Masonic circle, it seems unlikely that they would have been ignorant of the Guaraní episode. It was intimately tied to the earliest concerns about human rights and Ignaz von Born, who studied law in Prague, would have heard most of the arguments. His subsequent path from legal studies to experimental mineralogy, where he excelled, is more difficult to follow. During his lifetime, the transmutation of metals was still under the influence of alchemy. While his contributions were universally recognized, the culmination came on 24 April 1785, when von Born was appointed Knight of the Realm by Joseph II for his discovery of a new smelting process. The event was celebrated with a Mozart cantata composed specifically for the occasion: *Die Maurerfreude*, K. 471.

As we will see in subsequent chapters, there is a ritual link between mineralogy, alchemy and various forms of magic— all identified in Greek and Egyptian tradition with the 'mastery of fire', and in Freemasonry with the occult side of the Craft. If one additionally takes into account Ignatius de Loyola's *Spiritual Exercises*, borrowed from Ibn'Arabi's (11165-1240) alchemical conception of prophetic revelation, Ignaz von Born's seemingly disparate endeavors suddenly start to make sense.

Loyola was exposed to Ibn'Arabi's writings at Alcala de Hénarès. Ibn'Arabi's approach to 'initiation' was predicated on the notion of a *Deus absconditus*, or hidden principle always aspiring to be revealed.[41]

"This revelation gives rise to a dramatic situation in which the divine Being and the being in which and through which he reveals himself are simultaneously implicated, for God cannot look at an *other* than himself, nor be seen by an *other* than himself. The *Awliya*, the 'initiates', graduated in the different spiritual degrees, are precisely the eyes at which God looks, because they are the eyes through which He looks." [42]

There are many reasons to dwell on the Jesuit connection, since it will rear its head again throughout these pages. The educational theme has been duly noted, but there are others. All are tied to the Jesuit's transformation in the aftermath of their official demise at the hands of the Pope.

The last place where we would have expected the Jesuits to do well is in Protestant strongholds:

"Fabulous? Baroque? How can we describe the Company's itinerary from 1773 to 1796? The rescue of this most papalist of Companies, destroyed by the Pope, at the hands of the Lutheran Frederick? And then its welcome and revitalization at the hands of the schismatic Empress of Russia? [...] When one reflects on the enormous services [the Company] had rendered the world in terms of education, of the intellectual prestige it had enjoyed, of its influence over both monarchs and masses, this sudden collapse has something terrifying, almost biblical about it. [..] Yet no sooner had the Papacy issued its brief than the King of Prussia [...] handed his unofficial representative in Rome the following note addressed to the Pope: 'On the matter of the Jesuits, my mind is made up to preserve them in my States just as they have always been. In the Treaty of Breslau I guaranteed the status quo of the Catholic Religion, and I have never known better priests'." [43]

Russia's Catherine the Great had an even more brutal message for the Pope:

"I know that Your Holiness is most disturbed, but fear ill suits him... My motives in granting my protection to the Jesuits are founded on reason and justice, as also on the hope that they will be useful to my States. This band of peaceable and innocent men shall live in my Empire because, of all the Catholic Societies, theirs is best fitted to instruct my subjects and inspire in them feelings of humanity and the true principles of the Christian Religion." [44]

These monarchs were referred to by the *philosophes* of the Enlightenment as the Solomon and Semiramis of the North. There was nothing sentimental about their welcome of the Jesuits. In such moments, when the hidden machinery of history suddenly becomes visible for a brief period of time, many questions arise for which answers are not readily available. At what level was the deception orchestrated? How could such unlikely scenarios be executed so flawlessly?

The best path of inquiry is in the direction of prophetic revelation, that both Freemasonry and the Jesuits were pursuing. For the Masons, the impetus came from the Lost Word of Freemasonry. For the Jesuits it was part of Ibn'Arabi's legacy, by way of Ignatius de Loyola.

Henry Corbin speaks of the 'image-symbol' (*mithâl*) as the principal instrument of prophetic revelation. The transformation of an image into a symbol is, in and of itself, a revelation. The prophetic character of image manipulation was associated in particular with alchemy. Its so-called 'experiments' were magic rituals— or transformative operations— whose outcome was a 'vision'.

To approach the ***The Magic Flute*** along these lines requires no particular mandate. A large body of evidence exists that suggests that there is nothing wrong with an occult interpretation. But it also implies that Mozart's opera cannot be reduced to the simplistic dramatic templates favored by professional musicologists. Critical theory, as it exists today, is not comfortable with allegories centered on magic:

"The task of aesthetics," says Theodor Adorno, "is not to comprehend artworks as hermeneutical objects; in the contemporary situation, it is their incomprehensibility that needs to be comprehended. [...] the ridiculous elements in artworks are most akin to their intentionless levels and therefore, in great works, also closest to their secret. Foolish subjects like those of *The Magic Flute* and *Der Freischütz* have more truth content through the medium of music than does the *Ring*, which gravely aims at the ultimate." [45]

One does not have to like Wagner, but his operas are not that easily dismissed. They have disturbed minds much deeper than Adorno's— starting with Nietzsche— and will continue to exert their fascination on generations to come. Wagner and Mozart were equals in their ability to undermine reason. Mozart did it subtly; Wagner more violently. Some of their creations belong to the realm of magic.

Modern critics miss out on the obvious because their focus is usually on aesthetics. Their understanding is clouded by stylistic considerations that have nothing to do with what was intended. The subversive nature of the exceptional is part of Mozart's and Wagner's legacy:

"Even an arch-materialist like Helvétius had believed that the extraordinary individual, the genius, must be permitted to override the rules of established behavior if humankind is to progress, and Diderot had been very aware of the confusing aesthetic appeal of great crimes. Shortly after Mozart's death his former colleague, the Salzburg trumpeter Andreas Schachtner, confided his memories of Mozart to the erstwhile Nannerl Mozart. In one revealing recollection he stated, 'I think that if he had not had the advantageously good education which he enjoyed, he might have become the most wicked villain, so susceptible was he to every attraction, the goodness of badness of which he was not yet able to imagine." [46]

The 'criminal' Mozart is a subject well developed in Alexander Pushkin's mini-dramas **Mozart and Salieri** and **The Stone Guest**. Pushkin was a Freemason and had a pretty good idea of where he was going with this notion. When distilled down to its Masonic essence, it leads to yet another restatement of the Hiramic legend. Exceptional talent seduces. In the process it creates fatal attractions and passionate jealousies. The human condition is such that it cannot withstand perfection. The seducer, identified elsewhere with Lucifer— the 'light-bringer'— exposes intolerable shortcomings, which, in turn lead to murder. From a criminal standpoint, the victim and the perpetrator are not as distinct as one would like to believe. The victim just happens to have what the perpetrator wants. By 'having' he incites the crime and is therefore the real criminal.

The only valid alternative to imitation is imagination. Mozart's youthful esoteric creations, such as the 'Kingdom of Back', are intuitive expressions of this fundamental need for inner freedom. As a very young child, Mozart also composed a song which he sang every night, together with his father, before going to sleep. The wording he used (*Oragna figata fa marina gamina fa*) provides an indication of his early fascination with intentional speech.[47] A characteristic that would never fade with time:

"We know of his fondness for codes and ciphers and his love of secret tongues: in 1772 he even learned the sign language of the deaf. Then there was his attachment for secret societies and orders— to the imaginary 'Kingdom of Back' of his childhood, to the Masonic Lodges, and to 'The Grotto', about which his wife reported so reticently after his death. [...] Mozart loved wordplay of every kind, including neologisms, transpositions, reversals, puns, rhymes, word-salads, and the like. If *Fastnacht* [Shrove Tuesday] derives from '*faseln*'— to talk nonsense— it was a holiday season designed for Mozart,

for this was the mother tongue of his Kingdom of Back. The riddles display Mozart's antic disposition as clearly as do his letters to the Bäsle, his outrageous first person entries in his sister's personal diary, and his obscene canons of the 1780s."
[48]

The path to Mozart's world is crooked. To musicologists like Adorno **The Magic Flute** is just another *Oragna figata:* a foolish musical utterance that can only draw aesthetic reactions. Had it not been for Mozart's well-documented involvement with Freemasonry it would be difficult to argue against this position.

The 'absurdity' of **The Magic Flute** is in line with what one encounters in occult systems in general. The parallels are easily drawn. They include: the esoteric use of 'names', confusing journeys of initiation, an extensive application of rhythm and visual symbolism— all of which conspire to create an overexcited atmosphere in which one's imagination easily takes over. What happens next, depends on the spectator's receptiveness. To the closed individual this mysterious dimension is forever off-limits, but to a more free-wheeling spirit it offers many challenges.

James Curl (**The Art and Architecture of Freemasonry**) gives a good example of a Masonic imagination at work:

"At the very beginning of the opera the overture (in the Masonic key of E flat major [i.e. with three flats]) starts with one chord followed by two more, the latter with anacruses, making five in all in the rhythm o-oo-oo. Now five combines the Dyad and the Triad, and represents the flaming star of the female Order, or light itself. The following Adagio is a conventional representation of the Kingdom of the Night [...] The opening of the fugue is *Ordo ab Chao*, the Kingdom of Light, with a rhythm suggesting the blows or tapping of mallets, that is, Masonic work. The fugue breaks off for the thrice-three chords of its Master's Degree with dotted rhythms (used in French Lodges under the Grand

Orient which were about to be closed) [...] There are many parallels with Isiac religion in **Die Zauberflöte**. Isis transformed herself into an old hag and then into a beautiful girl, just as happens to Papagena.[...] Another point that completely eludes modern designers of this opera is the fact that roses played an important part in early productions: the flying machine of the Three Boys is covered with roses, and there was presumably scope for roses in the gardens, bowers and other sets. Roses were used in Isiac rites; Lucius, in Apuleius, eats roses during his initiation, and the flower of Isis was the unfading rose.[...] The point about the beginning and the end of the **Flute** is that it teaches us two important truths: first, that things are not always what they seem to be, and, second, that the man who is 'more than a prince' by being a man, learns to cast aside the darkness by venturing through the gates of hell into the Underworld, metaphorically dies, and is resurrected after initiation and undergoing trials, overcoming the very terror of death itself. He also, when playing the flute, standing with the instrument in its transverse position, becomes an enigmatical representation of a word or a name by suggesting a Masonic Square." [49]

The Magic Flute revolves around Egyptian Masonry, but this 'Egyptian Masonry' is nothing more than an eighteenth-century revival of ancient Greek and Jewish esoteric thought. There may have been a true Egyptian connection, but it is hidden so deeply within the corpus of **The Magic Flute** that it barely registers on the crude mental instrumentation we now use to measure such things.

The Egyptian discourse has many branches, but from a Masonic viewpoint the earliest Egyptian Rites emerged during the period immediately preceding the fall of the French monarchy. The most important Rite was established in 1788. The date corresponds to the foundation of the first Egyptian Lodge in Venice, at the time of Cagliostro's presumed visit to that city.[50]

Cagliostro has always been a controversial figure. He was involved with Freemasonry for more than a decade before his Egyptian Rite officially surfaced. Some say that he was influenced by the teachings of the Order of Malta and a number of chroniclers even claim that, during his stay in Malta, he was noticed by the Order's Grand Master, Don Manuel Pinto d'Alfonseca, who taught him alchemy, the significance of Illuminism and introduced him to occult pursuits.[51] The early record is sketchy, but there is no doubt that in 1777 he joined the Esperance Lodge of London, which followed the Rite of Strict Observance.[52]

Cagliostro was eager to promote himself as a *Doctor* who could miraculously cure the sick and turn lesser metals into gold. He was hardly a pioneer in adopting this disguise. It helps to remember that the Habsburg court was a patron of the arts by which alchemical transmutations were effected.

Physical processes were used to illustrate hermetic principles. The main emphasis was always on the 'image-symbol', not chemistry. The *Doctors* who worked at the Imperial court were Cagliostro's predecessors and their lineage can be traced to Renaissance Italy. From there it extends to ancient Greece and reaches all the way back to Alexandria, where the Egyptian connection suddenly becomes real.

Many hermetic actions were officially commemorated by the Habsburg court and a quick analysis of the symbolism involved shows that the people who performed the transformations had a sophisticated understanding of ritual.

"In 1675, after almost five years as commercial advisor at the Imperial court in Vienna [...] Becher transmuted lead into silver. From the transmuted silver he made a commemorative medallion bearing the inscription, 'In the year 1675, the month of July, I, J.J. Becher, *Doctor*, transmuted this piece of the finest silver from lead by the art of alchemy'. On the reverse side was portrayed a one-legged, barefooted Saturn dressed in the clothes of a German peasant, carrying a scythe over one shoulder and his bare, struggling child slung over the other. This depiction of Saturn referred to the process of assaying gold and silver by adding them to molten lead in a crucible. Saturn symbolized the base metal, lead, and the act of eating his children was analogous to the behavior of all metals (except gold and silver), which, on being added to molten lead in a crucible merged with the lead. The two noble metals were not absorbed by lead, but instead were left as a 'button' at the bottom off the vessel, separated from all impurities. Saturn could not digest these, the noblest of his children, and so he vomited them up again, purified." [53]

Ignaz von Born's intellectual ancestors relied on these manipulations for their image-symbol transformations. One does not have to be superstitious to see how these ritual processes actually worked. Cagliostro's or Becher's claims to be *Doctors* must not be confused with updated notions of what this particular science represented. In the traditional sense, a *Doctor* was anyone qualified to display hermetic knowledge. Within this scope, science in general, appears not as an advancement over the original art, but as an unknowing heir to a completely different tradition.

During Leopold I's reign (1658-1705), both opera and alchemy flourished in Vienna and the emperor's spending habits have since been invoked to explain his support for gold producing charlatans. Such explanations assume that he was a naïve individual with outrageous habits that only vast quantities of gold could fuel. A simplistic view, as later chapters will show.

The emperors of the Holy Roman Empire were not uneducated spendthrifts bent on dilapidating their inheritance. They understood economics very well and were just as aware of the advantages brought about by a thorough knowledge of metals. It just so happens that the metaphysical transmutations were performed by the same people who transmuted metals. Becher's officially commemorated action was not unique. Wenceslas Seiler, an Augustinian monk, was made Ritter von Reinberg and sent to Bohemia as an officer of the mint after he transmuted copper into gold.[54] Leopold's interest in the art was not an aberration. His ancestors had cultivated it for a very long time:

"It was probably [a] combination of financial woe and love of spectacle that caused Leopold to gain a reputation as a patron of alchemists, although the Habsburg court had long been known as a refuge for alchemists. Most lately, Leopold's predecessor Ferdinand III had patronized alchemy, and their common forebear, Rudolf II, had made the Habsburg court in Prague synonymous with the golden art [...] Leopold's love of the theater and display no doubt played a part in his appreciation of Seiler's artifice, but success in alchemical transmutation could be interpreted as confirming princely power and fitness to rule, for alchemical knowledge was revealed only to the most pious, and success in transmutation was granted only to individuals of exceptional moral probity [...] Patronage of alchemy as much as patronage of music, letters, or natural philosophy was a way to direct and sustain the representation of the prince." [55]

These are important considerations. They imply that alchemy, music and the theater could all be used to legitimize a ruling principle. During Mozart's time, the emphasis on legitimacy remained unchanged, but with the French Revolution just around the corner new realities had to be faced. The Habsburgs were running out of time. They could no longer afford to wait for magical confirmations of their fitness to rule.

Hermetic principles had to be applied directly to social engineering tasks. This, in turn, led to modern image making, with its assortment of mass manipulation techniques and more or less sordid deception. The media instruments assembled by the *Doctors* could be used to destroy as well as to sustain.

Cagliostro's notoriety, as far as ordinary historians are concerned, comes from his involvement in the famous and well-publicized Necklace Affair, through which the French monarchy was thoroughly discredited. This grand pre-revolutionary scheme will be discussed later, but Cagliostro's role in its ritual construction can be abstracted from a document retained in the case's archives. Right after his denunciation and arrest as a co-conspirator in the affair, Cagliostro wrote a **Mémoire contre le Procureur général**, [memorandum against the prosecutor] in which he characterized himself as follows:

"I am of no epoch and no particular place; outside of time and space, my spiritual being lives its eternal existence, and, if I dive into my thoughts retracing the course of the ages, if I extend my spirit toward a mode of existence distant from the one you perceive, I become whoever I desire to be. Participating consciously in the absolute being, I regulate my actions according to my surroundings. My name is that of my function and I select it, as well as my function, because I am free; my country is where my steps temporarily come to a halt [...] Here I am: a noble traveler; I speak and your soul trembles as it recognizes ancient words; a voice within you that fell silent long ago responds to my call; I act and peace returns to your hearts, health to your bodies, hope and courage to your souls. All men are my brothers; all countries are dear to me; I journey through them so that everywhere, the Spirit can descend and find its way to you. " [56]

The mystery of the character, his well articulated belief in a universal brotherhood, the formal identity of name and function are all Masonic traits that Cagliostro shares with Sarastro— Mozart's high-priest of the temple of Isis and Osiris. In the Masonic world— as James Curl has observed— things are not always what they seem to be. Egyptian Masonry capitalized heavily on ambiguities and the story of its birth in Venice is most likely fictitious. Cagliostro's legend would have placed him there, even if he had never set foot within its walls. Venice and Florence had strong ties to Byzantine culture and both were quite influential in reintroducing Europe to a long forgotten hermetic tradition, located 'outside of time and space'. Egyptian Masonry also appears to have been constructed purposefully for the dissemination of ritualistic forms of worship not tied directly to Christianity. A great deal of energy was expanded on the formulation of a solid pre-Christian— and even pre-Hebrew— foundation.

Since the purpose of ritual is to formally acknowledge subtle powers located 'outside of time and space', there is always a thin line between a well-executed ritual and the search for effective magic. Here again, Egypt is the most attractive source and the historical record suggests that its practices have always prevailed. Greek religion, in its pre-Christian incarnation, was never a threat to Egyptian cult forms:

"The personal participation of Greeks in native [Egyptian] cults did not necessarily make much difference to the way those cults were conducted, or to the behavior and beliefs of their native followers. It is instructive to examine the Sarapis cult as it was practiced in the culturally antithetical cities of Alexandria and Memphis. At [Alexandria] Sarapis was naturally enough treated as a Greek god [...] The priesthood and rituals were also largely Greek [...] various Egyptian objects were to be seen adorning the Sarapeum, including a couple of statues of Psenptais, a third century priest of Memphite Ptah, that perhaps suggests links between the clergy of the two cities. [...] But at Memphis, once the Pharaohs' capital and still strongly Egyptian in character, 'Sarapis' was but a name for Osor-Hapi, whose presentation was scarcely Hellenized at all [...] the Sarapeum itself, its priesthood and ritual, remained as Egyptian as ever, and in that the Greek community in Memphis , and (with some exceptions) their compatriots who came from afar to visit the sanctuary, were content to acquiesce." [57]

The philosophy of the **Hermetica**, first rediscovered at Cosimo de Medici's Florentine Academy (Marsilio Ficino translated the **Corpus Hermeticum** from Greek to Latin in 1471) and the association of Zoroaster with Hermes,[58] all point to Alexandria. Mozart's Egyptian framework cannot be divorced from these ancient sources. The cross-pollination of mystical cultures in a spirit of enlightenment, was— and still is— the model of choice promoted by Freemasonry. As a universal brotherhood, not limited by religious or national affiliations, it has inherited the basic Alexandrian syncretism. The search for a sophisticated, yet universally acceptable cosmology, was effectively pioneered in the **Hermetica**:

"Even the non Graeco-Egyptian elements that one can detect in the **Hermetica** are precisely those that one would expect in texts written in Ptolemaic or Roman Egypt.[...] If Iranian influences, emphasized by R. Reitzenstein in the later period of his hermetic studies, are best regarded as remote and indirect, still Egypt was certainly not innocent of them. And that hermetic writers absorbed Jewish ideas is anything but surprising when one recalls the wide distribution and (one assumes) numerousness of Egypt's Jewish population. The Hebrew creation-myth was bound to be of interest to anyone who, like the hermetists, regarded cosmology as one of the foundations of philosophy; and the **Poimandres**'s debt to **Genesis** was already remarked on by Psellus. Recent scholarship has elaborated on this perception, unearthed evidence for Jewish influence on other philosophical **Hermetica** too, and shown that the sources of this influence are to be looked for not just in the reading of the **Septuagint**, but also in personal contact with the liturgical life of Jews living in Egypt." [59]

The implications of an early Iranian connection are particularly interesting given the Zarathustrian character of the Brotherhood of Light depicted in **The Magic Flute**. Sarastro, its leader, wears the seven-rayed solar emblem on his chest and this reference to the world of Apollo indicates that the syncretism may have been intended— at least within the framework being considered here. René Terrasson claims that the 'solar circle', which the Queen of the Night reveals to her daughter as the source of all power (Act II, scene 8), came right out of the **Emerald Tablet**, attributed to Hermes Trismegistus:

"I am Hermes Trismegistus
For in me are the Three Wisdoms of the World
What I utter is Just and Perfect
For I speak from the Solar Circle master of the Work" [60]

Terrasson's translation may be a bit aggressive, but the overall meaning remains the same. If Sarastro is the legitimate heir to a hermetic wisdom previously protected by the Queen of the Night's husband, the alchemical dimension of **The Magic Flute** cannot reasonably be denied. We will see later where this leads. Just as important is the Jewish connection, which likewise fits the 'Egyptian' model found in the **Hermetica**. For this we must turn from Sarastro to Tamino.

Tamino's behavior fits that of a Noachite. As he stands in front of the Temple, waiting to be admitted, his ritual stance symbolically identifies him. Noachites are descendants of Noah and this designation is found in the second edition of Anderson's **Book of Constitutions**, where it is used to describe a Mason.

What distinguishes a Noachite from other people is his appearance as a 'proselyte of the gate'; that is a stranger, who in spite of his foreign origin, requests entry to the Temple. Albert Mackey, in his **History of Freemasonry**, explains the link between Freemasonry and the so-called descendants of Noah:

"But why, it may be asked, are the Freemasons called the descendants of Noah? Why has he been selected alone to represent the leadership of the Fraternity? I have no doubt that Dr. Anderson was led to the adoption of the word by the following reason. After Noah's emergence from the ark, he is said to have promulgated seven precepts for the government of the new race of men of whom he was to be the progenitor [...] These seven obligations [..] are held binding on all men, inasmuch as all are descendants of Noah [...] In consequence of this, the Jewish religion [before the destruction of Temple] was not confined during its existence in Palestine to the Jewish nation only, but proselytes of three kinds were freely admitted. One of these classes was the 'proselytes of the gate'. These were persons who, without undergoing the rite of circumcision or observing the ritual prescribed by the Law of Moses, engaged to worship the true God, and to observe the seven precepts of Noah." [61]

To which Claude Guérillot adds that the potential candidate was called *guér-tsèdèq*, or 'just stranger'.[62] The seven precepts— like the 'solar circle' and its seven rays— extend far beyond their exoteric manifestations. They hide complex esoteric allegories in which geometry plays a major role. Tamino, holding his flute, for instance, represents the Greek letter Ã, otherwise known as the *arkhan*, or one of the four immovable foundations of the Temple.

"Whence the attentive study of figures (the sphere and pyramid in particular) and their properties, so that geometric examples can be promoted to the level of symbols, by applying them to the physics of Light. It is then that something like a *topography of the spiritual universes* becomes possible." [63]

Light— in its esoteric form— controls the phenomenal world through a language analogous to music. Not a music that can be heard; but as sound perceived mentally in extreme forms of consciousness. This sound, often equated with a divine voice, was assigned a prophetic quality.

The significance of Tamino's flute can be further abstracted from Macrobius' **Saturnalia** [I, 21-22], where mention is made of the Soul of the World distributed among the seven spheres:

"Macrobius, who has transmitted many ancient mysteries to us, tells that this soul, distributed among the seven spheres of the world which it moves and animates and from which it produces the harmonic tones, was designated emblematically by the number 7, or figuratively by the seven-holed flute placed in the hands of Pan, the God of the Universe. This number, revered by all peoples, was specially consecrated to the God of Light. The emperor Julian speaks enigmatically of the god with seven rays, knowledge of whom is not given to everyone [...] the ancient Egyptians [...] imagined a boat steered by seven genii; and Martianus Capella, who acts as their interpreter, places the Sun god in the middle of this boat, holding in his hands seven spheres, which like so many concave mirrors reflect the light which he pours out in great waves." [64]

Pamina and Tamino are to replace Sarastro at the head of the solar priesthood. The fairy-tale setting of the opera makes their union look natural, but it is alchemical in every respect. The *neue Paar* is bound together by the power of names, about which there will be much to say as the argument progresses. Pamina and Tamino, like Noah, are magic progenitors of a new humanity rededicated to the Law of Sevens.

Sarastro's pseudo-Iranian heritage creates the indispensable link to a historically active prophetic tradition: that of the Prophet himself. As Zarathustra's namesake, he belongs to the final lineage of light, preserved by Islam in its *shi'ite* Iranian form.

"We must remember, " writes Henry Corbin, " that Jabir Ibn Hayyan, the famous alchemist, disciple of the Imam Ja'far Sâdiq, according to a pretty constant tradition that nothing invalidates, was nicknamed, from the very start, the *sufi*. Jabir's alchemy is inseparable from his *shi'ite* conceptions: the Imam is for the spiritual world what the Stone or the Elixir are for the world of Nature. And it is thus one of Jabir's most abtruse works that gives us the first elaboration of the Stranger, the spiritual expatriate (*gharîb*) who has come from distant shores. Yet the archetype of the stranger, in *shi'ite* gnosis, remains that of Salman the Persian (*Salmân Pârsî*): the pilgrim searching for the True Prophet, who belongs by birth to the Mazdean chivalry."[65]

The 'genesis' of a new seed requires special formulations. The book of **Genesis** is a repository of such formulas rather than a creation-myth. As a generator of Light its function is to tie subtle creative principles to the active power of names.

The imaginary cosmic space within which these names are operative is completely outside of the physical world we know and its relationship to that world is a subject that need not occupy us here. Names are bound together in rhythmic sets and incantation is always the intended mode of delivery. The original Hebrew gives a better idea of the underlying poetic vehicle.

At **Genesis** X.13, where Egypt (*Mitzeraîm*) is first mentioned, the original text reads as follows: "*W - Mitzeraîm îalad æth-Loudîm w æth - Whonanîm w æth-Le-habîm w'æth-Naphethuhîm.*" [66] The suffix *-îm* which recurs throughout the verse refers— according to Fabre d'Olivet [1767-1825]— to universal manifestation. The prefix *æth-* denotes a symbol, sign or mark. The root MTZ, of which *Mitzeraîm* is primarily composed, conveys the idea of 'that which attains an end[67] and the extension R brings to the name 'that which possesses in itself, a proper and determining movement'.[68] *Mitzeraîm* is thus the name of 'that which attains an end through a self-determined movement that manifests universally'. A better abstract definition of Masonry is difficult to find.

References to Jews and Greeks in a ritually potent Egyptian context are abundant. As many writers have already observed, the story of Israel in Egypt is full of subplots that refer directly to Masonic-type rituals. Joseph's story, for instance, unfolds like an initiation ritual and contains many familiar elements: death at the hands of his 'brothers', a journey to a hostile land, trials and confinement, emergence into the Light through divination, and finally reunion with his 'brothers'. While this is not the proper place to expand on the similarities, the basic pattern should at least be noted.

The Hebrew Scriptures also speak of Israel's Exodus from Egypt, while Greek legends describe Danaus' no less perturbing flight from the same country. In both cases, the break with Egypt is full of ominous overtones. The fifty Danaids must murder the sons of Aegyptus on the night of their mass wedding. The Hebrews, to escape the tenth plague, had to slaughter a lamb and smear its blood on their door posts as a sign of recognition. As Yahve moved from house to house, smiting firstborns, he would bypass homes on whose doorposts the sacrificial blood had been smeared. 'Passover' (*Pesah*) was instituted to commemorate this act of recognition.[69]

It is difficult to be part of a group that has to pass such stringent ritual tests. The flight from Egypt is not a self-validating, divinely assisted escape from a wicked enemy, but an oppressive nightmare that cannot be shaken off— even in the waking state of historical distance. At the end of the day, the fear of Yahve remains stronger than the fear of any earthly ruler and the two combine to create a feeling of tragic anticipation that makes being Jewish such a challenging experience.

Egypt represents the power of confinement: the power of the god Set, Osiris' tormentor. Osiris— like Dionysus— is a god of renewal. His 'seed' is imprisoned by chtonic forces and its flowering into life is poetically rendered as an escape from the Underworld— or world of spirits.

The Jews' time in Egypt can be viewed as a period of gestation during which the 'chosen seed' is held. The actual flight from Egypt results in a long journey through the desert: a phase representing the seed's emergence into the Light. As the process advances, the body of the Hebrew nation acquires very special characteristics. It becomes formally divided into 13 parts (the Tribes), 12 of which are gathered in a square pattern around the Tabernacle in the Wilderness. The mapping into 12 produces active correspondences with the zodiac (just like the 12 Imams of *shi'ite* tradition) and the ritual wanderings complete the magical emergence of Israel, by which the macrocosm formally replicates itself onto a living microcosmic structure. With the eventual dismemberment of Israel, the seeds are further scattered among the nations.

The power that immobilizes and confines is the power of the primordial snake holding life forces hostage. In Greek myth, the serpent Python is Apollo's ritual enemy and its slaying consecrates the oracular site at Delphi. The Delphic oracle was consulted whenever the Greeks thought of establishing new centers— thus extending and renewing their legacy.

A similar pattern can be found in Hebrew tradition. Jacob, the 'founding father' *par excellence,* is said to have fought with a man for an entire night, and yet the stranger was unable to overcome him. At dawn the mysterious opponent wanted to leave, but Jacob would not let him go until he received his blessing. Blessings are bestowed by name and the man had to ask Jacob for his. Upon hearing Jacob's answer, the stranger told him that from now on, his name would be 'Israel' because he had fought with both god and man, and prevailed. The name 'Israel' means: 'he who struggles with God'.(**Genesis**, 24-28).

In **The Magic Flute** Tamino is running through a strange, deserted country as he is being pursued by a serpent. His state of mind— if it can be projected at all—must be almost identical to that of Siegmund, in Act I of Wagner's **Die Walküre**. Siegmund tries to outrun Hunding's *posse*; but, by accident, arrives at his pursuer's house. One danger is escaped, only to be replaced by an even greater one. To this is added the need to rescue a sexually attractive female held prisoner by the very power one has to confront.

Wagner's Hunding is 'the hounder'— the fiendish foe who persecutes and pursues unpityingly. The hounder is a harbinger of hermetic transformations in which death plays an important part. It would be disingenuous to assert that in such trials death is purely symbolic. Whoever fails may remain physically alive, but it hardly matters. What counts is that the journey toward the Light is over.

The symbolism of 'hounds' has already been explored in this series and it is perhaps time to point out that hounds and snakes are associated with the figure of Hecate: the goddess of roads that are either blocked, or open. Hecate belongs to the world of witchcraft and E.A. Wallis Budge relates a significant story in which it is claimed that the goddess Isis—acting as the Egyptian Hecate— created the snake by which the sun god Ra was immobilized:

"Isis placed a snake in the path which Ra traveled in his boat 'at the head of his mariners'. Ra had become old, and Isis wanted to become 'mistress of the earth, and a mighty goddess'. This she could do if she could get possession of Ra's secret and ineffable name. She took some of Ra's saliva, moistened dust with it, and fashioned a snake, which she laid in Ra's path. His fang struck Ra as he went by unawares, and the god suffered terribly from the poison. Isis promised to help Ra if he would deliver to her his secret name. He finally consented, and his name, which was also his heart, left his body and passed over to Isis. Ra was now as good as dead; but Isis with an incantation expelled the poison from his body and brought him back to life. Isis is here a mistress of witchcraft, who, it is said, esteems the spirits even above the gods: that is, she is the Egyptian Hecate."[70]

Hecate is a 'light-bringer' (*phosphoros*) and her art is clearly tied to the power of names. In Act I of **Die Walküre** the drama also revolves around names. The fugitive Siegmund does not know his as he enters Hunding's house. He will receive it from his sister Sieglinde— Hunding's wife— as she becomes his mistress. Siegmund is literally victorious-mouth: *Wehwalt* the *Wölfing*; the solar hero concealed under a wolf-skin as he journeys through life. The sword he consecrates and names in turn, while ritually acknowledging his own name, is the royal instrument of witchcraft, bequeathed directly by Wotan. It will be used by his son Siegfried to slay the dragon Fafner.

The naming patterns in **The Magic Flute** and **Die Walküre** are very similar. It is Pamina and Tamino in Mozart's opera, versus Siegmund and Sieglinde in Wagner's. In the first case, the common radical is '-*min*'; in the second it is '*sieg*-'.

In German mythology, the linden tree's wood, when made into a cradle, becomes a magic incubator for a child fated to perform great deeds.[71] *Sieg-mund* and *Sieg-linde*, who give birth to *Sieg-fried* (the slayer of the dragon Fafner), are not ordinary parents; but magic progenitors of an exceptional offspring. An analogous procedure, down to fire-breathing dragons, is found in Goethe's sequel to Mozart's **The Magic Flute**, written in 1795.

Here Tamino and Pamina likewise give birth to a child. The young boy is stolen by Monostatos and confined to a golden sarcophagus, sealed with the Queen of the Night's seal. The story culminates with the liberation of Genius— the golden child revealed in his true essence:

> Conceived during midnight
> in the lordliest bed,
> then lost to all sight
> into nights filled with dread.
> The pointed spears threaten,
> the vengeance is seething,
> the army din deafens
> with dragons fire-breathing.
> Yet all of these dangers
> are nothing to me. [72]

Siegfried and Genius belong to the same species of exceptional children born to magic parents with the help of witchcraft. Goethe's Masonic background gives the sequel a certain stamp of authority— although there are problems with his resolution. Since it hinges on his interpretation of Mozart's opera, chances are that the extrapolation follows an occult pattern Goethe was familiar with. But more about that in a later chapter.

It is somewhat surprising that two operas, as different as *The Magic Flute* and *Die Walküre*, should revolve around similarly constructed rituals— bringing together male and female characters with 'structured' names. The mystery is puzzling unless one assumes that Wagner, Mozart and Goethe all had access to the same sources.

Act I of *Die Walküre* takes places in Sieglinde's house. The first scene of *The Magic Flute* is placed in the domain of the Queen of the Night. Both represent Hecate's realm, where the path through the world of shadows begins. The complete journey is conditioned by the generative use of names, but the identity of the magic offspring is determined by Hecate. It is the result of a necromantic transfer, which, in *Die Walküre*, takes place at the point where Hunding slays Siegmund. Siegfried is destined to learn the language of the birds because he inherits these prophetic powers from his father's corpse. Wotan's reluctant sacrifice of Siegmund— his own son—creates the conditions necessary for the transfer, which is executed through the inheritance of the sword. The word necromancy comes from the Greek *nekros*, which means corpse, and *manteia*, which stands for its prophetic powers.

In the *Ring* Wotan's integrity is on trial and the fate of the gods is at stake. James Curl mentions that the blows, or tapping of mallets— that is hammering— represents Masonic work. In *Das Rheingold*, as Wotan and Loge descend down to Nibelheim, where gold is extracted, that is precisely what one hears. Wotan, the principal protagonist of the **Ring**, who has fathered both Siegmund and Sieglinde, is elsewhere identified by Wagner with the historical figure of Titus, the Roman Emperor responsible for the destruction of the Temple of Jerusalem. This odd piece of information comes from a conversation on **Parsifal**, which Wagner's wife Cosima relates in her diary (**Diary**, 19 February 1878):

"'Who is Titurel?', Wagner asks Cosima. She reflects. 'Wotan', says Wagner. 'After his renunciation of the world he is granted salvation, the greatest of possessions is entrusted to his care, and now he is guarding it like a mortal god'— A lovely thought!

Cosima says that Wotan's name ought to be reflected in the name Titurel, and Wagner replies, 'Titurel, the little Titus, Titus the symbol of royal standing and power, Wotan the God-King'."[73]

Wotan— the God-King— is the Egyptian *Deus Pharaonis!* **The Magic Flute** and the **Ring** thus coalesce in their agendas. Both are promoting a royalty built on magic. As the hermetist R.A. Schwaller de Lubicz points out:

"The royal principle on which ancient Egypt was founded has nothing in common with our usual concept of 'king'. [...] The reigning king is a symbol, a guise embodying the mythical and the mystical as well as the hermetic sense of a ray of original Light's corporification, the Horian Logos. Through its fall into Nature the 'creative Word' is imprisoned in earth by Set. As *Neter*, this 'fire in earth' is Ptah, the Greek Hephaestus. The king is animated by the Horian or Luciferian aspect of the fallen archangel. The temple ritual explains the royal fulfillment of the Horian light through the phases it must undergo on the way to its corporeal exaltation, 'the philosopher's stone', as it was called in medieval times. This is the King of divine origin, almighty in things of created Nature." [74]

Wotan's access to his full solar nature comes as a by-product of his renunciation of the world. But it is a Jewish character who helps him achieve that renunciation. Wotan's court-Jew is Loge, the God of Fire. He thoroughly corrupts the God-King by encouraging him in his worldly ambitions. Yet Loge is the only character in the *Ring* who never loses his integrity. Throughout highly unethical dealings on behalf of his master, personal motives never surface.

Fire is the vehicle of the sacrifice. Loge, Hephaestus and Ptah are incarnations of the Word (*logos*) uttered exclusively to 'burn the hearts of men'— to use Alexander Pushkin's poetic expression. They represent a lost unity that can only be recovered through fire. Wagner's assimilation of Wotan with the Roman emperor Titus implies that Wotan, who presides over the destruction of Valhalla in *Gotterdammerung*, is equivalent to Titus, who orders the destruction of the Temple of Jerusalem. The two actions are esoterically congruent. In *The Magic Flute*, a similar blow is aimed at the forces of the Queen of the Night. It is over their ashes that Sarastro's Temple is to be turned over to the dual priesthood of Pamina and Tamino.

It was, of course, during Mozart's time that Wagner's hated Jewish bankers first appeared as a real force. They emerged as the 'power behind the throne'— like Loge— and their sudden rise to prominence has never been successfully explained. Niall Ferguson, who studied the subject in relation to the Rothschilds, comes up with the following assessment:

"Between 1754 and 1778 the Bethmanns floated loans totaling nearly 2 million gulden, and no fewer than fifty-four separate loans totaling nearly 30 million gulden in the following five years. Other Frankfurt bankers became involved in the same kind of business, notably Jakob Friedrich Gontard. Neither Bethmann nor Gontard was Jewish. Yet there is no question that, by the later eighteenth- century, it was Jews who had come to be seen as the most enterprising operators when it came to money-changing and all kinds of lending. After more than a century of scholarly reflection on the subject, it is still hard to say quite why this was." [75]

Money is the operative instrument of corruption. In the modern world it fulfills the same function as fire. Wotan and Loge's journey to Nibelheim, where gold is produced, is indeed Masonic work. It is the critical exposure to what must be renounced:

"To become a Freemason, one must start by giving up one's metals. Applied in all the Lodges, this rule seems to go back to a prodigious antiquity. In a Babylonian poem, which was already considered ancient five thousand years ago, the goddess Ishtar is depicted as compelled to deposit all of her jewelry in order to cross the seven thresholds of the infernal world and appear naked in front of her sister, the fiendish queen of the world of the dead.[...] Metal shines, it radiates attractively and lends itself to exchange, whence its buying power which stretches all the way to our conscience." [76]

Early Jewish bankers were not trying for world domination, as conspiracy theorists like to suggest. What counted most for them was Jewish emancipation. In Berlin, in 1778, court banker Isaak Daniel Itzig (1750-1806) founded a 'Jewish Free School' together with his brother-in-law David Friedländer (1750-1834). They were actually the first teachers there.[77] Their driving ideal was a complete integration of all Jews into German society. Their up-front work was paralleled by a less visible, but no less important involvement in organizations seeking to speed up the process. Most of these efforts were centered on Moses Mendelssohn's conception of the modern Jew and an important litmus test was acceptance into Masonic Lodges— since they supposedly taught tolerance and ascribed to progressive ideals:

"The generation growing in the shadow of Mendelssohn accepted his ideal of the removal of all barriers separating Jews from Christians, but did not inherit his virtues of patience and moderation. His disciples and followers desired to attain in practice what they had been taught to believe in, and sought to hasten the process of absorption into the cells of their social environment— and here the Masonic cells were held to be of basic importance.[...] Three or four such attempts took place around the end of Mendelssohn's lifetime (1786), the period of the enactment of the first laws aimed at the removal of civil disabilities from Jews and of the first agitation for the integration of Jews into the general society. The initial attempt led to the flaring up of the first controversy over the acceptance of Jews in Masonic Lodges." [78]

The earliest Masonic order created specifically for the purpose of accepting both Jews and Christians was the Order of the Asiatic Brethren (*Die Brüder St. Johannes des Evangelisten aus Asien in Europa*), founded in Vienna in 1780-81.[79] Several of Mozart's close associates joined that order and an entry in Kronauer's Masonic album suggests that Mozart may have been among them.

Mozart was close to Vienna's most prominent Jewish family, but that relationship has never been satisfactorily documented. He may have enjoyed the atmosphere of international intrigue surrounding these unusual Jews. Their uncertain allegiance in the battle of alliances pitting Berlin against Vienna— that is Protestant Germany against Catholic Austria— was as confusing as the Jesuit position at that mystifying moment in history.

Mozart's extreme fascination with corruption extended primarily to the power exerted by women. The symbolic transmutation of this power into fantastic male characters, like Don Giovanni or Don Alfonso, is, at a certain level, no different from Wagner's compulsive interest in Jews and money. Behind these intensely felt obsessions lies a genuine inquiry into the nature of 'fire' as a powerful erotic agent:

"We must [...] ask ourselves again about the relationship between Eros and magic, namely: where does Eros end, where does magic begin? The answer seems very simple: at the very moment Eros is made manifest, so is magic also. That is why erotic magic, at bottom, represents the starting point of all magic. We still have to go deeper into the definition of magic as a *spiritual manipulation*. In any case it is a question of a transitive assumption making it possible to say that every other spiritual manipulation is at the same time a magical one." [80]

An operatic composer is a manipulator of public passions. By subtly conniving with erotic forces, Mozart becomes their hidden accomplice. Wagner is quite open in his confrontations. Where Mozart skillfully grapples with the debilitating aspects of seduction, a revolted Wagner equates 'seduction' with the power of money 'before which all our doings and our dealings lose their force'.[81]

"Wagner relied on the stereotype already fabricated by his anti-Semitic predecessors such as Bruno Bauer and Karl Marx. The word *Jew* used in the singular as a representative of the whole of Jewry was an abstraction employed by Bauer and Marx, who projected the qualities supposedly characterizing the Jews onto a suprapersonal reification. [...] The notion of an art-commodity-exchange follows the Marxist critique of Judaism. Marx said, 'The bill of exchange is the actual god of the Jew'."[82]

In *The Magic Flute* seduction works both ways. The bothersome Noachite seeking entry to the Temple is as much on trial as the Temple's priesthood. How does one attract— or even seduce—from within, without at the same time being corrupted by outsiders?

In the dramatic rendition of this dilemma Mozart and Wagner faced the basic problem of art:

"Ah yes: art! How right the Buddha was when he called it the surest way to miss the path of salvation! It was in a long stormy letter written to Mathilde Wesendonck from Venice in 1858 that Wagner expounded this to his friend, after telling her of his plans for a Buddhist drama to be called *Die Sieger* [The Victors].

'Buddhist drama': there's the rub, for this is nothing less than a contradiction in terms— as he realized when he faced the problem of turning a man who is perfectly liberated and released from all passion— the Buddha himself— into suitable material for dramatic (and more specifically, musical) representation. That which is pure, holy, pacified through knowledge is artistically defunct: sanctity and drama are quite clearly incompatible. So it was a happy chance that Sakyamuni Buddha (according to the sources) was confronted with one last problem, entangled in one last conflict: he has to wrestle with the difficult decision whether to admit the chandala girl Savitri to the holy order, contrary to his earlier principles. Here— thank heavens— he becomes a possible subject for art. Wagner is delighted— but in the same instant his conscience is burdened by the guilty realization of art's dependence on life, and of its power to lead men astray." [83]

2

MOZART AND THE ENLIGHTENMENT

Young Mozart was billed as a child prodigy and the Enlightenment turned him into a cultural icon. He was the individual of exceptional ability who could effortlessly uphold the highest creative and moral standards. To this symbol of genius would be opposed the sorry figure of the idle aristocrat: privileged by birth, but unproductive in every other respect. Wolfgang Amadeus was forcefully cast into this mold. His father, Leopold, took him on travels all across Europe to take advantage of expanding opportunities ushered in by the Enlightenment.

One is thus hardly surprised to see him being handled by Baron Melchior Grimm during his first stay in Paris (1763-64). Grimm was an influential propagandist of the French Enlightenment and Leopold Mozart referred to him as 'our best friend, M. Grimm'.[1]

"Grimm was an important figure in literary circles; he was a friend of Diderot, Voltaire and Rousseau, and secretary to the Duke or Orleans, founder of the first Masonic Lodge in Paris."[2]

Whether he liked it or not, Mozart had become part of a larger experiment that extended far beyond his, or his fathers, musical ambitions. It would take a long time for him to recover from this early typecasting and David Schroeder suggests that the Mozarts were more than willing participants in the Enlightenment's high-powered game of image creation:

"Among their own friends, acquaintances and correspondents were three of the great *épistoliers* (or *épistlières*) of the century: Baron Melchior Grimm, Mme Louise d'Épinay and Christian Fürchtegott Gellert [...] The list quickly multiplies when one takes into account that Grimm and d'Épinay counted all the great *philosophes*, including Voltaire, Diderot, Rousseau, d'Alembert, Galliani and Holbach, as their colleagues on the **Correspondence littéraire**, or that Gellert, the leading epistolary stylist in Germany, had himself learned from Gottsched, had read numerous of the great English writers, and taught no less a luminary than Goethe." [3]

A talent of Mozart's caliber had to be nursed with special care and that was Leopold's task. Properly managed along the principles outlined by the philosophers, Mozart's talent could be used to influence the public at large. The Encyclopedists, Diderot and d'Alembert in particular, had strong opinions about the theater and expressed their normative views during the 1750s. They were extremely influential and displayed an intuitive grasp of the relationship between the theater, music, politics and a subtle 'magic' by which public opinion was effectively swayed.

During this pre-revolutionary period, political life, with its leading figures seen as actors, was evolving toward a form of public theater, where critics were becoming increasingly influential. Early adopters of authoritative opinion and its dissemination— like Grimm— created insightful newsletters designed to propagate the Enlightenment's point of view to selected and often distant readers. The main objective was to reach subscribers with real political clout.

Diderot's call for a serious theater came in 1757. His *Entretiens sur 'Le Fils Naturel'* suggested that plays be recast as dramatic exercises in moral instruction. The group with which he worked, the *Encyclopédie*, was composed of materialist philosophers who had no use for organized religion and its outdated conceptions of morality— even when their background suggested the opposite. That was certainly true of the Abbé Claude Yvon, usually described as the 'metaphysician' of Diderot's *Encyclopédie* (1751-1775).[4]

"Yvon had been a close associate of Diderot and he wrote some of the most important articles in the famous *Encyclopédie*. His article on the soul was far too generous in recapitulating the arguments put forth by materialists against its existence. Already under suspicion because of his association with Diderot and with philosophical heresy, Yvon and his close friend the abbé de Prades were forced to flee Paris in 1752 under fear of arrest. De Prades had submitted a blatantly materialist thesis to the Sorbonne, and it had been carelessly passed. When the authorities discovered they had been made to look foolish, the Parlement of Paris issued a warrant for his arrest. In the company of de Prades, Yvon made his way first to Amsterdam. Like so many itinerant men of the eighteenth-century, he then not simply joined but actually helped found a new Masonic lodge, *Concordia vincit Animos*." [5]

Freemasonry was not catering exclusively to rationalists and materialists. It also harbored those willing to speculate along more mystical or occult lines— like the Rosicrucians. Rosicrucianism originated in Regensburg during the 1750s[6] and propagated doctrines that were seemingly at odds with those of the Enlightenment. With its mix of esoteric Christianity and alchemical baggage, the Rosicrucian branch was often categorized as a bastion of superstition. Nevertheless, it was part of the larger Masonic family and served to attract people who would have never joined a purely materialistic order.

The royalty, to whom Grimm's **Correspondence littéraire** was addressed, was not entirely sold on Freemasonry. Catherine the Great, for instance, protected early Russian Masons, but secretly feared their influence. She wanted to uproot the primitive element in Russian culture and tried to initiate a major shift in the direction of rationality.

What irritated her most was the seemingly inconsistent stance of the *philosophes* with respect to paranormal subjects. As rationalists, they should have been squarely on the side of material realities— but they were not. The same fuzziness could be found in Freemasonry, which harbored completely contradictory tendencies.

"Shamanism represented to Catherine the Great a composite of all the dark, obscurantist forces conspiring against the advance of reason that the Enlightenment so warmly encouraged and so loyally supported. Catherine, who was determined to change the image of her empire once and for all from irrationally Asiatic, or female, to rationally European, or male, associated the purveyors of shamanic beliefs and their followers with drug addicts, homosexuals, convulsionaries, religious enthusiasts, and political fanatics— that is dissidents or assassins.[...] Catherine applied the tactics of revisionism and wrote opposing whatever connected her realm with shamanism. Her three-hundred-page **Antidote** refuted the Abbé Jean Chappe d'Auteroche's (1722-1769) **Voyage en Sibérie** (1761), which, among other things, damned Russia as a nation confounded by its shamans.[...] She even criticized the Encyclopedists for including in their work articles on [...] paranormal subjects, which she considered part of the dangerous contraband of the current passing fashion. Especially troubling was the article 'Théosophes', which, she thought, revealed for public consumption matters that would best have been left concealed. It reported on people who viewed human reason as pitiably limited rather than as supreme." [7]

Diderot's involvement with Catherine lasted from the early 1760s until his death in 1784, at which time she became the rightful owner of all his books and manuscripts. French intellectuals were particularly excited about her and Voltaire (1694-1778) exclaimed once: "What times we live in! France persecutes the *philosophes*, and the Scythians show them favor!" [8]

But Catherine had her own agenda and ended up blaming the Encyclopedists for spreading subversive ideas. At one point she wrote Grimm, her man in Paris: "Acquire for me all the works of Diderot. Of course they will not get out of my hands and will not harm anyone. Send them together with the library." [9]

Diderot was for a multifaceted approach to life's complexities. The fluidity of his thinking reflects the experimental nature of his philosophy, influenced in great part by Francis Bacon and more distantly by Spinoza, Giordano Bruno, Leibniz and Wolff. [10] In his eyes, the ultimate test of any phenomenon was its social relevance.

When Wolfgang Amadeus Mozart— the child prodigy— arrived on the Parisian scene, his existence had already been foretold by the philosophers. It was only a matter of anointing him as one of the 'events' awaited by the Enlightenment.

"Friedrich Melchior Grimm was a proponent of everything Mozart stood for. Grimm reported this in his **Correspondence littéraire**, a kind of journal in which he transmitted the latest cultural news from Paris to his subscribers in German lands and the Russia ruled by the notorious Catherine the Great. Again and again, he wrote that the Parisians were astonished by the young Mozart's musical gifts. To describe the phenomenon that was Mozart, he used words expressing the idea of genius, talent, prodigy, all precisely in the same way the theorists had used them. [...] Grimm [...] thought Mozart's musical improvisation demonstrated genuine inspiration and 'a mass of enchanting ideas, which moreover he knows how to connect with taste and without confusion'." [11]

Mozart was a working prototype for future generations of musicians and composers. In the meantime, here was proof that the Orphic model actually worked; that someone could produce charming music at will, the way normal people conversed. Mozart's early handlers wasted no time giving him subjects dear to their heart: "the Mozarts were introduced into Masonic circles by Dr. Mesmer, in whose garden the twelve-year-old Wolfgang's *Singspiel*, **Bastien and Bastienne**, based on a text by Jean-Jacques Rousseau (**Le devin du village**) was first performed." [12]

Dr. Anton Mesmer, the hypnotist, whose art is immortalized in the Act I finale of **Cosi fan tutte**, was a Rosicrucian. On the surface this appears to negate the influence of the secular and rational wing of the Enlightenment, but that would be too simple. Throughout his life, Mozart was associated with both Illuminists and Rosicrucians. Count Dietrichstein, one of Mozart's most important patrons, was a known Rosicrucian. So was Count Küfstein, who appears on Mozart's subscription list. "A further member of Küfstein's former Chapter of Clermont Lodge was Count Franz Joseph Thun, husband of Mozart's beloved Countess Wilhelmine Thun, and son of the dedicatee of Mozart's 'Linz' Symphony, Count Johann Joseph Thun, himself Grandmaster of the Bohemian Rosenkreuzer." [13]

Whether the modern Rosicrucians were conscious of it or not, their predecessors, the original Rosicrucians, had created the right conditions for the emergence of universalist movements. Their message emerged from the occult underground of Venice and Prague, near the end of Rudolf II of Habsburg's (1576-1612) reign:

"Emperor Rudolf II dealt with the external world— the rebellions, the petitions and demands which came pressing in on him from all sides— by shutting himself up in his castle at Prague and refusing to hear them mentioned. He was a man of sensibility, deeply interested in art and learning. The process of decomposition had gone so far and so deep in Europe that it very likely occurred to him that all this frenzied activity within the labyrinth in whose exitless mazes God and man seemed to have shut one another up for good was merely childish.[...] Rudolf was twenty-four when he came to Prague and found in it the landscape of his soul. A dreamer by nature, he created there for himself an art world full of mysteries as an antidote to humdrum reality. [...] Where other powers sent out agents to glean political and military intelligence, Rudolf was concerned only with tracking down great works of art. [...] In 1601 strong men actually carried Dürer's *Feast of the Rose Garlands* slung from poles all the way from Venice over the Alps to Prague, to avoid damaging the picture. [...] The emperor himself enjoyed working with his hands, for example as a stonecutter.[...] He looked to the works of art and nature to provide the meaning he could no longer find in churches or in the world of power. [...] In his flight from death and madness (though madness claimed him in the end), Rudolf immersed himself in the natural sciences, in particular the study of the stars." [14]

Under Rudolf, Prague became a center of both esoteric and scientific studies. Tycho Brahae and Johannes Kepler were the leading lights in the field of mathematics and astronomy; Michael Maier and Oswald Croll worked as physicians and alchemists; the Englishmen John Dee and Edward Kelley agitated the occult underground; Giordano Bruno published a book on magic. Many others worked alongside, corresponding with anyone of importance not physically located in Prague. 'Feminism'— of the kind found in the cult of Isis— was most likely part of this secret tradition of roses, philosophy and art.

Dürer's altarpiece of 1506, the *Feast of the Rose Gardlands*, which elicited such unusual precautions during its transportation, shows the emperor and the pope kneeling before an enthroned Virgin distributing rose garlands. At once a message and a program— both conveniently synthesized in a work of art. The political overtones of the message are hardly subtle and the

1. Dürer's Feast of the Rose Garlands

scene implies that it takes a feminine figure of power to work this difficult magic. This at a time when witches were actively hunted.

Dürer's works were commissioned by Maximilian I, whose views on the house of Habsburg were symbolically reflected in the paintings he ordered. As Robert Evans points out:

"In Maximilian's commissions to his beloved circle of Humanist artists [...] are reflected all the dignity and power of the house: the prophecies, the ancestors, the universalist role and the territorial claims, Caesarism and solidarity against the Turk, the Orders of St. George and the Golden Fleece. They are a precise prefiguration of the Rudolfine symbolism, though without some of the latter's intellectual underpinnings." [15]

In Maximilian's commissions, the symbolic dimension of imperial rule was still tied to images produced specifically to sustain its traditional conception. Maximilian's 'humanists' were working magicians and that is why Rudolf was so passionate about Dürer's canvases:

"His reasons for valuing them were no doubt various: emulation of Maximilian I must have played its part together with the Emperor's sympathy for the symbolism in Dürer's work, not only in its service to the mystique, but also through its wider occult and magical significance." [16]

Rudolf's anticlerical attitude and his desire to see the values of the state embodied in his person have been compared to Joseph II's ruling principles. The salient features of this form of government include a grassroots Catholicism (free from Papal control), an aristocratic hierarchy and natural resistance to foreign domination. Joseph II's progressive agenda was set by an elitist Freemasonry empowered by the emperor.

Although Giordano Bruno spent only six months at Rudolf''s court, in 1588, he dedicated his ***Articuli adversus mathematicos***— published in Prague— to the emperor. The title, 'Against mathematicians', really meant against the 'Aristotelians'.

"[Bruno's] message in its application to the times in which he lived is nowhere more clearly set out than in his dedication to

Rudolph II. Here are all his usual themes, the vicissitudes of light and darkness, the 'Mercuries descending from heaven' who, as we know from this familiar phrase in other contexts, destroyed the religion of the Egyptians, the natural religion which he himself follows and which does not break the *ius gentium* and the universal law of love as the fanatical sectaries do, the 'Aristotelians' who want to impose their prejudices on others."[17]

It was during the Wittenberg period, just before his stay in Prague, that Bruno wrote his *Lampas triginta statuarum* in which he discusses practical aspects of 'linking' with demons through interior images constructed on talismanic principles.[18] His conception of talismanic magic was completely conditioned by earlier interpretations of Egyptian ritual:

"These inner 'statues' are a transference into inner imagery of those statues which formed so essential a part of the religion of the Egyptians, as described in the *Asclepius*, which they knew how to animate by introducing demons into them. As we know from *De Magia*, Bruno believed that the most important and powerful of all ways of 'linking' with demons was through the imagination." [19]

Lampas triginta statuarum was preceded by earlier works on the same subject, dealing with other types of magic. Manipulation of the masses— as a black art— was considered in *De vinculis in genere*, where the science of bonds and attachments is expounded on in some detail.

It is a science based on transference and the insertion of operative imagery into the dreaming consciousness of ordinary individuals. Ficino had already observed that "the whole power of Magic is founded on Eros" (*Amore*, VI, 10)[20] and Bruno was ready to look at practical applications.

"*De vinculis in genere* ('Of Bonds in general') [...] is one of those little-known works whose importance in the history of ideas far outstrips that of more famous ones. [...] Without being aware of it, the brain trusts that dominate the world have been inspired by it, have put Bruno's own ideas to practical use. A continuity surely might exist, for Bruno seems to have exerted a certain influence on the ideological movement at the beginning of the seventeenth century, the Rosicrucian movement, which had great repercussions. [...] In the nineteenth century, of course, we find ideologues like Karl Marx and Frederick Engels who believe that religion is the 'opium of the people'. Therein they only repeat Bruno's statement in **De vinculis**, where religion is seen merely as a powerful tool for manipulating the masses. But while Marx and Engels have humanitarian and utopian ideals, Bruno shows little concern for safeguarding human dignity; the only right he envisages belongs neither to God, nor to man but to the *manipulator* himself." [21]

The link between Bruno and the next generation of manipulators is even reflected in the name the Encyclopedists were given. They were referred to as the '*philosophes*' and the implied connection to Bruno is certainly interesting:

"In Mocegino's delation to the Inquisition against Bruno," says Frances Yates, "he reports him as having said that he had intended to found a new sect under the name of philosophy. Other informers made the same insinuation, adding that Bruno had said that the sect was called the 'Giordanisti' and appealed particularly to the Lutherans in Germany. It has occurred to me to wonder whether these rumored 'Giordanisti' could have any connection with the unsolved mystery of the origin of the Rosicrucians who are first heard of in Germany in the early seventeenth century, in Lutheran circles." [22]

The first part of the Rosicrucian manifesto published at Cassel in 1614 is just a translation into German of chapter 77 of Traiano Boccalini's **Ragguagli di Parnaso**, which came out in Venice, in 1612-1613. The author was a friend of Galileo and belonged to a liberal group based in the Venice-Padua area. [23] We will see later that the Venice-Padua axis played an important role in the development of Egyptian Masonry, as it began to flourish during the second half of the 18th century.

The Rosicrucian phenomenon cannot be divorced from alchemical speculation. Venice was evidently in contact with Greek or Arab sources, who supplied the concept of 'orientation', so critical to a proper staging of the *mundus imaginalis* referred to in **De Magia**. The corresponding angelology, or demonology, cannot be taught outside of a tradition where knowledge of the awakened state exists and is acquired through initiation.

A historically accurate picture of its transmission to the Rosicrucian 'invisible order' is beyond the scope of this quick aside, but there are enough parallels between the Rosicrucian description of the order's purpose and Iranian statements about the tradition from which such notions issue:

"Thus, on the one hand, the angel Sraosha [the priest-angel of initiation (Pehlevi *Srosh*, Persian *Sorush*), equivalent to the angel Gabriel] watches over the sleeping world; he is the guardian angel and the head of a brotherhood of migrants who 'keep watch' on the world and for the world; they are described by a term referring to their holy poverty, the Avestan term *drigu* (Pehlevi *drigosh*, Pazend *daryosh*), the equivalent of which in modern Persian is *darwish*, 'dervish', the name by which all Iranian Sufis are still referred to today: the 'poor in spirit'. On the other hand this brotherhood represents a group which is invisible to ordinary men and which exemplifies the very image of the cosmos unfolded, resting like a tent on its axis and at its peak Sraosha's own adobe, the cosmic North 'secreting its own light'. The symbols of Taoism, Zoroastrianism, and Sufism are all in accord with this same representation." [24]

The power exerted by this group comes from its ability to relate to the cosmic North, recreated within the *mundus imaginalis* for the purpose of finding the real Light. Natural light does not 'orient' our existence. Meaning comes from the cosmic *pole*, toward which each journey is oriented:

"It would take a whole book to bring together all the evidence showing the significance of the Orient as supra-sensory Orient, Orient-origin, Orient that consequently has to be looked for in the heights, on the vertical axis because it is identified with the pole, the cosmic North, as being a threshold of the worlds beyond. This *orientation* was already given to the Orphic *mystes*. We find it in the poem of Parmenides where the poet undertakes a journey toward the Orient. [...] the great Iranian Sufi master, 'Ali-e Hamadani, in a treatise on dreams, speaks of the *Orient* which is the very ipseity of the world of Mystery, that is to say of the supra-sensory world [...] Elsewhere he speaks of this same Orient as the ipseity of the invisible world which is the source of the emanation of being, *descending* to the *Occident* of the world of bodies [...] the 'Orientals' are those who, coming from above, return there after passing through initiation." [25]

The Enlightenment was extending the hermetic laboratory. The *philosophes* were not so much interested in convincing people through rational arguments as they were in indoctrinating them through the growing power of the printing press. The instrument they needed had sufficiently matured. Technology could now be used to create and manipulate a collective *mundus imaginalis,* with an 'orientation' to be provided by the philosophers.

High publicity causes were used to inflame public passions and the philosophers kept the fires burning by fanning them with well organized campaigns. The war against social abuse was just a fight for the moral high ground from which the entire political edifice could be controlled.

In their role as arbitrators and reporters of public opinion, the philosophers decided what was acceptable and what was not. Their weapon of choice was exposition. Only through technology could a minority of intellectuals hope to challenge long established institutions. Behavior at court and the superstitions propagated by the Church were at last reviewable in public.

These were heady days for science and its worshippers. But its emergence owed more to the raw pursuit of power than the mere love of reason, as Nietzsche cleverly observed.

"Do you believe then that the sciences would have arisen and grown up if the sorcerers, alchemists, astrologers and witches had not been their forerunners; those who, with their promisings and foreshadowings had first to create a thirst, a hunger and a taste for *hidden and forbidden* powers?" [*Prelude to Science* (***The Joyful Wisdom***, 233-34)][26]

Mozart's time was a time of transition during which science overran magic based on effectiveness. The discourse on superstition was all about repeatable results and the need to fulfill the Promethean promise.

But science's biggest shortcoming was its overemphasis on material things. It had no way of opening windows onto the world of meaning. Meaning still had to be created, but an answer to that potential roadblock was soon discovered. Through a systematic manipulation of material circumstances an individual's self-image could also be controlled. It was just a matter of producing a new bourgeoisie that responded well to material impulses. Any leftover metaphysical cravings could be handled by creating additional fantasies.

"Behind Nietzsche's apparent diachrony [...] lurks a cynical and sinister synchrony, according to which he would attack science's privilege by wondering what it is that it is a prelude to, locating rather the 'will to power' as the primordial factor, for which science is simply the temporarily dominant expression, because, whatever its liberal veneer, it is a crueler, more savage, deadly and unscrupulous form than magic." [27]

In magic, the binding element has always been erotic and it

is therefore not surprising that sexual images were used to link a subject with another subject. "The way Magic works," says Marsilio Ficino (***Amore***, VI, 10)[28], "is by bringing things together through their inherent similarity."

When a spirit recognizes a kindred spirit, the bonding occurs. In the artificial world created by technology, only one side of the attraction is real. The other is faked entirely. The subject to subject relationship is turned into a subject to object dependency.

The Encyclopedists were the forerunners of today's manipulators. They focused on information, not knowledge. The types of communication they favored, complete with highly targeted mailing lists, were similar in concept— if not in scope— to tools of indoctrination we are all familiar with. Grimm's ***Correspondence littéraire*** was aimed at an influential elite:

"The ***Correspondence***, a periodical circulated in manuscript, was produced for the rulers of a number of German states to enable them to keep abreast of the latest social, intellectual and cultural developments in Paris, and in theory was only available to crowned heads. 'I made it a rule some time ago to give this correspondence to Princes only', Grimm was to declare in 1766 [...], and he allowed few exceptions to his rule (Catherine the Great of Russia, Leopold of Tuscany and the Queen of Sweden, to whom the ***Correspondence*** was also circulated, were all originally of German birth). The subscription lists for the years 1763-6 accordingly contain few uncrowned names: M.and Mme Necker (Necker was a fellow Alsatian, and subsequently to be the king of France's Minister); Grimm's colleagues Helvétius and Diderot (who as an occasional contributor got his copies free); Horace Walpole; the Marquis of Tavistock (who was probably a great deal more powerful, and certainly richer, than many petty German princes). Among these eminent names one finds that of 'Mozart, maître de chapelle'. Although not even dignified with the 'M.' given to other commoners, and although he subscribed only to a print to raise funds for the Calas campaign, the presence of Kapellmeister Leopold Mozart's name on this list indicates that Leopold must have received a certain degree of acceptance within the advanced circle of the *philosophes* in Paris, an indication that was to be borne out on Wolfgang's later visit to Paris in 1777."[29]

There is a great deal of overlap between the philosophies expounded by the Paris group and those endorsed by Mozart's later Masonic associates, such as Gemmingen. Mozart's relationship with his father, as portrayed in their official correspondence, is almost a blueprint for what the Encyclopedists had in mind. The foundation of authority in bourgeois society rests on family values:

"During the course of the eighteenth-century, family virtues became sacrosanct. The 'filial piety' of Hercules' son Hylas inspired Handel to one of his finest choruses in the oratorio **Hercules**, and filial piety became one of the catch phrases of the age, the title of numerous sentimental dramas. [,,,] To complement the frequent portrayal of filial loyalty, the Enlightenment promoted numerous images of the good and loving father, such as Diderot's **Le père de famille**, and Gemmingen's Diderot-inspired **Der deutsche Hausvater**, written the same year as **Idomeneo**." [30]

Leopold and young Wolfgang Mozart's trip to Paris was an advertising tour for family values. Under the loving guidance of his father, the son rises to the highest levels of achievement through self-sacrifice. In artistic circles this implied that the theater had moral standing— in perfect accordance with Aristotelian principles.

This was Hans Christian Gottshed's view of the theater. Considered the most important reformer of the German theater, he paved the way for three National Theaters to be founded in Hamburg, Mannheim and Vienna:

"Behind the Hamburg project was Lessing [author of **Nathan** *the Wise* and *Masonic Dialogues*, member of the 'Three Roses' Lodge in Hamburg, and Moses Mendelssohn's best friend], who as *Dramaturg* at the Hamburg Theater elaborated his programme for a moral German theater in the influential *Hamburgische Dramaturgie* of 1767-8. For the National Theater in Mannheim Mozart's friend, colleague and later Masonic Lodge-master Otto von Gemmingen wrote his *Mannheimer Dramaturgie* of 1779, in which he urged that the theater be taken seriously as a 'moral institution'." [31]

The theater was a convenient instrument for mass dissemination and bourgeois propaganda. There were, of course, others. The Calas affair, which prompted Leopold Mozart to action, was a *cause célèbre* of the 1760s, which showcased 'public opinion' as an effective moral weight. People did not have to confine their excitement to the theater. They could also sit as judges and critics in the theater of life. The Enlightenment kept them informed on current events and their developing opinions were voiced by the best minds of the age.

Voltaire's vocal and ultimately successful support of the Calas family demonstrates that "opinion governs the world and in the end the philosophers govern men's opinions." [32]

The Calas case represented a shocking miscarriage of justice. The family lived in Toulouse, where tensions between Protestants and Catholics ran high. They were Protestant shopkeepers and one of their sons, Louis, had converted to Catholicism, while another, Marc-Antoine, was subject to fits of severe depression. On 13 October 1761, while they were having dinner in their apartment, Marc-Antoine abruptly left the room. The family later claimed that they had found his body downstairs on the shop floor. He had died of strangulation and a rope, as well as a wooden rod, were scattered around the corpse.

It is believed that Marc-Antoine had either hanged himself, or that he was the victim of a passing thief. In any case the Calas family handled the subsequent interrogation rather poorly. In the light of Louis' recent religious conversion and influenced by furious anti-Protestant prejudice, the judges concluded that Jean Calas had killed his own son to prevent him from converting to Catholicism.

"Jean Calas, who steadfastly protested his innocence under torture, was found guilty by eight votes against five and broken on the wheel in Toulouse on 10 March 1762. As if in recognition of their own doubts about the matter, the judges then proceeded merely to banish one of Calas's sons and to acquit the other family members." [33]

Voltaire stated unequivocally that the trial concerned the human race and represented a benchmark in the fight between reason and blind popular prejudice. This should be kept in mind as some of Voltaire's other pronouncements are considered in a later chapter.

There is a complex relationship between the world of the theater (to which Mozart belonged), Freemasonry (to which he also belonged) and the moralistic tendencies of the Enlightenment (which he ignored). One would like to believe that the theater, as a sphere of influence, was only marginally relevant; but that was not the case. Goethe's **Wilhelm Meister**, whose action is set in the mid-1700s, shows that the desire to become an actor, to seek fulfillment in the mythical and mystical world of the stage, was particularly important.

The freedom to assume different identities and to act out powerful inner drives, has always been a prerequisite for Masonic mastery. That freedom appeared dangerous to a number of eighteenth-century philosophers. It was compared to freedom at court, which fueled all kinds of perversions. The actor— much like the aristocrat— was a false person: a morally bankrupt individual who pretended to be what he was not.

"Rousseau wrote his **Letter to M. d'Alembert on the Theater** in response to d'Alembert's article 'Geneva' in the

Encyclopédie, which, while praising the enlightened religious tolerance of the Genevans, deplored the city's puritanical ban on theatrical entertainment. The article prompted Rousseau to spring to the defense of his native city, producing the extended missive that marked his decisive break with the mainstream Enlightenment represented by the *Encyclopédie*. Beyond d'Alembert, Rousseau's polemic was aimed at Voltaire, whose lifelong passion for the theater revealed his profound cultural kinship with the literate— in Rousseau's view, corrupt— French upper classes. [...] 'What is the talent of the actor? It is the art of counterfeiting himself, of putting on another character than his own, of appearing different than he is, of becoming passionate in cold blood [...] What is the profession of the actor? It is a trade in which he performs for money, submits himself to the disgrace and the affronts that others buy the right to give him, and puts his person publicly on sale'." [34]

The Letter to M. d'Alembert was written in 1758— a year after Diderot's *Entretiens sur 'Le Fils Naturel'*. Soon thereafter Leopold Mozart could be found selling the talents of his son. Rousseau was farsighted in that Mozart's music-making followed most of the practices he had condemned. It was highly confrontational and consisted of demonstrating his prowess at the expense of others.

In 1762, during an early visit to Vienna, Mozart performed at court and accounts given by those present help establish many of these disturbing flaws:

"Anecdotes of the visit to Schönbrunn confirm that the [Mozart] children put on a diverting entertainment: one of the ladies of the court assured the biographer Franz Niemetschek that both children made 'a very great impression', recalling that people could hardly believe their ears and eyes at the performance'. It was said that the emperor teased the little 'magician', as he was dubbed: 'It is no great art to play with all your fingers; but if you could play with only one finger and on a covered keyboard, that would be something worthy of admiration'. Naturally, Mozart was not fazed by this suggestion, which could not have been altogether unexpected, for he had brought along a bagful of keyboard tricks from Salzburg. He commenced 'to play with one finger only, as precisely as possible; and then he permitted the clavier keyboard to be covered and performed with marvelous dexterity, as though he had long been practicing this feat'. Mozart also charmed the assembly by insisting that court composer Georg Christoph Wagenseil be sent for: 'Is Herr Wagenseil not here? It was understood that he would be here'. The emperor obligingly fetched Wagenseil to take his place beside Mozart at the clavier, and the boy said to him: 'I am going to play one your concertos and you must turn the pages for me'. The court showed its appreciation not only by its applause but in the manner that was most welcome— paying the Mozarts 100 ducats for providing so unusual an amusement." [35]

Consumers and providers of this sort of entertainment really deserve each other. Since the entire edifice of modern music rests on similar values, it is not surprising that young Mozart has grown into one of its greatest cult figures. The message is repeated and underscored in Peter Schaffer's contemporary **Amadeus**, where the composer happily demonstrates Salieri's ineptness in front of the emperor. As he brilliantly improvises on one of Salieri's supposedly dull numbers, our instinct for the jugular is triggered. Mozart is a winner, Salieri a loser.

At the core of much virtuosity and brilliance lies an uncanny ability to imitate. Shared by musicians and stage actors, this skill is seldom developed through gradual study. In most cases it is present from the start and will flourish only if exercised on a continuous basis. Childhood seems to be the optimal time for the acquisition of the basic motor skills. The extent to which an activity is engaged in on a continuous basis favors its unusual, almost pathological development— assuming, of course, that the basic talent is there.

Mozart's concertizing on the London scene, during the same general period, illustrates the point. The demons of brilliant falsification offer many tempting shortcuts:

"In London, Daines Barrington was as impressed by Mozart's ability to improvise 'vocal works in various affects, such as Song of Love, Song of Anger, Song of Rage', as by his skill at reading a five-part score at sight: 'nothing could exceed the masterly manner in which he sung'. The eminent music historian Charles Burney similarly was impressed by a performance at which Mozart imitated 'the several Styles of Singing of each of the then Opera Singers, as well as of their Songs in an Extemporary opera to nonsense words." [36]

Skill is indispensable, but inspiration critical. Young Mozart's genius consisted in producing music at will— any place, any time, on any theme. It was something he would eventually outgrow; but early on, the little 'magician' was all too happy to serve in the traveling circus organized by his father. His principal rewards were the messianic adulation of his audiences and the flattering zeal of his promoters.

Leopold Mozart did not hesitate to claim that his son was "a miracle, which God has allowed to see the light in Salzburg [...] *And if it is ever to be my duty to convince the world of this miracle, it is so now, when people are ridiculing whatever is called a miracle and denying all miracles.* Therefore they must be convinced. And was it not a great joy and a tremendous victory for me to hear a Volterian say to me in amazement: '*Now for once in my life I have seen a miracle; and this is the first!*'" [37]

Since Leopold Mozart attributed his son's gift to a divine origin, Wolfgang Amadeus could only reciprocate by placing his father on a pedestal next to the source:

"*Next to God comes Papa*, was my moto or axiom as a child," wrote Mozart in 1778, "and I still cling to it" [letter from Mannheim, 7 March 1778][38]

But Mozart soon became aware of his father's controlling ways and opposed them through well-disguised responses. The long-term effects of these manipulations, however, are difficult to measure. That they pushed Mozart in the direction of disguise and deceit is one obvious conclusion.

Most of Mozart's operas were based on popular themes of the time, which he treated astutely. In the second half of the eighteenth- century, a number of political events conspired to give women a bad name and these provided fuel for his lifelong warnings against the frailties of the weaker sex.

The corrupting power of women was repeatedly brought up to explain the decline of the French monarchy. There were many other causes, but it was felt that women provided the finishing touch. When Mozart traveled through Paris, as a child, France was already in trouble:

"A broad array of causes— including the personal unpopularity of Louis XV, the military fiascoes of the Seven Years' War, the writings of the *philosophes*, and especially the impact of the protracted struggles over Jansenism— contributed to the onset as early as the 1750s of what historians have termed the 'desacralization' of the French monarchy." [39]

In Rousseau's **Lettre à d'Alembert** a theatrical analogy was used to describe the King's court. The 'court as theater' pointed to a social microcosm through which life at court could be equated with life on the stage: at once closed and yet very public. This life was dominated by women, who exercised their sexual power over men, emasculating them in the process:

"[Louis XV's] notorious debauchery, the power wielded by his mistresses Mme de Pompadour and later Mme du Barry, the existence of a private brothel called the *Parc aux Cerfs*, where the monarch was provided with an unending series of nubile young women, were widely known secrets long before his death. Many a subject of Louis '*le Bien-Aimé*' shared the feelings of

Jean-François Le Clerc, a veteran arrested in 1757 for calling the king a 'bugger' and complaining that the kingdom was governed by 'two whores'." [40]

The stringent criticism of women associated with the French crown, extended well into the 1780s. Louis the XVIth Austrian wife, Marie-Antoinette, was given the same rough treatment at the hands of various pamphleteers. In 1783, a popular piece titled *Essais historiques sur la vie de Marie-Antoinette d'Autriche, reine de France*, drew parallels between Mme du Barry and the queen, suggesting that they were both driven by the same taste for power and debauched 'effervescence of passions'.[41]

"The phenomenally successful *Essais historiques sur la vie de Marie-Antoinette*— first published and suppressed in 1783, then a runaway success in 1789 and after— picks up the Queen's alleged fondness for nighttime walks in the gardens of Versailles in the company of her ladies-in-waiting; these nocturnal pastimes, according to the author, soon degenerated into orgies with the young princess and her friends and attendants swapping lovers in the gardens of the palace." [42]

The misogynistic tenor of Mozart's operas can perhaps be traced to this common perception of women in positions of power. But the original theatrical source for Mozart's antifeminist portrayals is still Beaumarchais' *Marriage of Figaro*, the runaway success of 1784:

"With Beaumarchais' *Marriage of Figaro* we have come full circle back to Rousseau's fulminations about 'public women'. The Genevan writer, it will be remembered, had already articulated in the late 1750s the cultural kinship between high society, court society and the contemporary stage: 'Look through most contemporary plays. It is always a woman who knows everything, who teaches everything to men'. Had Rousseau lived to witness the Diamond Necklace Affair or to see the *Marriage of Figaro*, he would have found his irate masculinist prognosis amply confirmed. In Beaumarchais' most famous play, Figaro, for all his self-dramatizing insolence, is duped in the end by a conspiracy of women. As for the Diamond Necklace Affair, it too was a women's business, down to its central object: in eighteenth-century licentious parlance, jewels, *les bijoux*, meant genitalia." [43]

The Diamond Necklace Affair developed through an extremely complicated plot, full of subplots in which the major themes of the age emerged. In this affair, the central character was an impersonator of royalty. Her name was Jeanne de Saint-Rémi and she belonged to a completely ruined family of provincial nobility. Yet she officially claimed descent from the French royal family and took the name of Jeanne de Valois. In 1780 she married a penniless member of fringe nobility, Count Nicolas de la Motte.

Three years later, the ever scheming Countess de la Motte met the fifty-year old Louis de Rohan, a prominent member of the powerful and well-established Rohan-Soubise family. Louis de Rohan was the bishop of Strasbourg, Grand Almoner of France, and a former ambassador to Vienna. His wealth was proverbial and he was actively involved in occult pursuits.

"His Eminence was one of the darlings of Fortune, whose choicest favors had been showered on him with a lavish hand. Of the most illustrious birth, exceptionally handsome, enormously rich, and undeniably fascinating, no younger son ever started life under more brilliant auspices. The Church seemed to exist solely for the purpose of providing him with honors. Bishop of Strasbourg, Grand Almoner of France, Cardinal, Prince of the Empire, Landgrave of Alsace— his titles were as numerous as the beads of a rosary. Nor were they merely high-sounding dignities. From the Abbey of St. Waast, the richest in France, he drew 300,000 livres a year, and from all these various sources combined his revenue was estimated at 1,200,000 livres. Nature had endowed him no less bounteously than Fortune. To the honors which he owed to the accident of birth, his intellect had won him another still more coveted. At twenty-seven he had been elected to the *Académie Française*, where, as he was particularly brilliant in conversation, it is not surprising that the Immortals should have 'declared themselves charmed with his company'. He possessed all the conspicuous qualities and defects which in the eighteenth-century were characteristic of the aristocrat. High ecclesiastic that he was, he had nothing of the ascetic about him. Like so many of the dignitaries of the Church under the *ancien régime*, he was worldly to the last degree. As he was not a hypocrite, he did not hesitate to live as he pleased. Appointed Ambassador to Vienna, he had scandalized the straightlaced Maria-Theresa by his reckless extravagance and dissipation. The Emperor, to her disgust, 'loved conversing with him to enjoy his flippant gossip and wicked stories'. 'Our women', she wrote to her Ambassador at Versailles, 'young and old, beautiful and ugly, are bewitched by him. He is their idol. [...] Gracious to all, he was generous to a fault. He dispensed favor and charity alike without discernment, giving to the poor as bountifully as to his mistresses. [...] Besides his weakness for a pretty face, [he] had a fondness amounting to passion for pomp and alchemy. 'On state occasions at Versailles', says Madame d'Oberkirch, he wore an alb of lace *en point à aiguille* of such beauty that the assistants were almost afraid to touch it'. It was embroidered with his arms and device— the famous device of the Rohans, *Roy ne puis, prince ne daigne, Rohan je suis*. It was said to be worth a million livres. [...] At his episcopal palace at Saverne, near Strasbourg, which he rebuilt after it was destroyed by fire in 1779 at a cost of between two and three million livres, he had a magnificent library. [...] His principal pastime, however, was alchemy. At Saverne, besides his library, he had one of the finest laboratories in Europe." [44]

During his stay at the Austrian court, Rohan had managed to

alienate Marie-Antoinette and since she was now married to Louis the XVIth of France, the rift stood mightily in the way of his ambitions. This was something the Countess de la Motte was able to capitalize on very quickly.

It was not long before Rohan started writing— through her— to her 'cousin' the queen, trying to redress past wrongs. Since the relationship was entirely fictitious, the letters obviously never reached the queen and the replies were forged by the Countess' lover, Rétaux de Villette.

As the missives went back and forth, the Countess conceived of an even more elaborate scheme. She had already received financial help from Rohan, who was happy to assist this destitute aristocratic relative of the queen, but she felt that the potential for a much bigger payoff was there. She therefore started searching the streets of Paris for a Marie-Antoinette look-alike, eventually finding her in the gardens of the Palais-Royal. The newly anointed queen was a young woman of light virtue, who went by the name of Nicole Le Guay. Carefully groomed by the Countess, she met Rohan in the gardens of Versailles on what, one assumes, was a dark summer night in 1784. The audience was short, but Rohan was fooled.

The earlier correspondence was thus authenticated and shortly thereafter the Countess was able to convince Rohan that the queen was absolutely enamored with an expansive jewel and that if he would just get it for her, his political fortunes were sure to improve.

"The most famous jewel in France, a diamond necklace made up of 647 flawless gems and worth over one and a half million livres, was the masterpiece of the jewellers Boehmer and Bassange. Louis XV had commissioned it for Mme du Barry, and then backed down because of the Jewel's price. [...] By 1785, however, Mme de la Motte was able to persuade Rohan that the queen had her heart set on this expansive bauble [...] A purchase order duly approved and signed by the queen was produced, and on the night of 1 February 1785 the object was delivered to Rohan and the Countess and handed over to a man purporting to be the Queen's valet. The necklace, which Rohan was to pay for in installments over the next several years, was promptly picked apart, and the gems sold on the black markets of Paris and London." [45]

By August, the confidence game had unraveled and France was stunned to hear of Cardinal de Rohan's arrest at Versailles. It was not long before the real villains were caught, but by then the damage had been done. The affair was being discussed publicly, driving up popular passions and the scandal would culminate on 31 May 1786, when the official verdict was read.

The Countess and her lover were given life imprisonment, but a furor erupted in court when the prosecutor requested a sentence of exile against Rohan, for his 'criminal temerity' and disrespect for the queen: [46]

"After hours of bitter dispute the *Grande Chambre* of the Parlement returned a verdict of not guilty by a vote of thirty to twenty. While Rohan left the *Palais de Justice* to the roars of a cheering crowd, the queen at Versailles wept tears of anger and humiliation." [47]

The Diamond Necklace Affair was the first major media event of the period. The **Gazette de Leyde**, the most successful of the foreign newspapers reporting French news, had a peak European-wide circulation of 4,200 by the mid-1780s. During the affair, through public lending institutions and authorized or pirated reprints, it managed to reach an estimated readership of close to 100,000. [48]

At the core of *l'affaire du cardinal* was the shadowy world of eighteenth-century intrigue. It is therefore not surprising to find the name of Cagliostro associated with these events. Cagliostro met Rohan during his stay in Strasbourg. A shared interest in alchemy brought them together and they had, according to W.R.H. Trowbridge "long, frequent and secret confabulations in the Cardinal's well-equipped laboratory." [49]

At the Cardinal's request, Cagliostro and his wife went to live at Saverne, Rohan's episcopal palace located near Strasbourg. Trowbridge claims that Rohan was not a Mason himself, but that he knew of Cagliostro's activities. If Rohan was not a Mason, members of his family certainly were. There is a reference to a 'Prince de Rohan, Master of the Grand Lodge l'Intelligence, Sovereign Prince of Masons, etc.' whose name appears at the bottom of the no less controversial Morin Patent, granted on 27 August 1761 in Paris, by the Grand Orient. [50] The patent was used to establish the Grand Lodge of Perfection at Charleston, South Carolina, in 1783.

During the same general period, the Grand Master of the Order of Malta was a certain Emmanuel-Jean-Marie-des-Neiges de Rohan. [51] The Baroness d'Oberkirch, who visited Saverne while Cagliostro was there reported that "she was stunned by the pomp with which he was treated." [52]

"So great was the confidence that Rohan placed in Cagliostro that he treated him as an oracle. He constantly consulted him, and suffered himself to be guided entirely by his advice. As the consequences of this infatuation were in the end disastrous, it is customary to regard the Cardinal as the dupe of Cagliostro."[53]

If Hermes is the god of swindlers, his modern priesthood was well represented in the Diamond Necklace Affair. But was the affair spontaneous or organized?

The quasi-theatrical characters of Cagliostro, Mme de la Motte and de Rohan would have been difficult to duplicate. If the objective was to undermine and further desacralize the French monarchy, that objective was clearly achieved. In his ***Forbidden Best-Sellers of Revolutionary France***, Robert Darnton shows that pamphlets written "under the cloak" were even more influential than the writings of the *philosophes*. They capitalized heavily on salacious events and served to manufacture a negative image of the monarchy. An image that implicitly argued for its demise. Intrigue and gossip were everywhere:

"The insistence on the fluid character of Mme de la Motte's social identity served to underscore her vocation for intrigue: she was the exact female equivalent of the protean Cagliostro, though her femininity made her the more dangerous of the two. She [...] had gathered [...] a *demi-monde* of fake Counts, Barons and Marquis, all of whom pursued social promotion by means of sexual and financial intrigue. It was exactly this sort of world, a degraded replica of high society, that had generated a Mme du Barry, fully equipped with ersatz nobility and threatening sexual powers." [54]

Rohan's secretary, the abbé Georgel, and his defense barrister, Guy-Jean-Baptiste Target, speak at length of the 'illusion' and 'artifice' used by the false Countess de la Motte in 'staging' the 'scenes' through which the Cardinal was duped.[55]

Yet by itself, Mme de la Motte's swindle could not have had such a powerful impact. It had to be recast in more threatening terms and tied to the elite's fear of the irrational— with which Cagliostro's name was associated. That a prominent individual of de Rohan's stature and intellect could have been caught in Cagliostro's net would serve as a warning for everyone else.

The recurring theme behind these magical dealings, in which reality was craftily distorted to create an even more compelling 'truth', was always that of Egypt. We have identified it in Bruno's conception of talismanic magic and find it again with Cagliostro— the high-priest of Egyptian Masonry associated with Cardinal de Rohan.

But what was Mozart's introduction to the 'Egyptian' discourse? We know that his first contact with the topic was through Baron Tobias von Gebler (1726-1786), vice-chancellor of the Austro-Bohemian chancellery.

"Gebler played a leading role in the promotion of the sciences, in the reorganization of the police and the judiciary, and in the development of the educational system. He was also mainly responsible for the banning, in 1770, of improvised theatrical farces, which were frequently of low moral standard. He is furthermore believed to have been the author of the memorandum ***Vorschllag zur Verbesserung der National-Schaubühne und des Theaters überhaupt***, probably written in 1775, which proposed that Joseph II should assume direct control over the national theatre; the emperor did so that same year." [56]

Gebler was an early champion of German opera and most of his ideas on the subject are expressed in letters he wrote to the Berlin bookseller and writer Friedrich Nicolai (1733-1811). Gebler was also a successful playwright and it is through his ***Thamos, König in Ägypten*** that Mozart was first introduced— when he was only seventeen years old— to the vast subject of 'Egypt'. ***Thamos*** was based on the novel ***Sethos*** (Paris, 1731), written by the already mentioned abbé Jean Terrasson, and we will now see that this work had other, more compelling ancestors.

Thamos promotes a number of Masonic ideals[57], and that is not surprising. Gebler eventually became Grand Master of '*Zum neuen Bunde*' and Master of '*Zur neugekrönten Hoffnung*', which Mozart joined in 1786. What is surprising is that someone pushing science and morals would be so interested in 'Egypt'. Cagliostro's use of 'Egypt' for his mystifications is understandable; but Gebler's attraction to the same subject is not that obvious.

At the root of it all is Plato's ***Phaedrus***: a treatise on the art of persuasion, where effectiveness depends on a correct recollection of Ideas. This leads to the esoteric Art of Memory, recently written about by Frances Yates, and already cultivated in Venice during the Renaissance by the likes of Giulio Camillo and Giordano Bruno.

Thamos' name is found in **Phaedrus** (274C-275B), where Socrates tells the following tale:

"Among the ancient gods of Naucratis in Egypt there was one to whom the bird called the ibis is sacred. The name of that divinity was Theuth [Thoth], and it was he who first discovered number and calculation, geometry and astronomy, as well as the game of checkers and dice, and, above all else, writing. Now the king of all Egypt at that time was Thamus [Thamos], who lived in the great city in the upper region that the Greeks call Egyptian Thebes [...] Theuth came to exhibit his arts to him and urged him to disseminate them to all the Egyptians. Thamus asked him about the usefulness of each art, and while Theuth was explaining it, Thamus praised him for what he thought was right in his explanations and criticized him for whatever he thought was wrong. [...] When they came to writing, Theuth said: 'O King, here is something that, once learned, will make the Egyptians wiser and will improve their memory; I have discovered a potion for memory and for wisdom'. Thamus, however, replied: 'O most expert Theuth, one man can give birth to the elements of an art, but only another can judge how they can benefit or harm those who will use them. And now, since you are the father of writing, your affection for it has made you describe its effects as the opposite of what they really are. In fact it will introduce forgetfulness into the soul of those who learn it: they will not practice using their memory because they will put their trust in writing, which is external and depends on signs that belong to others, instead of trying to remember from the inside, completely on their own. You have not discovered a potion for remembering, but for reminding; you provide your students with the appearance of wisdom, not with its reality. Your invention will enable them to hear many things without being properly taught, and they will imagine that they have come to know much while for the most part they will know nothing. And they will be difficult to get along with, since they will merely appear to be wise instead of really being so." [58]

Frances Yates points out that this passage was used by Alexander Dicson, a disciple of Giordano Bruno, who was trying to propagate Bruno's hermetic and 'Egyptian' notion of artificial memory in England.[59] Dicson was a native of Scotland, and Yates claims that he was a secret political agent.[60] His *De umbra rationis* [1583] follows Bruno's *De umbris idearum* in its promotion of an artificial memory based on occult principles.

"Dicson follows Bruno in making Mercurius [Thoth] the inventor, not of letters, but of the 'inner writing' of the art of memory. He thus stands for the inner wisdom which Thamus says that the Egyptians lost when external writing with letters was invented. For Dicson, as for Bruno, Mercurius Trismegistus is the patron of hermetic, or occult, memory." [61]

Dicson's work was reprinted with the title *Thamus* in 1597, by Thomas Basson, an English printer settled at Leiden.[62] Among others, it interested the Jesuits:

"Not the least peculiar feature in the career of this strange book is that the Jesuit, Martin Del Rio, in his book against magic published in 1600 [*Disquisitionum Magicarum, Libri Sex*], commends as 'not without salt and acumen the *Thamus* of Alexander Dicson which Heius Scepsius defends against the attack of a Cambridge man in the edition published at Leiden'. Why was the Egyptian 'inner writing' of the art of memory as taught by Dicson worthy of Jesuit commendation, whereas the master from whom he learned it was burned at the stake?" [63]

Together with other Masons— particularly Joseph von Sonnenfels, the Vice-Master of '*Zur wahren Eintracht*'— Gebler was trying to create an instrument of propaganda to be put under the direct control of the Emperor. The art of persuasion was certainly relevant to that enterprise.

"Joseph's personal interest in the theatre was extraordinary. As an historian of Josephinism has written, 'Joseph saw in the school, the pulpit, and the theater the three media for the fashioning of public opinion' [...] In the course of his frequent journeys outside Vienna Joseph was assiduous in talent-spotting for his theaters. On a visit to Pressburg in 1784 Joseph saw Schikaneder's company perform Schikaneder's new moralistic play, *Kinder, reizet eure Eltern, und Eltern eure Kinder nicht* ('Children, don't annoy your parents, and parents, don't annoy your children') which greatly appealed to him, and prompted him to invite Schikaneder to take over the management of the second court theater, the Kärtnertortheater." [64]

Schikaneder is officially credited with the libretto of *The Magic Flute*, and because of this it is important to realize that he was not the simplistic oaf that writers on Mozart often make him out to be. The Emperor's interest in him as a 'fashioner of public opinion' makes him a key player in Joseph's 'moral Mafia'. That position of trust was not earned on the basis of Schikaneder's personal morals. He was an incorrigible Don Juan and is portrayed in scenes of seduction on the *Bölzelschiessen* (air gun shooting) targets used in Mozart's home. The targets represented amusing or obscene scenes painted for the occasion.[65]

Much later, in Regensburg, Schikaneder fell out of favor in Masonic circles for the same reason. Mozart's friendship with him dates back to Salzburg, where he worked on *Thamos* for the second time, extending it by another chorus and five entr'acte interludes. Böhm, for whose company the original *Thamos* had been written, tried to tempt him with a performance, as did Schikaneder; but nothing came of it.[66]

The Emperor could recognize talent when he saw it, and the range of skills he was willing to enlist to accomplish his theatrical goals was pretty amazing. His collaborators were way ahead of their time, as Sonnenfels' case plainly illustrates:

"Joseph, Imperial Baron von Sonnenfels, came from a Jewish family— his father was the scholar Lipmann Perlin— and represented the second generation of Jewish-German emancipation. He became a prominent Freemason, was adviser on economic policy to Joseph II, and as an enlightened lawyer he campaigned against torture and the death penalty. His involvement in literary activities earned him the title of 'the Viennese Gottshed'. [...] He urged 'regular' plays; that is, the reasonable and appropriate works put on at the Emperor's 'enlightened' popular theater." [67]

But how does it all relate to 'Egypt'? Where is the link between morals, Plato's art of persuasion based on 'truth', and the Egypt of Thoth?

The answer is found in a thesis first advanced by John Spencer(1630-1693). Spencer was an English Hebraist, who postulated an Egyptian origin for Mosaic Law.[68] Since Mosaic Law is the foundation of Judeo-Christian morals, a scientific investigation into its origins effectively translated into a search for the historic roots of morals. The Enlightenment was trying to reach beyond the Bible. Its discursive explorations were based on ancient Greek texts and a well buried interpretative literature accessible mostly to university scholars.

Spencer's argument is summarized in two publications: his doctoral thesis, **Urim and Thummim** (1670) and the monograph **De Legibus Hebraeorum Ritualibus et Earum Rationibus Libri Tres** (1685).[69] According to Spencer, Moses merely 'translated' the Egyptian mysteries into the laws of the Hebrews.[70]

"Spencer's project was to demonstrate the Egyptian origin of the ritual laws of the Hebrews. In order to understand the novelty and the boldness of this undertaking, we must briefly consider how Spencer dislodged two crucial tenets of Christian theology. The first is the traditional Christian distinction between moral

Law, political Law, and ritual Law within the body of the 613 prescriptions and prohibitions contained in the Torah. Moral Law is the Decalogue, political and ritual Law is all the rest. Moral Law is eternal, political and ritual Law is temporal. The validity of the ritual Law is limited to the timespan between Moses and Jesus. The second presupposition is the orthodox view that every coincidence between a Biblical law and a pagan rite is a work of the devil, who is an ape of God. The Hebrew Law is the original model, and the pagan religions are diabolic institutions imitating this model. Spencer contradicted the second presupposition by showing that Egypt was the origin and the model of the ritual Law. Concerning the first presupposition, Spencer did quite a revolutionary thing: he shifted the focus from the timeless moral Law to the long abolished ritual Law, and, even more significant, he tried to use this body of prescriptions and institutions to reconstruct the long forgotten 'atrocities' of Egyptian idolatry. Notwithstanding his strategic professions of Egyptophobia, his extremely diligent and well-documented representation of Egyptian rites became one of the most important reference books for Egyptophiles of the eighteenth-century." [71]

Based on this outline one is surprised to hear from musicologists that Mozart's limited knowledge of 'Egypt' was all extracted from works like Terrasson's **Sethos**, which, they claim, was also Ignaz von Born's principal source. The subject is admittedly complex and the documentation sparse, but that is not sufficient grounds for rejecting **The Magic Flute**'s serious aspects, as some writers have done:

"The instinctive high-mindedness of critics who insist on serious interpretations of **Die Zauberflöte** stands very much at odds with what the librettist Emanuel Schikaneder and Mozart gave us. On a simple proportional level, Tamino, the focus of the mythical and symbolic studies, sings a part roughly two-thirds the size of Papageno's. [...] But where, one must ask, is the depth?" [72]

The answer is simple: it is hidden from those who are not equipped to perceive it. The Masons around Mozart were not people of the theater looking for exotic material. In Viennese Masonic circles, whose influence extended all the way to the Emperor, the preoccupation was with authenticity and in Ignaz von Born's elite group, the person directly responsible for advancing Spencer's thesis was Karl Leonhard Reinhold (1757-1825)— another former Jesuit:

"In 1788, Reinhold published a Masonic treatise under the pseudonym Br(uder) Decius that dealt with the same subject as Spencer's and Warburton's works: *Die Hebräischen Mysterien oder die älteste religiöse Freymaurery* (The Hebrew Mysteries, or the Older Religious Freemasonry). Reinhold wrote this book not as a philosopher, but as a Mason addressing his fellow Masons. Reinhold was first a Jesuit (Pater Don Pius Reinhold) and joined the order of the Illuminates (where his pseudonym was Decius). In 1783, at the age of twenty-six, he became a member of the Masonic lodge *'Zur Wahren Eintracht'* and passed all of the three degrees in only five months. Mozart, himself a member of *'Zur Wohltätigkeit'* , a sister Lodge, and Haydn frequented this Lodge. Ignaz von Born, one of the leading figures of the Austrian Enlightenment and like Rheinhold an Illuminist, was Grand Master. In November 1783, Reinhold fled from Vienna and from the order of the Jesuits to Leipzig, where he continued his studies of philosophy. He met Christoph Martin Wieland in 1784, became his partner in editing the journal *Teutsche Merkur*, and became Wieland's son-in-law in 1785 [...] Wieland was in close contact with the Vienna Lodge for some years before he himself became a Freemason. It was through the good offices of von Born and Josef von Sonnenfels that Reinhold was able to approach Wieland. Reinhold was converted to Protestantism by Superintendent Johann Gottfried Herder, a fellow Illuminist and Mason, in 1785. In 1787 he was appointed professor extraordinarius of philosophy at the University of Jena, where he became a friend and colleague of

Schiller (who taught history there). He wrote his essay on the Hebrew mysteries for von Born and his *Journal für Freymaurer*, where it appeared in two issues in 1786. Von Born had inaugurated this journal with a book-length treatise on the Egyptian mysteries." [73]

After the forced amalgamation of the Viennese Lodges, following Joseph II's decree's of 11 December 1785, von Born became Master of '*Zur Wahrheit*', into which '*Zur wahren Eintracht*', '*Zum Palmbaum*' and '*Zu den drei Adlern*' were recombined. He exercised a great deal of influence on Mozart and his Egyptian researches are therefore critical to a proper understanding of *The Magic Flute*.

Both Reinhold and von Born wanted to go beyond Mosaic Law, directly to its Egyptian sources. By studying Egypt as a historical civilization, these Masons proposed to rediscover the original tradition in its pristine state. The Illuminist angle, and its relevance to *The Magic Flute*, is found in the writings of Wieland and Adam Weishaupt's right-hand man, Baron Knigge:

"In Adolph Knigge's secret-society novel, *Geschichte Ludwigs von Seelberg* (1787), there is talk of a brotherly Order of Light that has 'in hand the surest means of guiding everything toward the great objective of restituting truth and freedom on earth *without violence or danger*'. The members of the order 'did much *in quiet*, bringing about revolutions which were attributed to other causes'. In 1789, six months after the storming of the Bastille, the metaphor of conquering darkness takes on a somewhat less peaceable tone in Christoph Wieland's novel *Peregrinus Proteus*: 'The light has broken forth from amidst the darkness, the kingdom of demons and their servants is nearing its terrible end. The City of God has already come down to us..., the people of the earth will be gathered to it, and each of its rays will be a lightning bolt which will consume the enemies of light'. History as a show of nature is now in progress; at its climax in 1791, the Queen of the Night and her attendants will perish in 'thunder, lightning, storm'. Their wail, in that now self-denunciatory rhyme *Macht/Nacht*, equates domination with annihilation." [74]

The first major Illuminist victory was won at the Masonic Congress of Wilhelmsbad (1782), near Hanau. At the urging of the Illuminist Dittfurth, the Congress declared that the Order of Strict Observance could not legally consider itself the successor of the Order of the Knights of the Temple.

"Templar Masonry, into which the majority of German Lodges were grouped until then, received a fatal blow and the Illuminists won everything it lost. [...] They were now the active and living force within Freemasonry, and this power they put in the service of light." [75]

Mozart made Christoph Wieland's acquaintance in 1777 and the Wolfgang-Leopold correspondence comments on the event:

Wolfgang:
"I have now added Herr Wieland to the list of my acquaintances. But he doesn't know as much about me as I know about him [...] He indulges in a sort of pedantic rudeness, combined occasionally with a stupid condescension [...] Everyone seems embarrassed in his presence, no one says a word, or moves an inch; all listen intently to every word he utters [..] Apart from that, he is what we all know him to be, a most gifted fellow." [76]

Leopold:
"The portrait you sketched of [Wieland] for my benefit I too could almost have given you, although I have never seen him. For M. Grimm and the two Romanzows gave me a most minute description of him during a walk we all took together." [77]

Reinhold, the theoretician of Ignaz von Born's tightly knit

group, became Wieland's son-in-law in 1785. It was he who introduced an Illuminist concept of initiation into Freemasonry. As Nicholas Till points out, this undertaking followed closely upon an outline provided by Wieland in **Geschichte des Agathon**, written in 1766-67. In it Wieland's young Greek hero learns to overcome the rule of religion and state "thence to become (the Enlightenment's highest aspiration) *'wie ein Gott über dem Chaos'* (like a God above Chaos)." [78]

"**Agathon** was one of the most widely read German novels of the period, and it made a huge impact on Adam Weishaupt, the founder of the *Illuminati*, who frequently cited it as one of the most important influences upon his own conception of the meaning of Masonic initiation." [79]

A concept that requires the initiate 'to see things as they are', and which was taught through the symbolism of the Tetragrammaton. The very same Tetragrammaton referred to discreetly in the original libretto of **The Magic Flute**— right at the point where Tamino's initiation takes place:

"'They [the armed men] read to him [Tamino] the transparent writing which is graven on a pyramid'. At the words 'fire, water, air, and earth' the holy Tetragrammaton JHVH was presumably shown[...] The solemnity of this part of the opera is thus remotely different from anything in the Austrian and Catholic experience, It is of Biblical solemnity— and by Biblical I mean literally derived from the Bible. See Isaiah 43/2: 'When thou passest through the waters, I will be with thee[...]; when thou walkest through the fire, thou shalt not be burned'." [80]

Wieland's influence can be underscored even further by referring to the work Schikaneder produced right before **The Magic Flute**. It was drawn from Wieland's **Dschinnistan** collection.[81] For the relationship between Egyptian symbolism and the Tetragrammaton we must again go back to Reinhold:

"Reinhold's personal and most important contribution to this discourse is his explanation of the Tetragrammaton. This passage is based on Voltaire's account of the '*rites égyptiens*'. But whereas Voltaire maintains that the Egyptians called the Supreme Being by a similar or even the same name as did the Jews, namely, 'I-ha-ho' or 'Iao', Reinhold bases his equation not on the sound, but on the meaning [...]:

> Brethren! Who among us does not know the ancient Egyptian inscriptions: the one on the pyramid at Sais: 'I am all that is, was and shall be, and no mortal has ever lifted my veil', and that other one on the statue of Isis: 'I am all that is'? Who among us does not understand the meaning of these words, as well as in those days of the Egyptian initiate, and who does not know that they express the essential Being, the meaning of the name Jehovah?" [82]

Reinhold declared that Mosaic legislation was a faithful copy of what he called 'the Egyptian Mysteries'.[83] His emphasis on Egypt was ritual— not intellectual. If the law of Moses could support Jewish ritual, a rediscovery of the Egyptian Mysteries might well lead to a truly 'illuminated' Freemasonry.

Jan Assmann points out that Renaissance grammatology was based on immediate signification and that Egyptian hieroglyphs were constructed on shapes and names. These 'signifiers' belonged to art rather than writing. In the old days they were used by craftsmen in much the same way as architectural symbolism was used by Masons.

"Thoth was the god of writing, but Ptah was the god of hieroglyphs. He did not write, but he invented the hieroglyphs by inventing the shapes and names of everything. Thoth, the god of writing did not *invent*; he merely found the script: thus in the ***Onomasticon of Anememope*** the notion of 'every word' is expressed as 'everything which Ptah has created and which Thoth has written down'. [...] To the hieroglyphic mind, things and signs are interchangeable [...] The Egyptian scribes, artists and magicians continued the work of their divine patrons Ptah and Thoth by constantly continuing the process of creation. These magic and mystical aspects of Egyptian cosmotheism remained connected to the vague notions of hieroglyphic writing that survived in European memory. In the hermetic tradition, hieroglyphs were associated with cabalistic and alchemistic notions of a magical control of cosmic energies." [84]

This pretty much captures the range of esoteric principles on which *The Magic Flute* is constructed. It is artists/craftsmen/ Masons extending the legacy of Ptah, but also twisting it to accommodate their new moral standard. There are, of course, many unanswered questions about their knowledge and its source. One must remember that *The Magic Flute* was written before hieroglyphic writing was officially deciphered.

Given the emphasis on Ptah and alchemy, it becomes clear that *The Magic Flute* was designed to bridge the existing gap between art and artifice. In so doing, it had to preserve Ptah's heritage and demonstrate a working knowledge of ritual method. The control of cosmic energies, achieved by the manipulation of signs and substances is part of that tradition. As the ultimate craftsman, Ptah is also the Master to whom the Word is known.

"The priest of Ptah was known as 'the chief artist' because Ptah himself was an artist and a demiurge. Alternately, the function of the priest was closely allied to the requirements of his particular god; for instance, at Coptos, the priest of Min was a chemist who could concoct a black dye called 'the divine substance' and which was painted on the statue of the god." [85]

The relationship between morals, 'truth' and the art of persuasion can also be derived from Spencer's investigation of Egypt. In his dissertation, *De Urim et Thummim* (1670), Spencer provides the critical bridge between Egyptian concepts of morality and justice, and their Hebrew or Greek equivalents. Urim and Thummim were the breastplates worn by the high priest and these were used for oracular purposes.

"Urim has nothing to do with Egypt, but Thummim is taken from Egypt. Thummim has a Hebrew etymology; it comes from *tam*, 'to be perfect', and means something like perfection, integrity, wholeness. But in the Septuagint it is mostly rendered not by *teleia*, 'perfection', but by *aletheia*, 'truth'. The explanation Spencer gives for this strange rendering is indeed most convincing: the translators were aware of the fact that in Egypt the supreme judge wore a figure of *aletheia* as a pectoral and that Thummim was just the Hebrew adaptation of this Egyptian custom. For this information, Spencer quotes Aelian and Diodorus, who in this case turn out to be reliable sources. The Vizier, who acted as supreme judge, indeed wore an emblem of *Maat*, the goddess of truth, on his breast. Spencer is thus referring to an authentic Egyptian custom." [86]

Spencer's investigation would open the door to additional possibilities. For promoters of the German Enlightenment, like Nicolai, Lessing and Mendelssohn, the path of reconstruction went through both ancient Greece and medieval Jewish rationalism. Moses Mendelssohn was practically raised on Maimonides (1135-1204). In 1742, a printing house set up by a branch of his family, the Wulffs, who descended from Moses Isserles of Cracow (1520-1572), had published a new edition of Maimonides' *More Nevukhim* ('Guide of the Perplexed') and Mendelssohn's biographer, Alexander Altmann, mentions that this particular work had not been reprinted since 1553.[87]

"Since the study of philosophy was still frowned upon by the pious (a ban pronounced in 1305 had made it elicit to engage in such study unless one was over the age of twenty five), it was all the more remarkable that the new edition of the *Guide* appeared with the tacit approval of the chief rabbi of Dessau: the cost of printing had been defrayed by a relative of the chief rabbi, and the reading of proofs had been supervised by Aaron Hirsch, a member of Beth Din. Prior to the publication of the *Guide*, the Wulffian press had already brought out [...] a whole series of works somewhat secular and scientific in character."[88]

Maimonides was looking for a rational explanation of Mosaic Law. A study of the arguments set forth in the **Guide** is not particularly relevant to the subject at hand, but the Mendelssohn connection serves to underscore the breadth of these rationalistic excursions.

They eventually developed into arguments concerning Spinoza, which both Mendelssohn and Lessing indulged in from the earliest stages of their long lasting friendship. The figure of Spinoza exerted a special fascination for Mendelssohn, since he was a Jew. He had wrestled with all of the metaphysical questions that were dear to Mendelssohn's heart and had come to the conclusion that God was the only substance in the universe, of which all beings were mere variations.

"Mendelssohn immediately felt at ease in Lessing's company. His own plan to rehabilitate the much abused Spinoza was akin in spirit to Lessing's **Vindications**, and the two young men must have spent many an hour discussing Spinoza. [..] To what extent Lessing had known Spinoza's thought prior to his friendship with Mendelssohn cannot be established with any degree of likelihood. [...] But it was undoubtedly Mendelssohn who introduced Lessing to a deeper understanding of philosophy in general and of Spinoza in particular." [89]

Lessing's prominent position in the ranks of the German Enlightenment makes his long, and by all accounts secret conversion to Spinozism an important one. Von Born and Reinhold conceptualized God as an abstraction of Nature, best characterized by 'all that is, that was, and that shall be'. Lessing, on the other hand, followed Spinoza onto a more Gnostic ground. If God was in all beings, then self-knowledge, rather than the knowledge of Nature was the correct path to wisdom. Behind the formula 'all is one and one is all', underlying Spinoza's metaphysics, lies the identity of macrocosm and microcosm on which all magic is based.

The temples of Reason and Nature, alluded to in Mozart's

The Magic Flute, are filled with the visions of Born and his group. Since Tamino is driven back from both temples, one may assume that Mozart had outgrown Reinhold's ideal of an anonymous godhead:

"Reinhold's contribution to the Moses discourse consisted of the equation of Jehovah and Isis (alias Nature). According to Clement of Alexandria, the last and highest initiation led to a point where all teaching ends, discursive instruction stops, and immediate vision takes over. [...] This is how Ignaz von Born, the Grand Master of True Concord, Vienna's most important Lodge [...] summarized the ultimate aim of the Egyptian mysteries: 'The knowledge of nature is the ultimate purpose of our application. We worship this progenitor, nourisher, and preserver of all creation in the image of Isis. Only he who knows the whole extent of her power and force will be able to uncover her veil without punishment." [90]

In 1791— at the time **The Magic Flute** was written— Mozart also composed a cantata for tenor and piano, **Die ihr des unermesslichen Weltalls Schöpfer ehrt** (K 619), which can be used to establish his vision of the godhead. The opening lines read as follows:

You who revere the
Creator of the boundless universe,
Call him Jehovah or God,
Call him Fu or Brahma.
Hark! Hark! to the words

Of the Almighty's trumpet call!
Ringing out through earth, moon, sun
Its sound is everlasting.

This characterization of the godhead as *shabda-brahman*, or the *logos* behind all audible sound, is Tantric in nature. It is sound as 'power' (Almighty = 'all mighty'), used in Hindu *mantras* as a binding agent between microcosm and macrocosm:

"In all cases it is the creative thought which ensouls the uttered sound which works now in man's small 'magic', just as it first worked in the 'grand magical display' of the World Creator." [91]

This is where the road followed by Lessing also leads: to the Temple of Wisdom, where God exists as 'creative sound' and as such transcends the anonymous spirit of Nature. Any believer in this conception of the godhead would also believe in ritual magic.

"On August 15, 1780 Lessing wrote the words *Hen kai pan* ('One-and-All') in Greek characters on the wallpaper of Gleim's garden house near Halberstadt, which was used as a guestbook. Five years later, after Lessing's death in 1781, Friedrich Heinrich Jacobi revealed the secret of this motto when he published his conversations with Lessing in a booklet called **On the Doctrines of Spinoza, Exposed in the Form of Letters Adressed to Moses Mendelssohn** (1785). The secret meaning of the motto was *deus sive natura*; it was a declaration of Spinozism." [92]

The news of Lessing's Spinozism exploded like a bomb.[93] It immediately influenced the ongoing debate on the nature of the godhead, which was central to the philosophy of the Enlightenment and the ritual framework of Freemasonry. There was something mysterious, however, in Lessing's usage of the motto *Hen kai Pan* and Jacobi's recognition of it as representative of Spinoza's philosophy.

The hidden path to the origins of this motto leads to Ralph Cudworth, another important Hebraist from Cambridge, who used it in his **True Intellectual System of the Universe**, which appeared in 1678.[94] The lengthy debate between Mendelssohn and Jacobi concerned the real nature of Spinozism, which was elsewhere identified with Cudworth's hermetic conception of Egypt.

In his work, Cudworth presents Egypt as the land of learning[95] and introduces the 'One-and-All' as central to the Egyptian education of Moses.[96]

"But Cudworth's subject was not the transmission of Egyptian wisdom to the Hebrews. He was interested in its transmission to the Greeks. In this respect, Orpheus played precisely the same role of mediator as Moses did in the Biblical tradition. Orpheus was generally believed to have been initiated into the 'Greater' Egyptian mysteries. Egypt was thus connected to Europe in two ways: to Jerusalem via Moses and to Athens via Orpheus. The 'Moses connection' informed European theology and religion, whereas the 'Orpheus connection' influenced European philosophy. Orpheus brought the idea of *Hen kai Pan* to Greece where it influenced the philosophies of Pythagoras, Heracleitus, Parmenides, Plato, the Stoics and others." [97]

The formula *Hen kai Pan* plays an important role in the Greek texts compiled in Alexandria, which make up the **Corpus Hermeticum**, the **papyri Gracae Magicae** and the alchemical tradition.[98] In **The Magic Flute**, Tamino appears as a contemporary recreation of Orpheus. His journey to retrieve Pamina is analogous to Orpheus' journey to the Underworld.

Further proof of the connection between *Hen kai Pan* and the **The Magic Flute** can be found in the special language used by Sarastro as he addresses the priests at the very beginning of Act II: 'consecrated servants of the great gods Osiris and Isis in the Temple of Wisdom'.

'Osiris and Isis' is precisely what the formula *'Hen kai Pan'* refers to:

"Casting the idea of cosmotheism into the formula *Hen kai Pan* meant tracing it back to its Egyptian origin. Spinoza did not use the phrase. It was Cudworth who had pointed out its Egyptian origin. Berkeley even translated it as 'Osiris [*to Hen*] and Isis [*to Pan*]'. The *kai* in the Greek formula has the same meaning as Spinoza's *sive*. It amounts not to an addition, but to an equation. In its most common form, the formula occurs as *Hen to Pan*,

'All *is* One', the world *is* God. This is what 'cosmotheism' means."[99]

Thus Isis is the 'All' whose oneness is represented by Osiris—perpetually torn to pieces by his enemy Set. The scattered pieces are to be painstakingly collected so that the primordial oneness can be restored. This notion plays an important role in Freemasonry.

3

RITUAL ACTION

Investigating Egyptian beginnings— Ignaz von Born's way— is fundamentally the same as looking for a stable foundation. One for which the 'Law' acts as a bond between human structures and an invisible, but inferred hierarchy charged with its enforcement. The existence of that hierarchy can, of course, be doubted; but in the past its presence had to be reluctantly deduced from the consequences of mindless transgressions. The entire edifice of Greek Tragedy speaks to that point and the message is echoed with uncompromising precision by ancient Hebrew and Egyptian sources. We have progressed in certain areas since then, but the basic concept of a harmonious order — equivalent to the Egyptian *Maat*— has never been invalidated. We may now believe in 'ourselves', in 'technology', or in 'progress', but none of this really matters if it cannot be integrated by means of a higher 'Truth' that effectively harmonizes the different parts.

"*Maat* designates the idea of a meaningful, all-pervasive order that embraces the world of humankind, objects and nature— in short, the meaning of creation, the form in which it was intended by the creator god.[...] The meaning of creation lies in its plenitude, which yields order and justice. [...] Plenitude was a matter of abundance and its just distribution. The former was a divine responsibility, and the latter was the King's, a division of labor that was expressed by means of an exchange. In the cult ritual, the king offered *Maat* to the divine, and especially to the sun god Re." [1]

Spencer's **Urim and Thummim** concentrated on the significance of the breastone worn by the Hebrew high-priest. That stone represented '*Maat*' as an active symbol of the 'Law'. The idea of looking back in time for meaningful insights, already inaugurated by Spencer, should be pursued to its next logical step if we wish to understand what lies behind these concepts. Archaic institutions relied on ritualized forms of government, where political activity was inconceivable outside of a well established ritual framework. As Walter Burkert points out:

"Whether in Israel, Greece, or Rome, no agreement, no contract, no alliance can be made without sacrifice.[...] Families and guilds organize themselves into sacrificial communities; so too cities at a festival, as well as gatherings of larger political groups.[...] The closer the bond, the more gruesome the ritual.[...] In a sacrifice, the circle of participants is segregated from the outside world. Complicated social structures find expression in the diverse roles the participants assume in the course of the ritual, from the various 'beginnings', through prayer, slaughter, skinning, and cutting up, to roasting and, above all, distributing the meat. [...] The sacrificial community is thus a model of society as a whole, divided according to occupation and rank." [2]

Today there is no room for primitive behavior and its complicated ethics. The ancients, however, needed no excuse to justify their sacrificial rituals. Their meat did not come shrink-wrapped and they had real decisions to make. They understood that city walls built to protect against outside threats were just as likely to be used for confinement.

The poets of old would have noticed that the only surviving homonym for the Greek word *polis*— used to designate a city— now happens to be the word *police*, which subtly betrays the essence of our modern social order. An order that relies on man-made rules instead of the 'Law'. The ancient Egyptians, or even the Greeks, had a totally different conception of the city:

"The city was the first and oldest work of creation, and it essentially preceded the actual creation, which was possible only through and from it. In an old text , the creator god described the primeval condition before creation 'When Heliopolis was not yet founded that I might be in it'. For the Egyptians a city was a temple located on the primeval mound, the home and domain of an autochthonous deity." [3]

Language always betrays its casual users and the same ambivalent pattern is again found in our use of the term *fraternity*, which outside of pure fiction refers only to groups of rowdy young people living together around an institution of higher learning. Such groups are survivors of ancient hunting societies through which suitably aggressive adolescents were brought into the ruling elite:

"Although the male societies that had been superimposed on the family structure lost their ostensible function when the hunt was abandoned, they were reestablished among planters as secret, or mask, societies. At the center was a secret sacrifice, and if the aggression there did not suffice, it was worked out within the society itself.[...] Likewise, the conflict between the generations became highly dramatized in the initiation rituals. Deprived of its hunting quarry, the secret society makes the initiand himself into a victim. The group's aggression becomes focused on this man and he is forthwith killed— symbolically, of course [...] However, the bloodshed and the refined methods of torture are very real and guarantee the seriousness of the ritual. The gruesome 'evil' at work in the ritual fulfills a function, i.e. to preserve a social structure over the course of generations." [4]

In antiquity, the mysteries of the *polis* were sometimes transmitted by means of riddles cast in stone. Foundation myths are full of sacrificial or building metaphors. The fiery character of the primordial foundation is emphasized throughout. Gregory Nagy mentions that the Greek 'hearth' (*hestia*) was a symbol for the generation of legitimacy and that, in Athens, the *arkhon*'s authority was derived from the Common Hearth (Aristotle, ***Politics*** 1322b). [5] He adds that this symbolism must be interpreted as an Indo-European legacy, since the hearth was identified with sacrificial fire (*Agni*).

The concept of illumination, or fire, was central to the establishment of a social unit, and it was just as present in geomantic aspects of the foundation process. In Greece, divination (*mantike*) guided the establishment of distant colonies and it was always the province of Apollo and his blind seers. Blindness indicated that the mode of perception had nothing to do with external light. It was the result of an inner illumination, granted by the universal Sun (Apollo) whose visible light informed only ordinary existence.

For the ancients, as a rule, true vision was exercised in time, not in space. It consisted in reaching for the beginning— for a 'first time', during which the phenomenon observed was not yet in motion. All foundation activity thus required a geomantic development of time into space.

At Delphi, the strongest verb used in oracular pronouncements was *semainein*, meaning to 'make known by signs, markings, references and indices'. As Marcel Detienne points out, this verb created a bridge between the spoken word and active wandering. [6] It corresponded to an initial impulse through which the journey was given its spatial characteristics:

"At the heart of the founder's activity, two terms are closely associated: the verb *ktizein* and the word *arkhé* [...] *Ktizein*, as we have already indicated, spells at the same time 'to clear the land' and 'to found' [...] the word *arkhé*, linked to the verb *arkhein*, seems to hold a double meaning right from the start: 'beginning' and 'command'; the first as a development in time, the second as it applies to a social hierarchy. That which the Roman world distinguishes as *prima*, beginnings in time, and *summa*, beginnings in the order of importance and dignity, the Greeks gather in the notion of *arkhé*, whose semantic complexity gains the attention of Aristotle in his **Metaphysics**. *Arkhé* would be said of 'the starting point of the movement of a thing': such as, for instance, the *arkhé* of a line (*mékos*) or of a trail (*hodos*)." [7]

Art and architecture were often by-products of this foundation activity. They were used to encode signs (*sema*) seen during the journey so that they could be preserved as visible and durable symbols. The language of signs provided a trail that could always lead back to the beginning— to the oracular word that started it all.

In construction the use of large building blocks implies a solid ritual foundation. As the distance to the 'first time' grows, less permanent structures start to appear. They are made of smaller stones and produce less durable landmarks.

To the increased structural instability of the modern *polis*, corresponds an injection of common materials, but also of common words. The ritual dimension of language is lost. The shift of emphasis from inner significance to objective reality is part of that transition. By abandoning forms of expression predominantly based on prophetic vision, we unwittingly reject the solid foundation on which our very existence depends.

The oracular word gives meaning to action because it comes from an established source. As a signifier it still has to be interpreted; but any errors of interpretation are just that. They cannot invalidate the original Word.

In the cryptic drawing chosen by Ignaz Alberti for the frontispiece of the first edition of **The Magic Flute**'s libretto (1791), we find the ambivalent symbolism of the cave. It indirectly refers to Hiram's assassins and their hiding place; but at the same time portrays the dying master (Hiram) lying in darkness as he gazes toward a barely visible acacia bush hanging near the ceiling. In Masonic symbolism, the acacia bush stands for the Lost Word and legend says that its flowering is an indication of the Word's imminent rediscovery.[8] Every rebirth comes in colors of light and fire:

"I close," says Gregory Nagy, " by citing once more a striking detail from the myth about the begetting of Servius, the Italic king par excellence, from the sacrificial fireplace.[...] To mark the moment that his kingship is revealed, the head of Servius literally lights up. The radiant visage of the king, the ideal human, is a theme that may be linked with the etymology that I have already suggested for the Greek *anthropos* 'human', that is, 'he who has the looks of embers'. In line with a ubiquitous theme of mythmaking, that the first human is the first king, this visage of the king with the visage glowing from the fire of the hearth is a symbol for the never-ending search of myth to grasp the celestial affinities of humankind." [9]

The 'look of embers' is congruent with the requirements for leadership found in ancient Israel as well. Whereas in Greece, the oracular Word is acquired by traveling to the *omphalos* at Delphi; in Hebrew tradition, the divine Word is forever encapsulated in the Torah, where it is also associated with light and fire, as well as the instruments of foundation:

"Two aggadot in Exodus Rabbah II connect the light of Torah with the light of creation: just as the process of creation commenced with light, so the process of constructing the Tabernacle began with making the Ark, which would enshrine the light of Torah that preceded even creation itself." [10]

Greek notions of 'beginning' and 'command', found in the word *arkhé,* are reflected in Jewish tradition by the inclusion of the commandments in the Torah, by whose light the human journey is informed:

"A Midrash in Deuteronomy Rabbah attributed to Bar Kappara [...] invokes Proverb 6.23, 'For the commandment (*mitzvah*) is a lamp (*ner*) and the Torah a light (*'or*) [...] Moreover, just as Moses, the paradigmatic sage, acquired his lustrous countenance through contact with the light of Torah, so the faces of the sages who study and expound Torah are said to be illuminated with radiance." [11]

There is no background to suggest that this light is to be interpreted as the light of human reason. Jewish and Greek illumination was tied to notions of renewed vitality:

"The Torah is more than the Law of Moses; it is the memorial attesting the deeds performed by the Lord for His Chosen People [...] The traditional lore of God's people was transmitted from parents to children, not as tales of a dead past but as a living and life giving force in the present. In order to remain vital, however, the past must be capable of being revitalized by every generation; every generation must be able to express its own fears and hopes in retelling the story of the forefathers [...] The rabbis called this work of actualization '*Haggadah*', a term that intimates that Scripture itself is telling its new meaning." [12]

The deeds performed are always inferred from oracular advice received during the performance of sacrificial rituals. The traditions of Apollo are in total agreement with Hebrew sources, right down to the language:

"For instance, the technical term *azkarah* in the sacrificial ritual was understood to derive from the verb *zakhar,* 'to remember', because it was considered to be a memorial for the one who offered it, and consequently was rendered in Greek by *to mnemosynon*. According to Scripture, the mysterious objects *urim* and *tumim* served for inquiring as to God's will; as the Septuagint translation of these words— *delosis* and *aletheia* shows, they were understood to mean 'command' and 'truth'."[13]

There is a high degree of consistency between the oracular traditions of the Jews and the sacrificial foundation rituals of Apollo. The final correlation is achieved in the visions of Ezekiel and the *Ma'aseh Merkabah*, or 'Work of the Chariot', which forms the material for early Kabbalistic speculation.

It is easy to understand how important Ezekiel's vision was in the context of Jewish foundation rituals. Ezekiel lived in the seventh century B.C., under the rule of King Josiah, at a time when Israel was trying to affirm its independence from the great empires of the time. The very existence of Israel depended on its ability to solidify its independence and maintain the continuity of the Davidic line to which King Josiah belonged.

Unfortunately, in 609 B.C. the Egyptian army invaded and killed King Josiah during a battle near the ancient town of Megiddo. As a result, the Jewish aristocracy was destroyed and the Kingdom of Judah would soon be incorporated into the growing Babylonian Empire. As a young priest, Ezekiel was forced into exile and warned rebellious Jews, who had secretly allied themselves with the Egyptians, to be weary of Babylon, which, based on his vision, merely acted as God's agent:

"Ezekiel's vision was not one of static majesty but rather of a mobile, world-conquering divinity, supported by the four bizarre figures propelled by fiery 'wheels', and blazing above an icy ceiling into the limitless depths of the sky. [...] Yet at the core of the vision was an astute political warning. As the exiles spoke of the coming triumphs of the Egyptians and the independent Judean people, Ezekiel knew that even greater disasters loomed before them. [...] For the time being the Temple still stood in

Jerusalem, but its days were numbered if the new king and court in Jerusalem persisted with their plans. Instructed by the spirit of the fiery Chariot to warn the People of Israel of the impending disaster, Ezekiel acted like a madman enflamed by the spirit, lying in the dust and prophesying doom for the Holy City and its leaders. [...] Yet the People of Israel didn't listen to Ezekiel— even as they also refused to listen to the prophet Jeremiah [...] Step by step the Babylonian armies advanced through the country spreading terror and destruction [...] The terrible cruelty of that Babylonian campaign, culminating in the destruction of Solomon's Temple, is commemorated by Jews all over the world in the solemn yearly fast of Tisha b'Av." [14]

The Cherubim supporting the Chariot seen in Ezekiel's vision had characteristics associated with the Greek Sun-god Apollo. This opens up an important topic that cannot, however, be investigated in this context. There is a solar tradition that spans many ancient cultures; but our understanding of its true nature is so deficient that it would take an entire volume just to correct existing misconceptions. Robert Graves spent a great deal of time searching for the common roots and has this to say on that particular subject:

"The color of these bright cloud-borne Cherubim was Apollonian amber, like that of the man whom they served. They might well be ministers of Hyperborean Apollo the Sun-god, whose sacred jewel was amber. What is more, each golden spoke of the wheel ended in the leg of a calf and the golden calf was the sacred beast of the god, who according to King Jeroboam, had brought Israel out of Egypt, as it also was of the God Dionysus, the changing part of the unchanging Apollo. This apparent identification of Jehovah with Apollo seems to have alarmed the Pharisees, though they did not dare reject the vision. It is recorded that a student who recognized the meaning of *hashmal* (amber— '*hashmal*' is modern Hebrew for electricity; 'electricity' is derived from the Greek work for amber) and discussed it imprudently was blasted by lightning (Haggadah, 13.B). For this reason, according to the Mishnah, the *Ma'aseh Merkabah* ('Work of the Chariot') might not be taught to anyone unless he were not only wise but able to deduce knowledge through wisdom of his own, and no one else might be present during the teaching." [15]

In their role as gatekeepers of the primordial oracular tradition, the so-called 'masters of truth' receive their inspiration from either Yahwe or Apollo. In archaic Greece, the authoritative Word was entrusted to the diviner, the bard, or the king. In Israel, the founding king was also portrayed as a bard, but diviners were replaced by prophets.

Greek scholars have recently redefined 'Truth' (*aletheia*) as an evolving concept that can be traced through early texts. They refer to a process of secularization associated with historical developments. The human journey, as a whole, has always been dedicated to the search for truth; but as the concept evolves, so does the purpose of the search.

Truth can only exist in notions of unity, since it has to apply equally to every aspect of the primordial foundation. It is everywhere, but gets lost as soon as one tries to translate it into rational concepts that do not refer to a common origin and a 'first time'. Martin Heidegger addressed this issue during lectures given at the University of Freiburg in 1942:

"The unity of locality and journeying is not a unity that consists in linking two things together; but a unity of origin. We will learn to grasp this unity when we attempt thoughtfully to reflect upon the essence of history. For Hölderlin, that essence is concealed in human beings' becoming homely, a becoming homely that is a passage through and encounter with the foreign. [...] For only when the foreign is known and acknowledged in its essential oppositional character does there exist the possibility of a genuine relationship, that is, of a uniting that is not a confused mixing but a conjoining in distinction. By contrast, where it remains only a matter of refuting, or even annihilating the foreign, what necessarily gets lost is the possibility of a passage through the foreign, and thereby the possibility of a return home into one's own." [16]

In **The Masters of Truth in Archaic Greece**, Marcel Detienne notes that for Heidegger and his disciples the meaning of *aletheia* is part of the history of being.[17] He criticizes Heidegger for deriving the word *polis* from *polein*— an ancient form of the verb 'to be'. What bothers Detienne even more is the distance between Heidegger's lofty world of metaphysics, where *aletheia* and *polein* find their meaning in the notion of Being, and the world of down-to-earth politics, where Heidegger's behavior is viewed with suspicion.

Detienne points to Heidegger's active support of National Socialism in the 1930s to explain the philosopher's subsequent avoidance of political subjects. In reality, things are not as clear-cut as Heidegger's critics would like to believe. The problem comes not so much from Heidegger's perceived political stance as from his critics inability to recognize the underlying commitment to an oracular framework. The Nazi machinery was not a purely human creation and its occult dimension remains puzzling to minds accustomed to simple explanations.

Nazism, as a modern day plague, belongs to the ritual world of Apollo, where Pied Piper-like patterns predominate. Ivan Nagel reminds us of one particular fairy tale that must be credited for bringing about the necessary mental changes:

"**Die Zauberflöte**, like no other work of art, helped the German bourgeoisie transform the 'better country' into a different one: the theatrical island of the good, true and beautiful, encircled by floods of pragmatic barbarity. Anyone who as a child listened to the 'Hallen' aria sung by the Reich's basses Strienz, Hahn, Weber in broadcasts from unholy national memorial halls, offering 'strength through joy' to a murderously triumphant *Wehrmacht*, will never again hear that tune without anguish or shame. The whole teaching then lay in the words of simplicity monopolized by the Order: 'Anyone not cheered by these teachings / Does not deserve to be a man'." [18]

Heidegger once explained Germany's attraction to Hitler as a 'drunkenness of destiny' (*Schicksalrausch*) and there is no need to show that he was familiar with Euripide's **Bacchae** to suggest that he knew what he was talking about. Dionysus *Bakkheios*, the changing part of the unchanging Apollo, produces the murderous 'drunkenness' that manifests as Apollo's oracular will.

"From one end to the other of the Greek world," says Marcel Detienne, "Apollo and Dionysus gladly exchange epithets and instruments, roles and masks, qualities and functions without ever being confused for all that. It is perhaps around murder and the implements of murder that a significant difference appears between two powers otherwise so obstinate in their complicity. Of course, Dionysus is no stranger to killing or murderous gesture; he loves to drive those who resist him to an intoxicated rampage, the mother tearing her son to pieces or the father hacking at his child with an axe. The madness injected by Dionysus leads to murder, but the blood is not spilled by the god's hand, and the consequences of the murder only weigh on the victims of Dionysus. The Apollo of Sikyon, accomplished murderer of Python, on the other hand, is himself possessed by a mixture of madness and pollution; impure god, he must become acquainted with flight, wandering, exile; he, the healer god, who can defeat plagues, is forced to seek refuge near purifying influences strong enough to free him from the demented and mortal anxieties that the spilling of blood generates." [19]

In Greek mythology, the wolf belongs to Apollo and 'wolf madness' is linked to child sacrifices conducted in retribution for the nurturing of the young Dionysus. Since Dionysus— like Osiris— is a god of renewal, Apollo, his double, is the god who initiates the sacrificial ritual through which the renewal proceeds:

"The transformation of the King's daughter into a goddess is always linked to the birth of Dionysus in Thebes: Ino took care of the young Dionysus and brought him up. To avenge herself for this, Hera struck Ino and her husband Athamas with madness. The story normally goes on to tell of a double infanticide through which the family of Athamas was annihilated. [...] the names Athamas and Ino establish a close link with the werewolf motif from Lykaon to Phrixos. 'Wolf's madness', ëÿóóá, is at work here, as it was with Lykurgus. And as with him, Athamas wields the double axe in his pursuit." [20]

In the first volume of this series we went over the motif of the 'wolf' in Nazi mythology, and Hitler's unending fascination with this occult image. From there to the double axe, the road is fairly straight. As a symbol, the double axe of antiquity is nothing more than a particular form of the *vajra*, or lightning, wielded by Indo-European gods of war. Its original form is the swastika which, as René Guénon points out, stands for cosmic forces manifesting in creative or destructive manner depending on the direction of rotation.[21] The swastika incorporates the symbolism of the 'four right angles' (*arkhan*) supporting any 'true' foundation, and that of the four keys (Ã) used in magically binding and dissolving cosmic forces (*potestas ligandi et solvendi*).

The power to dissolve or bind, known as *'solve'* and *'coagula'*, was the most important secret of the Royal Art, or alchemy. In the symbolism of the 18th degree of the Masonic Scottish Rite, the term *solve* is sometimes represented by a sign pointing toward Heaven, while the term *coagula* is rendered by a sign pointing in the direction of the Earth.[22]

In his commentary on the *vajra* and swastika, as instruments used to bind cosmic forces, René Guénon adds that "This is also the figurative meaning of certain two-sided cutting weapons, notably in the symbolism of archaic Greece of the double axe which can be brought into correspondence with the caduceus. On another level, since lightning and thunder in Scandinavian tradition were represented by Thor's hammer, which can be assimilated to the Master's mallet in Masonic symbolism; the mallet thus appears as another equivalent of the *vajra*, and like it, has the double power of giving life or death, as is shown by its role during the consecration phase of initiation on one hand and in the legend of Hiram on the other." [23]

In an article on "The Letter G and the Swastika" (***Symboles de la Science sacrée***), Guénon continues to explore the polar symbolism of the swastika. He mentions that its four branches represent the Greek letter Ã, which for many reasons must be assimilated with the Masonic symbol G. The swastika, like the letter G, stand for the Pole star, which for an Operative Mason represents the active seat of the hidden Sun of the universe, referred to as *Iah*. The divine name *Iah*, which in the ***Sepher Yetzirah*** refers to the King of the Universe, is in correspondence with the first of the three Grand-Masters in the 7th degree of Operative Masonry.

Since the hidden Sun of the universe happens to be Apollo in Greek tradition, and Iahve (or Yahwe) in Hebrew tradition, it follows that the Hebrew letter *iod* must be considered symbolically equivalent to the Greek letter *gamma*. *Iod* corresponds to the Solomonic metaphor for the construction of the Temple, considered as the foundation edifice of Jewish tradition. As in the case of the letter *gamma*, the underlying symbolism is associated with construction.

Ã also represents the Masonic Square, this time derived from a right triangle of sides 3-4-5 where the hypotenuse (the side of length 5) is missing. What makes this interesting is that this symbolism expresses the current situation of Masonry with respect to the Lost Word. In the legend of the construction of the Temple it is said that the Word was known to three Grand-Masters (Solomon, Hiram King of Tyre and Hiram Abi), but that its communication in ritual form always required the presence of all three Grand-Masters. Thus, the absence, or death, of one of the masters automatically invalidated the transmission of the Word and Ã thus refers indirectly to the Lost Word that must be restored.

Guénon points out that an Operative Lodge could only be opened with the cooperation of all three Masters (those of the 7th, or highest degree of operative Masonry, to which the Hiramic legend originally belonged). They had to produce sticks of respective sizes 3, 4 and 5, and it was only after these sticks had been assembled to form a Pythagorean triangle that the Lodge was declared open for work.[24]

From the standpoint of myth, the events of history are just reflections of larger supra-historical processes. References to this order rarely follow rationally decipherable patterns. Most include apocalyptic scripts, full of hidden invocations:

"Every magic tradition transmits the use of invocations, sacred words which serve as focus points and keynotes in the formation and realization of the celestial realm upon earth, opening new modes of perception. Music is closely related to— indeed intertwined with— the use of invocation or sacred words because magic, like music, is the result of variations upon a theme and of harmonization [...] The function of the sacred word— the invocation and music used in ritual— [is to] transmute the energy used in habitually recreating our mundane world each instant into a higher key." [25]

To every successful harmonization correspond effects that are plainly visible in the phenomenal world. Apollo's dark side is uncannily reflected in Adolf Hitler's occult profile. The wolf aspect, already explored in this series, addresses one of them; but there are others. Like Hitler, Apollo is a *prokathegemon*, a war-like 'leader' who blazes the path as a forerunner. The supernatural form credited for opening the road to marching armies was that of the Apollo known as *Karneios*.[26]

In the legends of the Heraclids (the descendants of Heracles) this dark Apollo-figure plays a central role. There are many parallels between the mythical plight of the exiled Heraclids, who must eventually return to their homeland and that of the Jews who had to follow a similar path. Marcel Detienne sums up the action in telegraphic style:

"One day, all of a sudden, the Heraclids are told by an oracle to return to the land of their fathers. But no sooner have they started that adversities hold them in check. Apollo is consulted and lets them know that they have started out too soon. [...] Fifty years later they again want to move. How should their return be planned? The oracle tells them to wait for 'the third fruit'. Convinced that it means three years later, they get under way. Failure— they are defeated and turned into slaves. The descendants of the losers come back to Delphi. Same answer. They become obstinate. Apollo explains to them the error of their interpretation. The 'third fruit' meant 'the third generation'. Another oracle surfaces: on the road that must be followed, 'narrow waterway', 'straights'. At the appointed time the Heraclids attempt to board their ships. Their leader is struck by lightning , the army is in shambles. At that moment a diviner suddenly appears, reciting oracles as if he were possessed by a god. The Heraclids believe it is a trap. One of them, a certain Hippotès does not hesitate: with his javelin he kills the false prophet. The consequences are immediate: the fleet is destroyed, a horrible famine follows, the Heraclids are routed. Once more back in Delphi: they have stupidly killed Apollo's seer, whose name was Karnos and who was supposed to show them the way. Ten years of exile for the murderer. Let the others take as guide, as *hegemon*, 'the man with three eyes'. He will be coming to meet them. It is still a challenge to identify him: a man mounted on a one-eyed horse. His name is Oxulos, he has committed a murder and is coming back from exile. The 'man with three eyes' accomplishes what Apollo's envoy, his *phasma*, was meant to do: to lead the Heraclids to victory. With the Peloponnese conquered, the descendants of Heracles go through the gestures of renewing its foundation: they raise three altars for the Zeus of their fathers, offer sacrifices and conduct random drawings for the conquered territories." [27]

These blundering wanderings need to be put in perspective if they are to be understood at all. It is perhaps time to take a quick step back and focus on the major principles involved. A historical excursion into eighteenth-century Freemasonry may also prove helpful.

Eighteenth-century Masons were well aware of the heritage they were trying to rediscover. As Joseph de Maistre wrote in his ***Mémoire à Brunswick***, sent to his Lodge Brother Savaron, who represented the Chambéry Lodge at the Wilhemsbad Congress: true religion is much older than eighteen centuries— it was born the day the days were born [*"Elle naquit le jour que naquirent les jours"*].[28]

Here again we find the critical reference to a 'first time', to which an unbroken ritual connection must be maintained. The entire edifice of Freemasonry was constructed solely to provide human raw material for this chain. According to de Maistre, the recruitment process was divided into three phases. The first consisted in building a large pool of common men from which potential candidates for more advanced initiation could be extracted. At that stage people were to be taught morals and political awareness. During the second stage specific objectives were set; namely, the unification of Christian denominations and the instruction of governments. Universalist themes provided additional motivation for this broad exercise, which stretches to this day, in one form or another.

The third stage dealt with the study of transcendental Christianity, revelation, the science of man and sublime knowledge. In the case of sublime knowledge, de Maistre went even further, stating that "everything is mystery in both Testaments and the elect of either Law are nothing more than true initiates." [29]

The purpose of the Scottish Rite was to provide a formal foundation for this quest. As Grand-Master of the Rite, the Duke of Brunswick had to decide how this could best be achieved. De Maistre's main argument was that Israel, through Abraham and Moses, had received the guardianship of a pure religious tradition, and that it had been separated from the other nations for that specific reason. Whereas for the Gentiles, initiation was an individual act; it was, for the Hebrews a collective phenomenon. As a nation of initiates, the Jewish people had been raised to a special status, best represented by the concept of *election*.[30]

The Hebrews and the Heraclids have a similar heritage. Their trials and tribulations take place in a totally different dimension from that of routine human existence. In Greek mythology, Heracles is also the 'chosen one'— the only mortal raised to divine status as a result of his heroic efforts. The lot of the elect is to be given life-threatening challenges. They are constantly being offered ambiguous choices, where the wrong decision can be catastrophic. That is because their actions are ritual actions affirming or denying the fundamental unity on which everything else depends.

In Freemasonry, the ultimate objective is reintegration within a living tradition. This requires an artificial extension of the sphere of election, usually accomplished by occult means— that is Kabbalistic practices.

In his review of de Maistre's **Mémoire à Brunswick**, René Guénon (**Vers l'Unité**, March 1927) mentions that de Maistre bundles the three symbolic Degrees with the Higher Degrees of the Scottish Rite and then breaks them up again into three *classes*: the first comprised of the three symbolic Degrees, the second of the capitulary Degrees and the third of the superior Degrees.[31] The detailed mapping of these classes to the Sephirotic Tree of the Kabbalah and its significance for the Masonic approach to initiation— as an extension of 'election'— will be covered in a subsequent section.

The idea of 'election' is virulently dismissed by a number of contemporary Freemasons and one must, of course, question their motives. The prolific French Masonic writer, Daniel Beresniak, for instance, insists that 'tradition' is a major culprit in fostering religious fundamentalisms and a general lack of tolerance. He suggests that the point is not to perpetuate the dead letter of Scripture— in parrot like fashion, passing it for the authoritative Word— but to look for meaning wherever it can be found. A siren song that modern seekers never tire of hearing; for it says that they can approach meaning on their own terms:

"The 'Here everything is symbol' heard at the moment of admission to the Temple and which, like a musical leitmotiv, has punctuated the ceremony between symbolic journeys, announces the method of initiation: which is to recognize what has been scattered so that it can be brought together again. To dismember in order to better reconstruct. To decompose each meaning into its meaningful parts, as numerous as possible, so that it can be recovered whole again. Or put differently, to learn how worlds can be created... how to become 'divine'." [32]

Interestingly enough, it is in Wagner's **Siegfried** that the method advertised by Beresniak is put into practice with the most striking effect. As the young hero files the shattered pieces of his sword down to dust, to better reconstruct it into an unbreakable weapon, he begins to transcend human limitations. Wagner's procedure, unlike Beresniak's, is magical at heart. It uses the ritual of the Smith (Hephaestus, Ptah) where the *solve* and *coagula* are part of the procedure.

An object constructed ritually is not a physical object. Behind its magic birth lies the reconstruction of the Word, whose impact is always difficult to predict. Early in this series, we mentioned that the original **Nibelungenlied** was composed of magical incantations. In its theatrical adaptation by Wagner, the dark Apollo imagery consigned into its folds emerges once again as mythical identities are projected onto living people:

"There was a collection of reproductions from Hanfstaengl's studio that caught Hitler's attention. These were paintings by Franz von Stuck, a follower of Böcklin's with an eye for striking effects, who became one of the Führer's favorite artists. Like Wagner before him and Hitler after him, Stuck painted mythological figures in stark contrasts of light and shade [...] Hitler hung Stuck's painting **Sin** on his wall, and the staring eyes of Stuck's **Medusa**, he said, reminded him of his mother. But there was another work to which he may also have been particularly drawn— a painting which, remarkably, revealed his own features, mask-like, with black quiff and moustache, an expression of grim, determined heroism on his face and the clenched fist of the orator raised aloft. On this, Franz von Stuck's first oil painting, done in 1889, the grim features belonged to Wotan, god of war [...] Like Hitler, Wagner's Wotan took the name of 'Wolf' [...] Jakob Grimm's **German Mythology** states that Wotan is accompanied by two ravens, called Hugin and Munin. These were the nicknames given to Otto Dietrich and Ernst Hanfstaengl, Hitler's two closest followers in Munich." [33]

However coincidental it all appears, the fact remains that these identifications were made. If one takes into account Wagner's own cryptic references to Wotan's transformation into Titurel— mentioned earlier— as well as his symbolic equation of Titurel with the Roman Emperor Titus, an entire program begins to emerge.

Attempts have recently been made to trace Wagner's use of Masonic symbolism and one of these efforts comes from Jacques Chailley *(Parsifal, opéra initiatique,* 1979), who bases much of his analysis on Paul Legardien's work. Legardien reviewed *Parsifal* for the *Bulletin du Grand-Orient de Belgique* (1968, p. 19-47) and followed it up with a notebook sized evaluation of the *Ring*, titled *Symbolisme et Franc-Maçonnerie dans la Tétralogie Wagnérienne* (1995). In it, Legardien makes an interesting observation concerning Wotan. An observation that brings us back to the subject of the 'Law':

"Wotan who had wanted to assume both temporal and spiritual power by means of the 'Law', is thereby conscious, perhaps not of the real nature of spiritual power; but at least of its existence, and thus of the fact that it differs from temporal power. In other words the sovereign understands that the 'Law' he imposes, because it is fundamentally an imposition, alters the excellency of the power he wields and that of the 'Treasure' from which this power derives. This represents his 'inner thought', his 'will' and his 'divine element'. Wagner incarnates this idea in the character of Brünnhilde, Wotan's daughter, who *is* his thought"[34]

This is equivalent to Greek representations of Athena as the daughter born of Zeus' mind alone. Set free by Hephaestus, who split Zeus' forehead open with an axe, she represents the spontaneous spirit by which 'truth' unfolds.

Chailley argues that *The Magic Flute* is ritually equivalent to *Parsifal*, and that Parsifal himself is Tamino's older 'Brother'. He notes that Ingmar Bergmann, in his film version of the opera (1975), had a scene in which the singer playing Sarastro is shown going over the score of *Parsifal* during an intermission. The part he would have been studying is that of Gurnemanz and this subtly implies that the two operas are related.[35]

Bergman's intuitive grasp of the underlying correspondences was never converted into an explicit analysis. Chailley, however, proceeds with a side by side comparison of *Parsifal* and *The*

Magic Flute. But his method is crude and one is left with the impression that the facts can be stretched only so far.

Chailley's best moment comes when he shows, after Newman (IV, 40), that Wagner's most intimate circle fantasized a great deal about **The Magic Flute**. Much of it had to do with Malvina Schnorr's spiritist delusions, but there were curious angles that cannot be completely attributed to Malvina Schnorr. She was Wagner's first Isolde and went mad after a total breakdown:

"To present **Parsifal** as **The Magic Flute** according to Wagner is not an exaggeration. It is common knowledge that he had a particular predilection for Mozart's work. In a curious coincidence, it was the day after 11 November 1884, when, back from Italy, and after seeing a performance of **The Magic Flute** in Munich, he gratified Ludwig II with two successive auditions of the prelude to Parsifal, writing for him the famous notice concerning the Three Virtues [Faith, Hope and Charity] for which we have already established a kinship to Masonic ritual. In February of 1867, when her influence on Wagner was at its peak, Malvina Schnorr corresponded with Peter Cornelius giving Wagner the name of Sarastro and equating Ludwig II with Tamino. Cornelius was Papageno and she herself was the Queen of the Night." [36]

The ritual bridge between the **Ring** and **Parsifal**, is in Wotan's unexpected reappearance as Titurel in **Parsifal**. Wagner identified Titurel with 'Royal Power'. A power that had to be reintegrated with 'Spiritual Power' in order to get back to the rule of 'Law' for which Wotan was responsible.

In **Wagner's Hitler**, Joachim Köhler, concludes that Hitler was following stage directions set by Wagner's Bayreuth. Hitler's activities complied with Wagner's revolutionary, German centric and anti-semitic blueprints. But Köhler's conclusion is a bit too simplistic and raises Wagner to the level of an omnipotent magician. Wagner's 'magic' was not really his own. It was the timely activation of a much older magic already encoded in the

Nibelungenlied. A solar magic that Wagner never fully understood.

"Hitler's ability to cast himself simultaneously in the roles both of the young Siegfried and of his grandfather Wotan derived from their function in the *Ring*, where the hero carries out the acts of redemption that the god has decreed [...] Untainted by Old Testament influence, Wotan shows the same favors to his Wälsungen— and to their racial incarnation, the Germans— as did Yahweh to the descendants of Abraham." [37]

The unspoken link lies in the identification of Yahweh with Apollo, proposed elsewhere by Robert Graves. Wagner's anti-semitism was full of contradictions. *Parsifal* was his last opera (just as *The Magic Flute* was Mozart's) and its performance was originally reserved for Bayreuth— where it was to be performed as a ritual. It was therefore something of a surprise that the anti-semitic Wagner would select Herman Levi to conduct the premiere of *Parsifal* at Bayreuth:

"By all accounts Levi was visibly shaken when Wagner told him in January 1881 that he would be conducting *Parsifal*. There were many others who Wagner could have selected and the appointment of this particular Munich conductor was not a requirement (in 1876 Wagner chose Richter to conduct the *Ring* when only a few years earlier Ludwig had ordered his dismissal from Munich for refusing to conduct *Rheingold*). Contrary to popular belief Wagner was not forced by the king to accept Levi or lose the Munich orchestra. His decision in favor of Levi was made almost three years before the performance. However, as a ploy and a way out of an embarrassing predicament Wagner would have enjoyed the popular rumor that it was Levi or no Munich orchestra." [38]

Without going into long arguments concerning Wagner and the Jewish question, we can approach the matter on ritual grounds alone. In ancient Israel, for a ritual to be legitimate, it had to be performed by a Levite. Wagner was well aware of this requirement:

"Wagner had the highest opinion of the young conductor's abilities. Weingartner remarked upon the spiritual nature of his interpretations [..] But although Wagner declared his respect for a Jew who clung to the Biblical *Levi* and did not change to *Löwe* or *Lewy*, this was about the extent of his enthusiasm for installing Israel in the Bayreuth pit." [39]

Installing a Levite— even symbolically— in the Bayreuth pit would have been perfectly in line with Wagner's ritual objectives. The interaction between Levi and Wagner, during the sixteen performances of *Parsifal* at Bayreuth, was much deeper and affecting than anything commonly associated with a conducting assignment:

"Repetitions of the work with changing casts continued until August 29, when the sixteenth presentation closed the festival. During this final presentation of *Parsifal* Wagner slipped into the pit and conducted the closing act from the twenty-third bar of the transformation music to the very end. A legend quickly grew; Wagner, it was said, sensing that Levi was ill, had hastened to relieve him. But Heckel confirms suspicions that the composer planned to lead the final scene, as does a letter to Rabbi Levi of Giessen from his son. It relates just what happened in the deep pit beneath the stage into which Wagner rarely descended. Herman [Levi] wrote to Giessen on August 31, by which time he had completely recovered his health. A nervous fatigue, he related, had seized him *after* the final performance of *Parsifal*. This performance had been an overwhelming emotional experience. 'During the transformation music, the master came into the orchestra, grabbled his way (*krabbelte*) up to the podium, took the baton from my hand, and conducted the performance to the end. I remained standing next to him because I feared he might make mistakes; but this was an idle fear; he conducted with the certainty of one who might have spent his entire life only as a *Kapellmeister*. At the end of the work, the public broke into a jubilation defying description. But the master did not show himself, remained sitting among us musicians, and made bad jokes. And when after ten minutes the noise would not abate, I cried out with all my might, 'Quiet, quiet!' [...] The Festspielhaus curtain then fell before Wagner's eyes for the final time." [40]

Levi was one of the pallbearers at Wagner's funeral and that gives a surrealistic feel to the entire picture. Ritual action is the process by which mythical powers are brought to life and induced to dwell in the Temple. There is a necromantic aspect to this magic and Wagner's dealings with Parsifal expose some of the principles involved. It also gives some idea of what Mozart and his Brethren may have been up to in **The Magic Flute**. As subsequent chapters will show, there are similarities between what Wagner was trying to achieve and what Mozart had set out to do.

"The principle of plenitude that made the world a flourishing paradise was *Maat*, the 'Right'. Its opposite devastated the world, because the gods renounced their dwelling, not only in the temples of the local dimension, but also in the life-giving powers of nature in the cosmic dimension." [41]

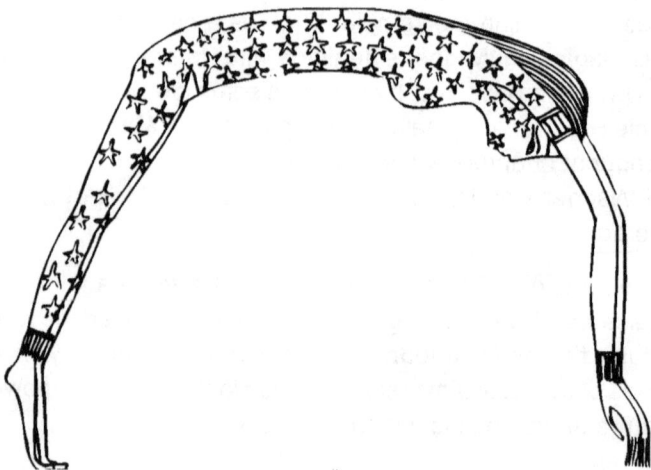

4

TOWARD EGYPTIAN MASONRY

Tamino's trials take place in a Masonic Temple where Isis and Osiris are invoked as protective deities. This means that Egyptian Masonry warrants further investigation. Here we join the raging controversy still pitting proponents of Mozart 'the rationalist' against those who suggest a more esoteric inclination. Valid positions are articulated by both sides and this makes a definitive conclusion difficult to reach.

'We would do well to remember," writes Maynard Solomon, "that Mozart was firmly associated with rationalist and Illuminist Lodges rather than with those of the Rosicrucian or Asiatic Brethren, that his close Masonic Brothers were anticlerical and believers in natural law, and that he nowhere expressed even veiled sympathy for occult or pseudo-scientific currents." [1]

A statement which Nicholas Till counters with the following reminder:

"Rosicrucianism had a strong following in Vienna. Count Dietrichstein, the Grand Master of all the Lodges in the Habsburg territories and one of Mozart's most influential patrons, was well known as an active Rosicrucian. Mozart's Lodge '*Zur Wohltätigkeit'* was, we have seen, a Catholic Lodge. [...] '*Zur Wohltätigkeit'* had attracted a number of members also interested in the esoteric Christianity of Rosicrucianism.[...] **Die Zauberflöte** is littered with Rosicrucian and esoteric Christian symbolism." [2]

In the face of such contradictory assertions it becomes clear that the issue cannot be resolved on the basis of fact alone. The problem has to be restated in such a way that Mozart's options can at least be understood. Occultism is not necessarily at odds with anticlerical sentiments, or a well-grounded belief in natural law. Nor are anticlerical sentiments above suspicion when they are voiced by former Jesuits massively present in Illuminist Lodges.

As the official custodian of a knowledge that could not be disseminated freely, Freemasonry had to protect its symbolic infrastructure. There are still people who argue that there is no Masonic secret and that all of this so-called knowledge can be culled from books, otherwise available to anyone who cares to read them. That may well be true, but there are patterns pointing to more complex developments that span centuries, if not millennia, in which Masonry plays a significant role.

In the days of Operative Masonry, many secrets consisted of building techniques. The Guilds protected them and there is little doubt regarding their existence or efficacy. But it is toward the symbolic side of the Craft that we need to turn our attention. With the advent of Speculative Masonry, the emphasis was placed squarely on rituals and the secrets associated with their performance were communicated strictly through initiation.

The complexities of ritual are such that it is very difficult to explain how they relate to everyday life. There is also the outstanding question of the relationship between Masonic ritual and religious ritual. At the heart of the matter is a nagging suspicion that religion did not start with a warped legacy and that Masonic ritual was originally designed to emphasize symbolic aspects of man's relationship with the world, as opposed to his relationship with the deities of various religions.

Mozart could not have bypassed the elementary teachings of his Craft and it is doubtful that they would have escaped the attention of his closest Masonic associates. The issue is not their collective dedication to reason and science in the face of rampant superstition; but the root cause of their zeal. Mysticism is not Masonic at heart. Esotericism is, because it focuses on problems of ritual behavior.

The main theme of the Enlightenment was universalism coupled with tolerance. Freemasonry differed from organized religion in that it required nothing more than a professed belief in a superior being. The battle against superstition was just a chapter in the fight for tolerance.

In Mozart's day the perennial outsiders were predictably women and Jews. Several branches of Masonry attempted to do something about these exceptions. The 'Egyptian Masonry' of Cagliostro promoted the admission of women. The Order of the Asiatic Brethren was open to both Christians and Jews. Founded in Vienna in 1737, the Order of Mopses, was governed jointly by a man and a woman.

"The problem of a female Masonry took on a new aspect when, about 1784, the renowned adventurer Cagliostro founded, as the 'Egyptian Rite', his own Freemasonry made up of Lodges admitting both sexes and mixing magical rites with alchemy, spiritualism, and witchcraft. He had taken the title of 'Grand Copt' and had promoted his companion, Lorenza Feliciani, to the rank of Grand Mistress of feminine initiation under the name of 'Queen of Sheeba'." [3]

The final scene of **The Magic Flute** showcases Tamino and

Pamina in 'priestly vestments'. Mozart was obviously willing to open the Temple of Wisdom to women. But what about the Jews? How big a consideration was that? Mozart had direct contacts with members of the Asiatic Brethren and we can only assume that he was aware of the problem.

Official Lodge affiliations did not preclude experimentation across the entire Masonic spectrum. Many Masons cumulated initiations and there was a very diverse network of Lodges in constant contact over most of Europe and even the rest of the world. In his summation of these interactions, Charles Porset (**Hiram Sans-Culotte? Franc-maçonnerie, Lumières et Révolution — Trente ans d'études et de recherches** [1998]) hints at Mozart's almost inevitable emergence as a 'noble traveler' in the Cagliostro tradition:

"The university library of Poznan offers a Masonic repository of the highest interest, where one finds numerous Masonic texts from eighteenth-century France, seized in the Lodges by the Nazis during their occupation of Poland. The catalog, in the form of cards, transferred to microfiche by the publisher Olms from Hildesheim (Germany), gives a good idea of the important value of this fund which, according to researchers who have been there, has not been completely inventoried. [...] one can [also] imagine that the systematic exploration of the archives of the USSR's former satellites (I am thinking, in particular, of the State Archive of Mersebourg— ex-GDR— now transferred to Berlin for what concerns the Masonry and movement of the *Illuminaten*) should yield many documents that can shed new light on the history of French Masonry, given the numerous relationships established throughout the eighteenth-century between the French Lodges and those of eastern Europe. The travels of a Cagliostro, Casanova or Mozart give a hint of this activity." [4]

The emphasis has generally been on Mozart's music making and no one has ventured to look at his journeys as anything other than the travels of a touring artist. That they may have served as a cover for Masonic activity has seldom been suggested. Mozart's present day status has obscured his real standing in the society of his time. Masonic associations would have brought him greater social recognition than his music.

As Casanova, himself, asserts in his biography:

"Any young man who travels, who wants to know the world and yet does not want to feel inferior to others and excluded from the company of his peers in the times we live in, must be initiated into what is called Masonry." [5]

As an ambassador for Viennese Masonry, Mozart would have been exposed to the most controversial questions of his time. His trip to Berlin in 1789, for instance, occurred at a time when major changes were taking place:

"Frederick II died in August 1786 and was succeeded by his nephew, Frederick William II, whose ascent to the throne prompted considerable anxiety within the Berlin Enlightenment. In the early 1780s, Frederick William had been drawn to Christian mysticism and was increasingly influenced by opponents of the Enlightenment, such as his most trusted adviser, Johann Christoph Wöllner." [6]

Both Wöllner and Frederick William II were somehow associated with the Asiatic Brethren (see below) and Mozart's mysterious visit to Berlin— no one was ever able to justify the trip on musical grounds alone— seems perfectly timed with Wöllner's rise to power:

"Despite Wöllner's revulsion against the Enlightenment, the first two years of Frederick William's reign were difficult to distinguish from that of his uncle [Frederick II]. The break came only after Wöllner had consolidated his position within the court, eventually replacing Zedlitz as minister of justice on 3 July 1788 and assuming responsibility over the Ecclesiastical Department. Six days later he issued his Religion Edict, which criticized

Protestant clergy for reviving 'the miserable, long-refuted errors of the Socinians, deists, naturalists, and other sectarians' and disseminating them among the people in the name of '*Aufklärung*'." [7]

The Edict initiated a spirited debate on religious fanaticism and its consequences. A flood of pamphlets, critical of Wöllner's action, argued against restrictions placed on the Enlightenment. To combat this tide, Wöllner issued a Censorship Edict in December 1788. Any writings on religious subjects now had to be reviewed for approval prior to publication. This forced two of the major organs of the *Aufklärung* to leave Berlin. One was the **Berlinische Monatsschrift**, the other Friedrich Nicolai's **Allgemeine Deutsche Bibliothek**.[8]

That Mozart's trip to Berlin was under the aegis of the Asiatic Brethren is further suggested by the linkage of Count Thun to the cast of characters involved. Count Thun had joined the Asiatic Brethren (see below) and his son-in-law was Mozart's companion on that particular trip:

"Count Thun had been a member of '*Zur wahren Eintracht*' in the early 1780s, but after the Masonic reform of 1785 he had, like Mozart, joined the Rosicrucian Lodge '*Zur neugekrönte Hoffnung*'. A member of Mozart's former Lodge '*Zur Wohltätigkeit*' who is not recorded as a member of '*Zur neugekrönte Hoffnung*' was Count Thun's son-in-law, Prince Karl Lichnowsky (later to be Beethoven's closest and most loyal patron). In 1789 Mozart traveled in the company of Lichnowsky to Berlin, where he was welcomed by the Rosicrucian monarch Frederick William II. [...] The most likely explanation is that Lichnowsky and Mozart traveled to Berlin at Frederick William's invitation as Rosicrucian emissaries from Vienna." [9]

That the trip was commissioned by the Rosicrucians is very unlikely for a number of reasons. The Asiatic Brethren and the Rosicrucians were at odds over the admission of Jews into

Masonic Lodges. The characters referred to so far (except for Lichnowsky) all appear as Asiatic Brethren in one Masonic publication or another. Then there is the recently discovered mystery [1991] of a lawsuit that Lichnowsky filed against Mozart in November of 1791. It was officially to recover a debt of 1,435 florins 32 kreuzer.[10]

"It was not unheard of for a Prince of the Holy Roman Empire of German Nations to sue a commoner, but for Lichnowsky to sue Mozart in the circumstances does seem extremely odd. Even odder is the fact that the debt was patently 'hushed up' immediately after Mozart's death. [...] How was it possible that the debt is never mentioned again? That Constanze was paid the last part of her late husband's salary? Did someone pay off the debt between 12 November and 5 December, thus avoiding the need for attachment of Mozart's goods and chattels?" [11]

There are no answers to these mysteries, but one senses that they are all related: the trip to Berlin, the Asiatic Brethren, Frederick William's esoteric agenda and Mozart's financial indebtedness to Lichnowsky. At the tail end of it all, *The Magic Flute* resurfaces, and Nicholas Till argues that Frederick William may well have planted the seeds of what eventually flowered into Mozart's last opera.[12] There is evidence that he got involved with *The Magic Flute* some time after the composer's death:

"Shortly after Mozart's death Frederick William made a personal effort to give Constanze financial support by buying items from Mozart's estate, and four years later was to command that Constanze be given a benefit performance of *La clemenza di Tito*. Furthermore, in March 1792, only three months after Mozart's death, the king attempted to get *Die Zauberflöte* performed in Berlin. He sent the score to the director of the National Theater for examination, and received the reply that the work would be incomprehensible to an audience 'ignorant of certain mysteries, and incapable of seeing through the dark and heavy veil of allegory'." [13]

The founder of the Asiatic Brethren, Baron Hans Heinrich von Ecker-und-Eckhoffen (1750-1790) was quite a controversial figure. Excluded from the Golden Rosy-Cross for insubordination,[14] he seems to have thrived on confrontations with the established Masonic hierarchy. His Order was founded in Vienna and Jacob Katz (**Jews and Freemasons in Europe, 1723-1939**) notes that shady personalities were involved from the very beginning.

Legend has it that one of the enigmatic originators of the order was a Franciscan monk named Justus (civil name Bischoff), who lived in Jerusalem, where he had met a group of Jewish Kabbalists and was given access to their manuscripts and rituals. In the order, Justus went by the name of *Ish Zaddik* and he is mentioned in both versions of the history of the Asiatic Brethren published by Franz Molitor.[15] The next, no less enigmatic figure, went by the name of Azariah, and it was he who supposedly gave Justus the manuscripts. Azariah, according to another associate of Ecker's, Ephraim Joseph Hirschfeld (1755-1820), belonged to a Kabbalistic sect identified as a vestige of the Sabbatai Zevi movement.

Jacob Katz mentions that "even though the connection of the Asiatic Brethren with the Sabbatian movement is conclusively proved by another source [...] the personality of Azariah lacks substance; information about him is too meager and full of contradictions." [16] The other source referred to by Katz is Baron Thomas von Schoenfeld, the third original participant in the foundation of the Order. Schoenfeld was an apostate Jew and a prolific writer who filled the function of copyist and translator of Kabbalistic works. He was born Moshe Dobruschka and had been an active follower of the Sabbatian movement.[17]

In 1781, Ecker published a book (**Der Rosenkreuzer in seiner Blosse**) in which he denounced the Rosicrucians, taking issue with them for not accepting Jews as members unless they were extremely affluent.[18] In 1782, he tried to present his new order at the Masonic congress of Wilhelmsbad, convened by Duke Frederick of Brunswick, the head of all German Masons. His main supporter was the Landgrave Karl von Hessen, who administered the province of Schleswig for the Danish monarchy. The Berlin Lodge opposed him and filed a protest against his appearance at Wilhelmsbad:[19]

"Had Ecker, even then, included in the opening of his constitution any paragraph providing Jews with the prospect of being accepted on an equal level with Christians, he could never have hoped to have his constitution ratified by the conference at large. The tenor of the Berlin protest, too, proves that the Jewish question had nowhere been placed on the agenda. [...] Ecker [...] had been denounced as a magician consorting with occult powers." [20]

Accusations of this sort are sometimes too easily dismissed and the timing of Ecker's movement indicates that it was part of a much larger effort aimed at incorporating the Jews of Europe into its society.

By 1782 the Jews of Austria had won their emancipation. The Edict of Toleration, proclaimed in January of that year, shows that the winds of political change were starting to pick up. Ecker had settled at Innsbruck and that was where he met Hirschfeld, who would become one of his closest collaborators. Hirschfeld was working as a bookkeeper and a teacher. He had met Baron Schoenfeld, who used him as a copyist.[21]

Hirschfeld had extensive contacts with 'Enlightened' Berlin Jews, but did not ascribe to their philosophy. His father was a cantor and a Talmudic scholar who had serious connections in German power circles. He dedicated one of his works to the Margrave Karl Friedrich of Baden[22] and his son, Ephraim, obviously benefited from that:

"Johann Georg Schlosser, Goethe's brother-in-law and a leading official in the Margrave's service, provided for the son's education, perhaps after the elder Hirschfeld had died. He enrolled him in the local gymnasium and later sent him to the University of Strasbourg to study medicine. [...] After his sojourn in Strasbourg, Hirschfeld moved to Berlin, taking with him the recommendation of his benefactor, Schlosser, to Moses Mendelssohn. There he obtained employment as tutor and bookkeeper in the household of David Friedländer. According to the testimonial given to him by Mendelssohn when he left Berlin two years later, Hirschfeld had been a frequent visitor." [23]

Mendelssohn was Hirschfeld's mentor, but Katz claims that Hirschfeld never subscribed to the rationalistic doctrines of Mendelssohn and that he turned against them in the end. It is interesting to note that the legend of the Asiatic Brethren's foundation— with its claim to high Kabbalistic patronage from Jerusalem— is not reflected in its published rituals.

Katz attributes the Order's deviant practices to Sabbatian influences. Some are identifiable in Moses Dobrushka-Schoenfeld's background, others come from the secular outlook of the Haskalah.

"The theology of the Asiatic Brethren has been subjected to a critical analysis by Professor Gershom Scholem. His study has revealed that on its theoretical level this theology was a conglomeration of principles drawn from Christian and Jewish sources, Kabbalistic and Sabbatian ideas were jumbled together with Christian theosophic doctrines. The same applied to symbols and festive and memorial days, which were fundamental to the activities of the various degrees of the Order. [...] The Christian Asiatic, however, did not have to suffer pangs of conscience. He could easily have regarded himself as completely faithful to the tenets of his religion [...] The Jew, on the other hand, could hardly remain oblivious to the fact that he was trespassing beyond the boundaries of his own traditions. The adoption of Christian symbols could on no account be reconciled with the doctrines of Judaism. And if these acts were not a sufficiently serious breach of his faith, he was also required, as a member of the Order, to eat pork with milk as part of some solemn celebration. Even the most ignorant of Jews was fully aware that he was thereby violating a law of his own religion. [...] [Some] members of the Order [were] adherents of the disintegrating tendencies of the Haskalah which, explicitly or tacitly, provided the justification for abandoning Jewish traditions. The histories of the Itzig and Arnstein families in Berlin and Vienna respectively furnish a clear example of this process of alienation, which impelled many to forsake Judaism altogether."[24]

Mozart lived in the Arnstein household for an entire year. He also owned a copy of Moses Mendelssohn's **Phaedon**— a treatise on the immortality of the soul. Whether that makes him an Asiatic sympathizer is open to debate. The master of his Lodge (*'Zur Wohltätigkeit'*), Otto von Gemmingen-Hornberg, is on Katz's list of Asiatic Brethren and Katz mentions Molitor's reference to Count Thun as a member of the Order.[25] Gemmingen was not a casual figure among Mozart's Masonic relations: "Indeed, it may well have been Gemmingen-Hornberg who suggested to Mozart that he should become a Mason." [26]

Count Thun's wife, Wilhelmine, was one of Mozart's principal patrons in Vienna. And to this mostly circumstantial evidence we can also add an entry in Johann Georg Kronauer's album which suggests that Mozart was an Asiatic Brother.[27]

The origin of these 'Asiatic' influences is important to trace. There is no doubt that they lead back to Jewish sources, but there is much confusion regarding their orientation. On the side of the rational Enlightenment, we find Moses Mendelssohn; on the Kabbalistic front, his protégé, Hirschfeld.

Moses Mendelssohn was Lessing's best friend and the most important companion in his search for 'truth'. This brings us to the subject of Lessing's conversion to Spinozism which is at the heart of the Egyptian discourse that so interested Austrian

Freemasons.

Mendelssohn pretended not to care for Freemasonry. His correspondence on the subject shows that he kept using a clever trick in his discussions with Lessing. He voiced his contempt for any institution willing to conceal its 'truths' from qualified seekers. In the process, he was able to engage Lessing— the author of **Dialogues for Freemasons**— to better promote the idea of universal inclusion, which the Order of the Asiatic Brethren tried to implement. Speaking to Lessing, he had this to say:

"From our early youth we have been seeking the truth. Ever since we became friends we have sought it jointly, with all the faithfulness [with which] it wants to be pursued. Now there might be truths that Lessing swore in the most solemn fashion not to reveal to his friend of twenty-five years standing, and yet I am supposed not to be even curious to know these truths. However, if it is not truths that the Order transmits to its adepts, you will all the more concede that I— [can have little respect for Freemasonry]." [28]

Mendelssohn had very little need for the so-called 'truths' known to Lessing. He was himself a member of the *Mittwochsgesellschaft* (the Wednesday Society), a secret society composed of 'friends of the Enlightenment', closely linked to the **Berlinische Monatsschrift**. It was a para-Masonic organization whose activities extended well beyond intellectual debates:

"The *Mittwochsgesellschaft* was a recent addition to the host of secret societies that flourished in Prussia and other German states in the last half of the eighteenth-century. Such societies satisfied a number of needs. In an age in which many individuals no longer found meaning in the rituals of orthodox religion, the ceremonies associated with some of these societies may have well provided an appealing and powerful substitute." [29]

Secret orders maintain a separation from the profane world in which everyday activities take place. In that context the argument between Mendelssohn and Lessing can be viewed as inclusion versus exclusion.

For Mendelssohn, whose argument is outlined in **Jerusalem** [1783], Judaism was defined by Mosaic legislation, which he considered forever binding on the Jews. The point is easily conceded; but it also underscores a fundamental difference between the Jews and other people— as Joseph de Maistre pointed out. A difference that militates strongly against their inclusion.

The paradoxical stance adopted by Mendelssohn glances over the fact that a priestly nation cannot compromise its fundamental values for the sake of social acceptance. The forerunner of this type of thinking was Spinoza, who in his Theological-Political Treatise of 1670— published anonymously— encouraged a positivist outlook on the subject of 'Revelation', which he tried to put on a par with natural knowledge.

"When they [people] speak of prophetic knowledge, they wish to exclude natural knowledge. Nevertheless it can be called divine with as much right as anything else, since God's nature, insofar as we participate in it, and his decrees, as it were, dictate it to us. [..] But though natural knowledge is divine, nevertheless those who spread it cannot be called prophets. For the things they teach other men can perceive and embrace with the same certainty and excellence as they do, and that not by faith alone." [30]

By making everything subservient to reason Mendelssohn followed Spinoza and effectively stifled forms of consciousness based on ritual knowledge— of which Judaism is one of the most important. His 'Judaism' consisted of an unstable mixture of rationalist doctrines that departed from tradition as much as the letter of the Law often departs from its spirit.

"*Moshe mi-Dessau* [Moses of Dessau], as he signed his name in Hebrew, and Moses Mendelssohn did not always seem to be identical. He lived in two spheres as it were, and the drama of his life and its achievements is caught within the dialectic of these two realms. Whether he ultimately succeeded in merging them into a unified whole is a moot point. The philosopher and the Jew in him were felt by his opponents to be hardly compatible. He was the acknowledged leader of the German philosophy of the Enlightenment in the latter half of the eighteenth-century. He was also the first spokesman of the Enlightenment in modern Jewry. Yet his philosophic stance is one thing, his Jewishness another." [31]

A strictly enforced ritual mode of life points to an underlying system created to maintain inner states through which a dialogue between microcosm and macrocosm remains possible. The quality of that dialogue depends on the effectiveness of the rituals used at any given time. Their faithful observance is part of a self purifying process through which access is given. The modalities are archaic because rituals create their own worlds. Worlds that are not necessarily consistent with what secular rationalists recognize as their 'reality'— and over which they lay questionable claims of understanding and control.

It is easy to portray Orthodox Jews as anachronistic followers of old superstitions; but it is a lot more difficult to understand why these rituals— as absurd as they may seem— support a framework dedicated in its expectations to the return of the protector of the Law— the mediator through whom working connections between macrocosm and microcosm can at last be reestablished so that the Temple can be rebuilt.

Considerable efforts have been expanded on defeating this conception of *Maat*. The forces of militant humanism and universal consciousness, always dedicated to the eradication of religious superstitions and the promotion of social causes, have concentrated entirely on form. Universal brotherhood is strictly a legalistic concept. Modern systems rely more than ever on exploitation and indoctrination. Their commitment to human rights is just a smokescreen deployed to disguise culturally invasive practices through which more dubious values are promoted. What remains stunning, however, is the righteous hypocrisy with which such campaigns are still waged.

Intellectuals in countries like France, where the Enlightenment was born, like to take Heidegger to task for his Nazi associations, but remain silent as contemporary publications of Voltaire's **Dictionnaire philosophique** are carefully sanitized to remove his passionate pronouncements:

"This [Jewish] nation," wrote Voltaire, "is only an ignorant and barbarous people who have long united the most sordid avarice with the most detestable superstition and the most invincible hatred for every people by whom they are tolerated and enriched." [32]

The target is precisely Orthodox Jews and not emancipated visionaries like Mendelssohn. Voltaire's accusations of Molochism make Richard Wagner's or Adolf Hitler's anti-Semitic harangues sound tame by comparison. Here is Voltaire again:

"Did the Jews eat human flesh? Among your calamities which have so often made me shudder, I have always reckoned your misfortune in having eaten human flesh. You say that this happened only on great occasions [...] Either renounce your sacred books [...] or acknowledge that your forefathers offered up to God rivers of human blood unparalleled by any people on earth." [33]

Voltaire's stature in progressive circles is such that his removal from the humanistic pantheon is practically unthinkable. His statements, however, indicate that the 'Jewish problem' predates Adolf Hitler by many generations and is by no means confined to 'barbarous' Germany. Today, that same intellectual elite uses racism and anti-semistism as a test for deviation from its broad cultural agenda.

Mozart was not a fan of Voltaire and chose strong language to announce his death to his father in a letter from Paris on 3 July 1778:

"Now I have a piece of news for you which you may have heard already, namely that godless arch-rascal Voltaire has pegged out like a dog, like a beast! That is his reward!" [34]

This comment has puzzled Wolfgang Hildesheimer, whose biography of Mozart handles the matter rather defensively:

"If Mozart had been asked, 'Reward for what?'," writes Hildesheimer, "he probably wouldn't have had an answer. One wonders what Voltaire meant to Mozart." [35]

One wonders not so much what Voltaire meant to Mozart— since the letter makes it perfectly clear— but what Voltaire meant to Hildesheimer, who is obviously miffed at Mozart's reactionary slap at his idol.

"Voltaire did not die like a dog," continues the apologetic Hildesheimer, "though that might have been the version current in bigoted Paris circles. He died, at least to all appearances, a repentant sinner, in the lap of the Church. We will never know whether this return was a last diabolical brainstorm or a true confession. On the other hand, Mozart himself, if he did not die like a dog, died in circumstances that make us almost suspect Voltaire of a posthumous revenge for the slander." [36]

Shortly before his death, and presumably as a reward for his contributions to universal enlightenment, Voltaire was initiated into the Lodge of the Nine Sisters, amidst incredible pomp and circumstance. Forty Masons had come to his house on foot, followed by their carriages, to invite him to the Lodge. He was given Helvetius's apron for the ceremony and was formally seated in the Orient in deference to his wisdom.[37] The Nine Sisters was the Lodge to which Benjamin Franklin belonged.

As a Freemason, where did Voltaire stand? The question is really designed to challenge our narrow notions of consistency. In general one joins an organization because one believes in its stated objectives and ideals. In Freemasonry, however, that approach is rarely encouraged. Freemasons never allow themselves to be confined to a definable position. That was certainly true for Ignaz von Born and his associates. Daniel Beresniak shows that Goethe followed the same practice.

Goethe was received into the Lodge Amalia, at Weimar, where he was raised to the 4th Degree (*Écossais vert*) of the Order of Strict Observance, in December 1782. This did not keep him from joining Adam Weishaupt's Bavarian *Illuminati*— an organization condemned and despised by the order to which he formally belonged— as early as 11 February 1783.[38] Weishaupt, an ex-Jesuit, built his organization entirely on practices of secrecy and obedience borrowed from the Society. His rituals were modeled on the ancient Greek and Egyptian Mysteries.[39] How that makes it an anti-Jesuit organization is difficult to see. If anything, it puts it completely in line with what is commonly referred to as 'Jesuitism'— that is the art of being all things to all people.

"The *Illuminati* were never strong numerically, but they were a powerful force in moulding the moral and social ideas of the age. Among their supporters in Germany were Goethe and Herder. In Austria, their leaders included Joseph von Sonnenfels [...] and Ignaz von Born [...] There is some evidence that [Mozart] may have attended gathering of the *Illuminati* before his initiation as a Freemason. The topographer Lorenz Hübner, writing in 1792, reported that meetings of *Illuminati* were held by night in a lonely grotto at Aigen, near Salzburg (now known as the '*Illuminaten-Höhle*', or 'Cave of the Illuminati'), attended by Count Gilowsky, one of the Illuminist leaders, 'with his friends von Amann, Mozart and Barisani'." [40]

The dark 'light' of reason, endorsed by the *Illuminati,* is well suited to the propagation of totalitarian terror and one only has to read Christoph Martin Wieland's (1733-1813) formal answers to questions about the Enlightenment— written on the eve of the French Revolution— to realize that the ultimate purpose of these 'illuminations' was the complete destruction of private thought:

"The most infallible means of making [the Enlightenment] become brighter is to increase the light, to remove as many dark bodies as possible that block its passage, and especially to illuminate painstakingly all the dark corners and caverns into which the light-shy person drives himself. All objects of our knowledge are either events or representations, concepts, judgments, and opinions. Events become enlightened when one investigates, to the satisfaction of every impartial researcher, whether and how they occurred." [41]

As the editor of the influential **Der Teutsche Merkur**, Wieland was a major opinion maker. But how can one reconcile his sermons about shining light into caverns, when that was precisely where the *Illuminati* held their secret rituals.

Examples of this sort abound and can be multiplied beyond anyone's capacity to follow them in tedious detail. Beresniak justifies Goethe's behavior by saying that the Masonic journey cannot be steered in any particular direction. He even cites Goethe's own writings in support of his conclusion:

"If you wish to reach the infinite
Turn first in every direction within the finite"

and

"Whoever forgets the 'Die and become'
Is only a dull passenger on a darkened earth"

At the crossroads of **Wilhelm Meister** and **Die Geheimnisse**, we meet Goethe's wretched actor who has to sort out reality as he tries to come to terms with what it means to be human. The road Mozart followed would have been just as crooked. His friends among Freemasons belonged to every conceivable denomination and his 'Egyptian' education was undertaken fairly early.

But what was the relationship between Egyptian Masonry and the *Illuminati* inspired explorations of Egypt, extensively documented in the previous chapter? Ignaz von Born's circle was tilling the ancestral ground for insights into ritual. Lessing's *Hen kai pan* had definite Egyptian connotations. But how could Egyptian Masonry surface at a point where these lofty metaphysical speculations suddenly intersected with Cagliostro's deceitful art?

Jan Assmann mentions that one of the immediate consequences of Lessing's *Hen kai pan* was its adoption as "a motto in the writings of Herder, Hamann, Hölderlin, Goethe, Schelling, and others (many of them Freemasons)."[42] The extreme popularity of the formula remains puzzling, based on Lessing's pronouncement alone. It becomes easier to understand once we are told that its original source is the **Corpus Hermeticum**:

"None of the numerous authors who wrote on the famous pantheism controversy seems ever to have asked the question of where Lessing got his formula *Hen kai pan*. Why did he not say '*deus sive natura*' if he wanted to refer to Spinoza? [...] If we look for a source, we are led to Cudworth, thus to Egypt and to Hermes Trismegistus. In a study on **Empedokles and Hölderlin**, Uvo Hölscher had already pointed to Ralph Cudworth as the most plausible source for Hölderlin's *Hen kai pan*. Cudworth's **True Intellectal System of the Universe** went through several editions in the eighteenth-century, one of them published in Germany. There is not the slightest doubt that this book was still accessible and well known in Lessing's time. Yet to link the names of Gotthold Ephraim Lessing and Hermes

Trismegistus is very strange. [...] As I pointed out earlier, Cudworth had carefully collected all the occurrences of this formula. It never appears exactly as *Hen kai pan*, but only occurs in more or less close approximations, such as *Hen to Pan, To hen kai to Pan*, and so on. The formula plays a very prominent role in Greek texts that were written in Egypt: the texts that constitute the **Corpus Hermeticum**, the magical incantations and ceremonies known as **papyri Graecae Magicae**, and the texts of the alchemical tradition. Plotinus, the most prominent exponent of Neoplatonism, whose teaching is most closely associated with All-Oneness, was an Egyptian and a native of Assiut (Lykopolis)." [43]

A path toward the infinite cannot be bound by reason. Mozart would have realized this, along with Lessing and the other luminaries investigating the ancient hermetic arts. The **Corpus Hermeticum** was more than a conversation piece in Masonic circles. It dealt with the world of magic, accessed exclusively through ritual, and unveiled only to those who are trusted.

Secrecy was there to protect invisible processes that have their roots in darkness. Subtle swirls of meaning that condense into hovering mists as their controlling power emerges. Birth remains a fragile moment during which dependencies are broken. Creation and magic are two forms of the same force that thrives in shadowy spaces where manipulations cannot be seen.

Modern Freemasonry, in Mozart's time, had to preserve its ritual secrets. Some authors dismiss that idea out of hand. Paul Nettl, in his **Mozart and Freemasonry**, downplays the secret side of the Craft:

"Secrecy is not the key to Freemasonry. Everything concerning its aims and rituals is available to the public in books and manuals. Indeed some well-informed insiders know more about the Craft than many a Mason of lower degree who should not have and does not wish any premature knowledge. Masonry keeps no secret from the uninitiated! Yet there is a Masonic secret, a mystery, an experience that cannot be taught or explained because it lies, like every mystic experience, beyond the realm of controlled consciousness.[...] The secret of Freemasonry is the secret of experiencing true love for all mankind, a positive attitude towards man and life, and broad affirmation of God." [44]

'True love for all mankind' has become such a hollow slogan that experiencing it today is symptomatic of one's inability to come to terms with social realities. There is nothing lovable about mankind anymore. The species is now mostly composed of self-centered, predatory individuals who will stop at nothing in their pursuit of self-gratification.

Mozart did not have to join the Order of the Asiatic Brethren to become aware of the thorny issues raised by its existence. The first paragraph of the general constitution of the Order, completed in November 1784, establishes its focus and militancy:

"Any brother, irrespective of his religion, class, or system, may join the Order, provided he is an upright person in thought and deed. Since the good and welfare of mankind are the sole purpose of our approach, these cannot be dependent on any other circumstance, be it a man's religion, his birth, or the class into which he has been bred." [45]

Mozart officially became a Mason on 14 December 1784, at which time he was admitted as an Apprentice in the Viennese Lodge '*Zur Wohltätigkeit*'. This was only a year before the Emperor's *Freimaurerpatent* of 11 December 1785, which severely restricted the operation of Masonic Lodges within the Habsburg territories.

"One of the regime's stated goals was to curb the influence of the secret order of the Rosicrucians (including the Rosicrucian offshoot, the Asiatic Brethren), and to limit the diversity of proliferating Masonic sects. By so doing, the Josephinian government took its stand on the side of the enlightened and rationalist Masons as against the adherents of unorthodox and occult tendencies. The decree referred disdainfully and provocatively to Masonic 'mysteries' (*Geheimnisse*) and 'impostures' (*Gaukeleien*). Because they sympathized with the alleged aim of purging Masonic ranks of Rosicrucian, alchemist, and other mystical tendencies, leaders of the rationalist wing of Freemasonry helped to promote and afterward saluted the imperial decree. It was not long, however, before the decree was turned against them as well." [46]

The Asiatic Brethren were not an offshoot of Rosicrucianism. Their common interest in ecumenical activism and secret doctrines constitutes a tentative link that should not be used to equate these organizations. The ecumenical ambitions of the Rosicrucians never reached beyond Christianity. That of the Asiatic Brethren extended across all religions.

After Joseph II's promulgation of the *Freimaurerpatent*, Ecker felt threatened in Vienna, but soon found a new protector in Schleswig, in the person of the Landgrave, Karl von Hessen, with whom he had previous contacts. Karl believed Ecker's assertion that the Asiatic Brethen possessed the key to the secret doctrine of Masonry and thus accepted to become the titular head of the Order. He also invited Ecker and Hirschfeld to come to Schleswig. The Order would spawn other Masonic organizations based on Jewish membership. These ecumenical ambitions were the principal point of intersection with Egyptian Masonry, which can now be surveyed from a pure historical perspective.

Here is what Gérard Galtier has to say about its origins and its most likely sources:

"The first Rites of initiation in modern times, that refer specifically to an Egyptian tradition, appear in the second half of the 18th century. These were times during which new Masonic systems flowered every day [...] The majority of these Rites were created by people who either lived in Mediterranean countries, or had been on the road for a very long time. In this zone of religious conflicts, these Rites often tried to become a meeting ground for Christians, Jews and even Muslims. One frequently encounters, at the origin of these Rites, mysterious Greeks— merchants, military men or professors; as, for instance, the count of Mélissino, general officer in the service of the Tsar who had founded, around 1760, within the Lodge 'The Silence' of Saint-Petersburg a mystical system made up of four Degrees [...] one can also cite professor Carburi, from Padua" [47]

Readers of this series already know that Greece, under Turkish occupation, was the last flourishing bastion of Operative Masonry. Its Byzantine traditions survived untouched until modern times.[48] What is interesting about these Greeks, is that they brought Speculative Masonry back to their native lands: opening new Lodges founded on charters issued by established European Lodges. Here again, cross-pollination was at work.

The modern Egyptian Rite eventually evolved into the Rite of 'Misraïm'— which means 'Egypt' in Hebrew (*Mitsraïm*). In the Bible, *Mitzeraïm* was the name of the eponymous ancestor of the Egyptians and Fabre d'Olivet (***The Hebrew Tongue Restored***) translates '*Mitzeraim*', at **Genesis** (X, 6) by 'subduing, overcoming power, compressing bodies to their narrowest bonds'.[49] This is consistent with the model of Egypt developed so far and the abstract definition of Freemasonry derived earlier from the same source. As the dark subterranean layer holding esoteric seeds, Egypt is indeed a power that cannot be overcome without special assistance.

Gérard Galtier mentions that Misraïm first appeared in Paris in 1814,[50] where it was introduced by the brothers Bédarride. The Masonic writer Claude-Antoine Thory had this to say about the order (*Acta Latomorum*, vol. I, 1815, p. 327):

"This institution, which in France dates back only a few years, was well established in Venice and the Ionian islands [...]Several *Harams*, or very knowledgeable Rabbis, claim that the Rite of Misphraïm is the true Masonic tree and that all other systems, whatever they may be, are only branches sprouting from this institution, respectable— they say— because of its high antiquity and its birth in Egypt. They add that they are in possession of the Statutes of this Order, written in Chaldean [...] All of the Degrees, except for the 88th, 89th and 90th, have different names which can be read in our nomenclature. As far as the three last ones are concerned, we do not know their titles: they were marked as veiled in the manuscript that was communicated to us and those who possess them are known in this Rite as *Absolute Masters*; they claim the privilege of governing indistinctly all branches of Freemasonry."

If this sounds like a page out of the **Protocols of the Elders of Zion**— a century ahead of time— it is because the implications are fundamentally the same. The distance in time between Thory's **Acta Latomorum** (1815) and Nilus' **Protocols** (which supposedly revealed secret decisions taken at the first Zionist Congress in 1897) precludes historical comparisons.[51] What remains, however, is the theme of occult 'control' within a well-defined globalist perspective.

In Mozart's time, the Itizgs in Berlin and the Arnsteins in Vienna were hardly great conspiratorial figures. They were, however, wealthy bankers with enough clout to influence European political events. Mozart had close contacts with this Jewish elite:

"Not a single biography of Mozart", writes Volkmar Braunbehrens," records that he lived for almost a year in the same house as this notable Jewish family [the Arnstein family], although virtually all them mention this address [No. 1175] on the Graben." [52]

The Arnstein family was heavily involved in the cause of Jewish emancipation and was part of a large European network of Jews committed to the same ideals. A brief history of the movement is given by Walter Röll:

"Every attempt to understand the great innovations in the life and culture of the Jews of Central Europe during the second half of the eighteenth-century starts with Moses Mendelssohn. [...] In the early 1780s some of the new ideas of the century had taken hold among groups of young Jews, and a movement began that was a Jewish analogy to the German Enlightenment. The Haskalah and its first periodical, *Ha-Meassef* (The Collector), cannot be understood without consideration of their roots in the European Enlightenment and especially in its Prussian variety. The model for the *Ha-Meassef* was the *Berlinische Monatsschrift*, 'the most important forum for the German Enlightenment in its last and highest phase'. But even before the first issue of the *Berlinische Monatsschrift* appeared, a group of young Jews in Königsberg, Prussia, took the first step toward the publication of their journal. In December 1782 they formed the Society of the Friends of the Hebrew Language. [...] Their *Ha-Meassef* was to become 'the most important organ for Haskalah writers'. In a letter to Naphtali Wessely, these young *maskilim* explained that some of them were 'Torah scholars and some commanded foreign languages— Greek and Latin, as well as modern', and went on to say that 'their entire goal and wish is to spread our holy language among our people as much as possible and to demonstrate its beauty to all nations'." [53]

There were seventeen *Ha-Meassef* subscribers in Vienna. Among them was Mme. Fanny Arnstein, daughter of Daniel Itzig, *Oberlandesältester* of the Jews of Prussia. Her husband, Nathan, was the son of Imperial Court Purveyor Adam Isaac Arnstein, who with his household of at least thirty people lived right next to Mozart at No. 1175 on the Graben:

"The exceptional feature of this house can be described in a single sentence: it was the only house in Vienna that a Jew had freely selected and rented as a place of residence. Though a few Jews had residency permits, none except Arnstein had this privilege, which extended to his family[...]" [54]

We know that the elder Arnstein lived strictly according to Jewish laws and customs and that his son was as a high-spirited socialite.[55] But there is very little information about Mozart's social intercourse with the Arnstein family:

"We know nothing about Mozart's personal contacts with the younger Arnstein and his wife, but they were among the subscribers to his concerts. It was very possibly through Fanny Arnstein that Mozart happened upon the book **Phaëton, or On the Immortality of the Soul**, by Moses Mendelssohn. The fourth edition, of which Mozart owned a copy, appeared the year Fanny Arnstein moved from Berlin to Vienna. It is known that she brought copies of this important work with her and introduced it to her Viennese acquaintances. [...] Most of our scanty information about Mozart's social contacts has come to us by chance [...] However, we can say categorically that Mozart counted numerous Jews among his friends." [56]

Braunbehrens mentions that the Graben was a fashionable promenade in Vienna during Mozart's time. The farce **Der Teufel in Wien** (The Devil in Vienna), long attributed to Schikaneder, casts it in a totally different light:

> In the long Kärtnetstrasse
> Girls are everywhere—
> In the narrow Naglergasse
> You can choose them as you care.
> But if in dozens you desire them
> Go every evening to the Graben."
> [*Wer sie aber Dutzendweis will haben*
> *Der geh'alle Abend auf den Graben.*][57]

Ambivalence was in Mozart's character and one should not be surprised to find it in every other aspect of his life, right down to some of the places where he lived. The Jewish circles around which Mozart gravitated all belonged to the Order of the Asiatic Brethren:

"The Masonic orders were not local organizations," writes Jacob Katz. "Their tentacles penetrated into numerous cities and countries. [...] The center of the movement remained in Vienna until the end of 1786, or the beginning of 1787. There the 'Sanhedrin' which governed the Order had its seat. It was a body composed of seven members as well as several officeholders and salaried employees. The 'Sanhedrin' delegated powers to the heads of the districts— four in number— for all of Europe and these heads conferred authorization on the individual cells in their respective regions.[...] We know of the existence of Asiatic Lodges in Prague, Inssbruck, Berlin, Frankfurt and Hamburg. The *Encyclopedie der Freimaurerei*, published in 1822, mentions that the cities of Wetzlar and Marburg were teeming with devotees of the Order.[...] In Innsbruck the society was composed of the local aristocracy. As for Berlin, the sources yield only the name of Itzig, but other relevant literature mentions Bischofswerder, Wöllner, and even the Crown Prince, who was later to become King Frederick William II of Prussia." [58]

How this squares off with secret conspiracies is not particularly important. The controversy will go on for a long time and people will continue to argue about the political impact of Freemasonry. In the case of the Asiatic Brethren, the international dimension is supplemented by a somewhat unusual set of qualifications for admission.

Gérard Galtier quotes from the Marquis de Luchet's note concerning the Asiatic Brethren (*Essai sur la secte des Illuminés*, 1789, p. 159-160):

"Is received without consideration of birth or religion any

honest man who believes in God and acknowledges it publicly. It is only asked that he should have been initiated into the first three grades of Freemasonry in a Lodge of St. John, or of Melchizedek. It is known that the Lodges of Saint John are for Christians only; those of Melchizedek, which are just as good and in conformance with the law, exist in great number in Italy, Holland, England, Portugal, Spain and receive Jews, Turks, Persians and Armenians. This Order is for all Europe destined to the great objective of union [...] The Order has five degrees, with the following names: the Seekers and Sufferers, which are only trial degrees; after which come the three principal ones, the Knights and Initiated Brothers of Asia and Europe, the Masters of the Wise [and] the Royal Priests or true Rose-Croix Brothers or grade of Melchizedek." [59]

Since the Asiatic Brethren used a system of Higher Grades, which required a regular Masonic initiation (Apprentice, Companion and Master); and since that course could only be completed in a regular Lodge— from which Jews were still barred— the entire proposition appeared doomed from the start.

The objective of union, with ecumenical ambitions reaching far beyond Christian boundaries, would have been perceived as subversive. Depending on whose commentaries one reads, one learns that the Order was either designed to further undermine Christianity, or else detract Jewish members from their true faith.

Modern Jewish experts, who have written extensively on the subject, particularly Jacob Katz and Gershom Scholem, have voiced a great deal of skepticism toward the real intentions of the founders.

"The ideology of the Asiatic Brethren has been subjected to a critical analysis by Professor Gershom Scholem. His study has revealed that on its theoretical level this ideology was a conglomeration of principles drawn from Christian and Jewish sources. Kabbalistic and Sabbatean ideas were jumbled together with Christian theosophic doctrines. [...] The Christian Asiatic, however, did not have to suffer pangs of conscience. He could easily have regarded himself as completely faithful to the tenets of his religion— and even look upon himself as reverting to the same pristine form of Christianity which was preserved within Judaism. The Jew, on the other hand could hardly remain oblivious to the fact that he was trespassing beyond the boundaries of his own traditions." [60]

One must note that the esoteric designations employed by the Asiatic Brethren were fairly consistent. Different rituals may have been jumbled together, but the occult foundation is pretty solid. St. John the Baptist was to Christianity what Melchizedek was to Judaism. Both were initiators who controlled the flow of cosmic waters running down the Sephirotic Tree— through Malkuth.

Such considerations escape Katz's attention as he sifts through the Order's historical documents, painfully looking for slights against the Jews. There were undoubtedly many of those, but that does not negate the soundness of the symbolism involved. The Asiatic Brethren may have misled their followers, but someone in the Order knew a lot about ritual.

Mozart's contacts with the Asiatic Brethren are undocumented and therefore controversial. Some things, however, we can infer. We have already noted that Mozart lived alongside the Arnsteins, who, according to Katz, were Asiatic Brethren. We know that the Eskeles family was also active in the Order.

It was through these social contacts that Mozart was drawn into an untenable situation where state secrets were involved:

"It was possibly in the Arnstein house," writes Volkmar Braunbehrens, "that Mozart met one of the emperor's closest aides, Johann Valentin Günther, who was a kind of private secretary to Joseph II. In this capacity he traveled with the emperor in 1780 to meet with Catherine II. At the time, the empress was still an ally of Prussia, and the sensitive mission of this journey was to make her a partner of the Habsburgs. Only the most trusted associates could help carry out such a difficult assignment. [...] Mozart called Günther a 'very good friend' by which he was surely implying more than just 'connections'. Günther was unmarried but had lived for a number of years with Eleonore Eskeles, who was born to Jewish parents in Vienna, grew up in Amsterdam, married in Berlin, then separated from her husband (Moises Fliess) and moved to the home of her brother, Bernhard Eskeles, in Vienna. [...] Bernhard Eskeles was a banker and merchant in Vienna, and together with Arnstein he later opened a banking and retail business; thanks to lucrative international connections, it soon became one of the largest and most important firms in Vienna. Fanny Arnstein was a distant relative of Eleonore Eskeles and became her closest friend." [61]

To make a long story short, we know that Mozart dined with Günther on 27 June 1782 and that the very next morning Günther was arrested. He was accused of spying for Prussia. Eleonore Eskeles was implicated and a letter of Mozart's dated 11 September 1782 gives the composer's version of the incident:

"The Jewess Eskeles has no doubt proved a very good and useful tool for breaking up the friendship between the emperor and the Russian court— the day before yesterday she was taken to Berlin so that the King might have the pleasure of her company. She is indeed a sow of the first order."

Braunbehrens mentions that Mozart's version of the events was incorrect and that he was just trumpeting the official story endorsed by the emperor. That may well have been, but there is no doubt that politics and commerce played an important part in the extended activities of the Asiatic Brethren. It was at around that time that Frederick of Prussia signed a most favored nation treaty with the future United States of America. An international game of alliances that had strong Masonic overtones.

It would be, to say the least, disingenuous on Braunbehrens' part, to affirm that Eleonore Eskeles did nothing more than gossip about the emperor's extra-marital affairs. That she owed her deportation to such trifles is highly unlikely. The stakes were much higher than that.

in 1780 Joseph II had traveled incognito to St Petersburg to re-establish Austria's prestige at Catherine's court. He went by the assumed name of Monsieur de Falkenstein and missed his rival, who would become King Frederick William II of Prussia, by a few months. Catherine sums up her early impression of both monarchs in the following way:

"I have no lessons to give to M. de Falkenstein, his education is complete and will produce a very clever master; but the apprentice with high pretensions [the Prussian Crown Prince] who just got under way from here will have to take a long journey before he becomes a companion... One says that he thinks well; that may be, but the same can be said of a turkey." [62]

In 1791, when she was told that Frederick William II, who was by then involved with Spiritism, had successfully conversed with Jesus Christ, she wrote to Grimm:

"If I could ever meet the Jew— and he must obviously be one— who impersonates the Savior on such occasions, I would gladly make his fortune, but on one condition, that at the second encounter he give him a thorough lashing, and this from me." [63]

After Frederick the Great's death, Prussia moved into the direction suggested by the Asiatic Brethren. The rivalry with Austria shifted to a different front, where international intrigue played an important part. Waliszewski concludes that Catherine the Great was attracted to Joseph II and that he tried to convert this advantage into political capital, but without any luck. He points out that Catherine's letters to Joseph were reviewed by

André Chouvaloff, a poet; while Joseph's were read by the old Prince Kaunitz.[64]

Catherine was even ready to take a step back and let Joseph be the leading Royal figure in Europe:

"I know a man in this world to whom heaven has destined the first place in Europe, without argument the first, I say, for glory. He must live; he must survive a couple of his contemporaries." [65]

But revolutionary climates have a way of affecting charmed predictions. A king cannot become a legend when monarchy is destined to fail. In the eternal fight against darkness the enemy is identified by his 'otherness', as Ivan Nagel thoughtfully observes:

"The metaphor of light and darkness answers the favorite riddle of today's enlightened critics who choose to ignore what the Enlightenment was. How does it happen, they ask, that Sarastro preaches pardon but, at his first action on stage, orders that Monostatos's feet be lashed 'seventy-seven' times? If the critics had seen something more in this incident than their chance to display verbal brotherhood with slaves and blacks, they might have added a deeper puzzle: why is *the* programmatic deed of **Die Zauberflöte**, the pardoning of the Queen in the *Hallen* manifesto, followed nonetheless by her descent to hell? Such lack of logic leads to the heart of the Enlightenment's revolutionary logic. The enemy, black as night, is unreal; therefore he can be whipped, damned, annulled. Humanity is valid only for humans, not for monstrous nonhumans— valid, that is, only within one's own party. 'Anyone not cheered by these teachings / Does not deserve to be a man'. The *terreur* soon showed that splintering off from the Party (that heir to the Order of Light) meant expulsion into nothingness. Death on the guillotine was not the consequence but the verification of an annulment that virtually had already been carried out by the apostate victims themselves." [66]

The Haskalah and the Asiatic Brethren sided with the forces of light, but they should have been more careful. In the fight against darkness history tends to repeat itself— particularly Jewish history. Moses Mendelssohn and his followers were forced into too many compromises. When in his *Jerusalem* Mendelssohn says: "I recognize no eternal truths other than those that are not merely comprehensible to human reason but can also be demonstrated and verified by human powers,"[67] he enters dangerous territory.

Spinoza, in his critique of traditional religion, had already stated that "prophecy is inferior to natural knowledge, which requires no sign, but involves certainty of its own nature."[68] This type of thinking conforms with the tenets of the Enlightenment and Speculative Masonry. But as far as speculation goes, to reflect is not necessarily to reason:

"The authentic meaning of 'speculative' is lost unless we bear in mind its etymological origin: *speculum* = mirror. [...] In the words of Franz von Baader, '*Spekulieren heisst spiegeln*' (to speculate is to reflect).[...] The speculative state, in its mystical sense, is when the human being has become a mirror in which the *gesta divina* are accomplished. However, because this mirror is the place of the soul contemplating itself in contemplation, it is also true to say that the mirror is itself the divine Being." [69]

At some point language intervenes. It describes what is seen in the mirror and that is where the prophetic dimension begins. The difficulty with this dimension comes from the cultic forms used to reflect divine meaning.

For the Egyptians, 'radiant power' (*akhu*)— light— was synonymous with 'spiritual power'. "As a verbal power that emanated from speech, *akhu* was a means that deities, especially deities of knowledge had at their disposal."[70] We are now far from Spinoza's natural knowledge and quickly approaching a language through which divine commandments are expressed.

This language injects meaning and provides cultic access to higher spheres involved in the maintenance of *Maat*. "*Maat* designates the idea of a meaningful, all-pervasive order that embraces the world of humankind, objects, and nature— in short, the meaning of creation, the form in which it was intended by the creator god."[71] It is also a language of power whenever it is wielded with the appropriate skill and spirit.

"In spells containing name formulas, the name serves to create a relationship between the two spheres, the cultic sphere 'here' and the sphere of the divine realm 'there'.[...] The relationship between the present and the distant was spun from the most basic material of language— phonemes. In the overwhelming majority of instances, the name and the word that designates the ritual act related to one another by assonance.[...] The wealth of wordplays demonstrates how those who composed spells for the cult worked self-consciously with language— with substance (sound) and with form (phonemic structure) of expression— to bring the cultic and divine spheres into a relationship with one another. They testify to a belief in the possibilities of language, a consciousness of language that is foreign to us. [...] We speak of 'plays' on words because we experience such a use of language, which undermines the conventionality of signs in a cunning and unusual manner, as playful. In Egypt, however, wordplay was regarded as a highly serious and controlled use of language, for language was understood to be a dimension of divine presence." [72]

In **The Magic Flute**, Tamino enters the Temple of *Maat* to assume its priestly functions together with Pamina. It is an Egyptian Temple, and although light vanquishes darkness in the end, the very nature of things Egyptian precludes an immediate rush to a happy ending. Mendelssohn, who studied Maimonides at length, apparently never payed attention to the following passage from *The Guide of the Perplexed* (1190) [Part III, chapter 24] which deals with man's relationship to an active solar deity:

"Know that this notion [fearing God] is corroborated and explained in the *Torah*, in which it is mentioned that the final end of the whole of the *Torah*, including its commandments, prohibitions, promises and narratives, is one thing only— namely fear of Him, may He be exalted." [73]

Egyptian Masonry cannot be separated from its implied Jewish leadership. The Rite of Misraïm originated in the Republic of Venice, where it was promoted by a gentleman who went by the name of Parenti. According to Galtier, Parenti was a Sephardic Jew. He is mentioned by Marc Bédarride (*De l'Ordre maçonnique de Misraïm*, 1845, vol. II, p. 125-126) who introduces him as an initiate of the 66th Degree, from the 'Valley' of Zakynthos. Parenti traveled to Belgium and France in 1782.[74]

Galtier uses these scraps of information to assemble a fairly credible picture of the origin of the Rite. He remarks that Zakynthos and Corfu were among the principal Ionian islands, controlled by the Republic of Venice at the end of the 18th century. He also recalls Thory's statement about the existence of Misraïm in Venice and the Ionian islands. To this he adds that there is a report authored by the Austrian secret police in Venice, in 1818, that speaks of a 'Secret Egyptian Society' established in Italy, Egypt and the Ionian islands.[75]

Marc Béddaride, who brought the Rite of Misraïm to Paris, claims that his father, Gad, was raised to the 90th Degree in Naples, in 1799.[76] The family hailed from the Jewish community of Cavaillon, near Avignon: a thriving survivor of the medieval Jewish settlements of Provence and Languedoc.

"Gad Bédarride, according to his son Marc, received the Masonic light at Avignon around 1771-1773 [...] He would have subsequently been received into the Rite of Misraïm in 1782, at

Cavaillon, by the learned Patriarch Ananiah [...] The figure of Ananiah should, in our opinion, be closely identified with that of the famous Kabbalist Hayyim Joseph David Azoulai [...] who hailed from Jerusalem, was an adept of the mystical school of Isaac Luria, and traveled extensively through Europe." [77]

The earliest exponent of Luria's doctrine was Hayyim Vital (1542-1620). He was born in Safed, Palestine, the son of a scribe who had come to Israel from Calabria, in southern Italy. In 1570, when Luria arrived from Egypt, Vital became his chief disciple in Safed.[78]

"Vital's interest in magic and alchemy has been underplayed to such an extent by the historians of Jewish mysticism that one has the impression that they were embarrassed by the fact that this great Kabbalist devoted much of his attention to such subjects." [79]

Even at this early stage there was already a link between Southern Italy and Egypt, through Vital and his master Isaac Luria. It is also known that from 1598 onwards, Vital served as rabbi of the Sicilian community in Damascus, which indicates that the connection to Southern Italy was not spurious.

Subsequent linkages with the kingdom of Naples show how easily Masonic Orders cross-pollinated during the second half of the 18th century. As early as 1773 Naples' Lodges consolidated into two obediences. One was the Grand Provincial Lodge for the Kingdom of Naples and Sicily, formed under British jurisdiction, and whose Grand Master was Duke Cesare Pignatelli della Rocca e di San Demetrio; the other was the independent Grand National Lodge, led by Prince Francesco d'Aquino di Caramanico.[80]

Prince d'Aquino had close ties with Queen Marie-Caroline of Austria, the wife of Ferdinand IV, who had succeeded his father in 1759, when the latter became king of Spain under the name of Charles III. Marie-Caroline had joined a Lodge of adoption and was very instrumental in blocking the Marquis of Tanucci, Ferninand's Prime Minister, in his attempts to shutdown Freemasonry within the kingdom. Tanucci thought that the Lodges interfered with the authority of the king and the church.[81]

The Duke of San Demetrio was a friend of Cagliostro. Cagliostro had created his Egyptian Rite on 24 December 1784, in Lyon, under the auspices of the Lodge *La Sagesse Triomphante*. He had been initiated into the Duke of San Demetrio's principal Neapolitan Lodge, The Perfect Union, in 1783. Prince d'Aquino's Grand National Lodge had already joined the German Order of Strict Observance in 1777, at the urging of Baron F.L. von Eyben, Denmark's Consul General in Naples. During that same year, another Lodge was founded on a charter received by the Mother Lodge of the Philosophical Scottish Rite of Avignon. This Lodge, 'The Mysteries of Hermes', was led by Prince Pignatelli di Strongoli.[82]

Luigi d'Aquino, the brother of Prince Francesco d'Aquino, Grand Master of Neapolitan Masonry, allegedly brought three mysterious high-degrees from Malta to Naples some time between 1767 and 1775. They were inspired by Egyptian-Hellenic hermeticism and called the *Arcana Arcanorum*. They were later incorporated as such into the Rite of Misraim.

The occult connection between the town of Safed, in Palestine, and modern Egyptian Masonry is not surprising if one takes into account its early history. The *Arcana Arcanorum* could have only come from there, and the people entrusted with these degrees would have indeed been the heirs to the esoteric traditions of medieval Masonry:

"Visitors still come to Safed in the hundreds of thousands hoping to taste the forbidden fruit of the Tree of mystical knowledge, in the synagogues and cemeteries that have been hallowed by the footsteps of saints and sages for hundreds of years. [...] Ironically, the Crusades, which had played such a bloody and formidable role in the crystallization of Jewish culture in Europe, were also responsible for Safed's sudden transformation from its traditional agricultural way of life. After the conquest of the Holy Land in 1099 [...] the city and the surrounding region were eventually handed over to the Order of the Knights Templar. [...] It is an extraordinary historical coincidence that around 1170— precisely at the time when the first Kabbalists of Provence and Aragon were responding to Cathar ideology and formulating their complex theories of the sephirotic powers— Templar Knights in the Holy Land were clearing the summit of Mount Canaan in Galilee and unwittingly building a city that would become the Kabbalah's most famous home." [83]

5

THE MAGIC FLUTE AND ITS SYMBOLIC STRUCTURE

The Magic Flute looks like a simple fairy tale, but its symbolic structure points to a more ambitious agenda. Conscientious investigators of its mysteries have been surprised by the complexities one immediately encounters as soon as one tries to fit it into a particular mold. Uncertainties over authorship abound and controversies regarding source materials make it difficult to come up with a definitive interpretation. There are standing arguments over the extent of Mozart's, Schikaneder's, and even Giesecke's participation in the libretto's creation. Judith Eckelmeyer [*The Cultural Context of Mozart's Magic Flute* (1991)] identifies more than 50 places where Mozart made visible alterations to the text and suggests that the Masonic material does not come from a single source.

A number of investigators assert that the basic plot was borrowed from Terrasson's *Sethos* (1731). Others prefer Gebler's opera, *Thamos, König von Aegypten* (1774). Naumann's *Osiris* (1781) is occasionally mentioned as a possible contributor. There is talk of collaboration between

Schikaneder and Giesecke, as both worked on Wranitzky's opera **Oberon der Elfenkönig**, another fairy tale sometimes viewed as a predecessor to **The Magic Flute**.

All in all, there is no shortage of suspects when it comes to the opera's ancestry. Classical sources listed include: Herodotus' **Histories**, Apuleius' **Golden Ass**; the writings of Hecateus, Strabo and Diodorus Siculus; Horapollo's treatise on the Egyptian hieroglyphs, Plutarch's **Isis and Osiris**, the **Corpus Hermeticum** and numerous other commentaries dealing with the above mentioned works.

There is no way out of this maze and a more direct approach recommends itself if we are to develop a meaningful interpretative framework. A structure— if structure there is— means that there are building elements from which it can be constructed. A correct identification of these basic elements is therefore essential.

Because Masonic subjects are by definition esoteric, we will assume that the foregoing chapters have provided a sufficiently broad introduction. That may be stretching it a bit, but there are no easy access roads into the topic.

Rather than settle for a working outline of the plot, which would only serve to trivialize this exercise, we plan to approach the problem by examining individual pieces of the puzzle. They are intriguing items in their own right. Judith Eckelmeyer claims that the plot follows a dialectic outline. The opposition of darkness and light comes as a precondition for their alchemical synthesis, achieved through the ritual union of Pamina and Tamino:

"Tamino and Pamina are identifiable as the purified alchemical King and Queen, gold and silver respectively, which when joined in alchemical processes produce the Philosopher's Stone, the eternal substance which confers immortality on whatever and whomever it touches." [1]

The union of the daughter of the Queen of the Night with the adopted son of the Temple of Light provides a reconstructed foundation on which a new humanity can build. That new humanity is prefigured by Papageno and Papagena, whose reproductive ambitions require an updated institutional setting. One in which Freemasonry plays an important role.

In trying to project Mozart's alchemical allusions onto a working Egyptian model some people have been tempted to identify the figures of Isis and Osiris with the Pamina/Tamino couple. A more realistic solution is proposed later in this chapter. It combines the alchemical symbolism of the three pairs of planets, conceived as 'couples' in the hermetic tradition (see volumes one and two of this series), and the Kabbalistic idea of the 'one-and-all' (*Hen kai Pan*) on which the Masonic Higher Degrees are constructed. Pamina and Tamino's union takes place at the level of intentional language, where substitutes for the Lost Word are manufactured.

In the chapter on ritual action we examined the basic connection between foundation rituals and solar divinities (Apollo, Horus, Yahve). The subject is both vast and difficult. It cannot be covered adequately in a study focused exclusively on *The Magic Flute*. It is therefore encouraging to find an independent corroboration of its applicability:

"The principal thrust of *The Magic Flute* is a message of struggle toward a better world, a regenerated and transformed society. The image of the spiral [Hegel's dialectic spiral] is apt, for it corresponds to the theoretical stasis/upheaval/resolution-to-new-stasis motion of the dialectical plan of the opera. [...] Six years after *The Magic Flute* premiere, Haydn completed his version of the same ideal, peaceful world as the conclusion of his oratorio, *The Creation*; in it, Adam and Eve live unspoiled in a new world teeming with beneficial and beautiful creatures of a benevolent God, without need of Christ's sacrifice or Second Coming. The recreation of all of nature, including the First

Parents, is another solution to the search for the Millennium in Haydn's work." [2]

THE KING

Ancient Egypt was always concerned with the perpetuation of 'enlightened rule'. The *Deus Pharaonis*, in whom priestly functions are combined with secular authority, embodies that principle. During the eighteenth-century, an important action item on the list of the occult establishment was a return to this type of rule. The convergence of priestly and secular authority was to take place within the context of a new millennium dedicated to light and the final removal of darkness.

In Goethe's sequel to ***The Magic Flute***, the birth of Genius is right in line with the Messianic expectations of Freemasonry. By indirectly giving birth to a new 'King'— to a 'genius' representing the Horian Logos, or 'the ray of Light's original corporification', to use Schwaller de Lubicz's terminology— Tamino and Pamina fulfill the promise of their Masonic masters.

Ignaz von Born's circle approached Egypt and Mosaic Law as a single subject. Goethe's sequel appears as a knowledgeable— though theatrically weak— extrapolation on the same perennial theme.

The attitude of Austrian Freemasons toward Joseph II betrays their attempts to transform his reign into a working symbol of ancient Egypt. Politics undoubtedly played a part in this, but the main purpose was to project enlightened rule as a return to past standards. A reformation contemplated in other European countries as well:

"Bossuet's discourse on universal history was undertaken to enlighten the dauphin and to improve the political situation. This project was shared by large parts of the Enlightenment, for example by the circle of British intellectuals who wrote the

Athenian Letters and by the Austrian Freemasons who pinned their hopes on Joseph II and wrote on the Egyptian Mysteries. They found what they sought in Diodorus' description of ancient Egyptian monarchy, which was based on Hecateus' account. Hecateus had pursued the same project, wanting to enlighten Ptolemy I. The 'ancient model' was so important in early

1. Triumph of Joseph II's liberal idea

Hellenism and in the Enlightenment not because it was historically correct but because its concept of an enlightened monarchy was politically useful." [3]

Born's essay on the Egyptian Mysteries, published in the first

issue of the **Journal für Freymäurer** and Reinhold's **Die kabirischen Mysterien**, found in the same series, are not random efforts. In spite of their rationalistic and politically motivated positions, they also point to a collective interest in hermetic image making. There is a good reason why alchemy was called the 'Royal Art'.

Music was the instrument of choice for the celebration of hermetic themes associated with the Royal Art. The basic blueprint is already found in *Libellus* XVIII of the **Corpus Hermeticum**:

"The aim of my endeavour is the glory of kings [...] the melody that the musician makes will sound the sweeter by reason of the greatness of his theme. Since then his lyre is tuned to treat of kings, and is set to the right pitch for songs of praise, he first uplifts his voice to laud the supreme King of the universe, and comes down thereafter to those who hold their sovereignty after His likeness.[...] The virtue of a king is shown in making peace; nay, the very name of *king* confers peace; for the king is so called for this cause, that with *smooth tread* he plants his feet upon the topmost heights, and prevails by means of reason [the Greek writer assumes that the word âáóéëåýò (king) means by derivation *one who treads smoothly*)].[4]

In earlier times, the king was at the center of every mystery and a Golden Age was inconceivable without his presence. The mythical relationship between an earthly Golden Age and a vanished King, who shall one day return, is expressed in every culture. In Egypt, it was associated with Ptah, the divine *architekton* of the cosmos.

"Whatever the word *mysterion*'s etymology may be, there can be no doubt that from the time when Herodotus wrote of the rites of the Kabiri of Samothrace [...] it always meant gaining esoteric wisdom after the endurance of ordeals, some of which might be painful. [...] The association of Isis with the Kabiri is a fascinating problem. The Kabiri were originally demi-gods, sons of Hephaestus, who could themselves share in the chtonic rites of Demeter and Kore [...] their main haunts were Lemnos and Samothrace. Herodotus, identifying the Greek Hephaestus of Lemnos with the Egyptian Ptah of Memphis, was convinced that the great Egyptian fire-god and Architect of the Universe had the Kabiri as his sons and that they were natives of Egypt." [5]

Reinhold's work on *Die kabirischen Mysterien* and Born's rediscovery of Egypt have to be understood in this context. The Great Architect of the Universe stands at the center of the Masonic edifice and his mythical association with blacksmiths and other masters of fire, places him squarely within the realm of alchemy where rites of purification by fire are conducted.

Given Reinhold's lifelong railings against superstition, it remains difficult to reconcile his academic expositions on the subject with the magical strata on which his investigations depended. There are undoubtedly many solutions to this problem, but they are difficult to verbalize unless one is willing to postulate the primacy of inwardly held hermetic convictions over philosophical statements targeted at profane audiences. In an age of reason, 'superstition' is anything that does not conform to known facts. The Jesuit in Reinhold would have been able to discriminate between the gross superstitions propagated by Catholic monks and priests and his own fascination with an enlightened ancient Egyptian priesthood.

Jan Assmann thinks that *Die kabirischen Mysterien* was a confession of pantheism in the Spinozic form of *deus sive natura*, but there are obvious problems with this explanation.[6] Spinoza, whose aversion to superstition was as acute as Reinhold's, was not a stranger to Kabbalistic lore. One must therefore wonder how far his reliance on reason really extended when ritual considerations were involved:

"The Kabbalah is the science of the Soul and of God in all their correlations and correspondences. It teaches and proves that *all is one* and that *one is all*, allowing one, thanks to analogy, to move from image to principle, or contrastingly, from principle to form." [7]

This Kabbalistic appropriation of *deus sive natura* shows that other avenues existed. They predated Spinoza's philosophy by centuries and offered systems that were far more complete than anything available in modern times.

Ignaz von Born's ***Journal für Freymäurer*** was an open account of a much larger investigation into the esoteric. Who knows where things would have gone if *Zur wahren Eintracht* had not been closed. Jan Assmann's conclusions regarding Reinhold's beliefs does not preclude Kabbalistic developments:

"Reinhold does not see any difference between the Egyptian, or hermetic, idea of the One and Biblical monotheism. He thinks that Moses believed in God as the One-and-All and instituted a new mystery religion which can be interpreted as the oldest form of Freemasonry." [8]

This is where Kabbalists tend to agree with Reinhold. Their mysteries correspond to the oral tradition left behind by Moses and they have always argued that the Scriptures cannot be accessed directly. In the Kabbalah, the symbolism of the King dominates the Sephirotic Tree. That tree conducts divine emanations from the higher world of *Kether* (the Crown) down to *Malkuth* (the Kingdom).

The Kabbalah is also tied to the Higher Degrees of Freemasonry in ways that have yet to be described here. That relationship existed in Mozart's time, but how much of this knowledge was available to Mozart is difficult to ascertain. When the ***Journal für Freymäurer*** folded, strange things began to happen.

"In 1786 Born gave up his membership and activities as a Freemason and left the Lodge, for what mysterious reason we do not know. When ***Die Zauberflöte*** was being written, he was already dangerously ill, and he died at the age of forty-eight on July 24, 1791. His death, too, is shrouded in mystery, and seems to have passed without comment, like his departure from the Lodge. There is no report of his death, no ceremony, no mention in the gazettes." [9]

In the end we are left with a couple of ex-Jesuit Illuminates— von Born and Reinhold— whose collaboration with a lukewarm Freemason (Wieland) produced most of the material on which *The Magic Flute* is based. Nettl mentions that Wieland's views on Freemasonry constantly fluctuated between recognition and rejection, and that he waited until he was 76 years old to formally apply for membership in a Lodge.[10] Then there is Reinhold's conversion to Protestantism in 1785. Johann Gottfried Herder, a fellow Mason and Illuminist, apparently convinced him.[11]

This leaves a fairly complicated picture, but little doubt about the Egyptian framework intended for *The Magic Flute*. The battle between the forces of light and darkness gives a ritual dimension to yet another battle whose participants were neither as remote nor mythical as the fairy tale suggests.

DARKNESS AND LIGHT

Light has many forms and one feels for Tamino as he hesitates in front of the three Temples. Information plus reason do not usually amount to knowledge and nature's secrets are not that easily penetrated. Darkness is the domain of evil because it hides the higher truths on which real knowledge is based. Evil's tool of choice is superstition, which propagates falsehoods and maintains people in a constant state of ignorance and dependency.

The linguistic dimension of 'enlightenment' is expressed in the Masonic conception of the Lost Word of Freemasonry, already developed in previous sections. But it is the Egyptian angle that interests us here. In Mozart's time it concerned the recovery of the original Word through which truth and meaning could be attained.

"The dream of early modernity was a reconciliation of nature and Scripture or, to put it in the words of a book title of the eighteenth-century: ***Naturae et Scripturae Concordia***. Traditionally, this project found its expression in the theory of the two books of God, the book of nature and the book of Scripture. Now, a different, but related, solution presented itself in the possibility of a 'Scripture of nature', a writing which would refer not to the sounds of language, but to the things of nature and to the concepts of the mind. Egyptian hieroglyphs were held to be such a script [...] This explains the enormous interest which early modern Europe invested in ancient Egypt and its hieroglyphs." [12]

It is only by stressing the equivalence of 'Light' with Scriptural language that one arrives at a correct understanding of what was intended in ***The Magic Flute***. In the rush to apply these principles to an ever evolving political situation, in which social renovation looked like an increasingly remote prospect, Mozart and a number of his Masonic collaborators graduated to the use of ritual magic. Who the collaborators were cannot be deduced from the available historical facts. Who they were not is somewhat easier to determine. Judith Eckelmeyer mentions that Gottfried van Swieten, as Prefect of the Court Library, was once involved in a minor controversy in connection with a requested addition of Kabbalistic books to the library's existing section of Judaic and rabbinical works. In reply to the request, van Swieten forwarded the following opinion to the Emperor: "Kabbalism and magic are, regarded from the least harmful point of view, the fruit of a sick and disturbed brain, and belong in the domain of insanity. The sound head and orderly man will never make them his study or his amusement." [13]

This pretty much dents Eckelmeyer's central argument, which claims that van Swieten was one of the hidden formulators of **The Magic Flute**. While it is true that van Swieten was one of Mozart's main supporters in 1790 (Constanze's correspondence refers to his generosity after Mozart's death), the relationship was evidently based on common musical interests. Van Swieten was an important 'educator' with strong Jansenist and anti-Jesuit convictions, but his open critique of magic hardly makes him a candidate for the formulation of Kabbalistic rituals.

After Joseph II's death, Freemasonry was no longer in a position to assert itself as an open guiding influence. The Brothers had to move underground. The role of Egypt during this new phase can still be visualized, but only if one sticks to basic principles:

"Since 1822, the date of Champollion's publication of his decipherment of hieroglyphics, we have known that hieroglyphs refer both to the concepts and to the sounds of language. But the grammatology of immediate signification did justice to a property of Egyptian hieroglyphs that is notoriously left unexplained by modern Egyptology: the systematic iconicity of hieroglyphs. Why did Egyptian hieroglyphs keep their pictorial character? Warburton's answer is: because they referred to things and formed a virtually complete inventory of all the 'figures' that constitute the created world. [...] Ptah, the Egyptian creator, is the god of plastic arts, of image-making." [14]

As the god of hieroglyphs, Ptah embodied the Egyptian principle of creative emanation that, in turn, translated into the Kabbalistic concept of *Keter* (the Crown) through which these emanations could trickle down to *Malkuth* (the Kingdom), where human affairs were conducted.

The Magic Flute ends with apocalyptic expectations:

> *Die Strahlen der Sonne vertreiben die Nacht,*
> *Zernichten der Heuchler erschlichene Macht"*

> [The sun's radiant glory has vanquished the night,
> The powers of darkness have yielded to light]

Sarastro's concluding words before the chorus cuts in for a final tribute to Isis and Osiris have a liturgical significance. They refer to an objective already achieved outside of time, which has yet to be realized in the realms below. But 'darkness' is here equated with hypocrisy (*Heuchelei*) and a surreptitiously obtained (*erschleichen*) power. Is this a political statement referring to Freemasonry's ultimate victory over its enemies, or are there other possible explanations?

The 'triumphant sun' of beauty and wisdom is to bring comfort to the Papagenos and Papagenas of this world. One has the distinct impression that Tamino and Pamina, who are to assume Sarastro's powers, have absolutely no idea of what their function really is. They have been 'joined' by their trials, but lack human substance for all their romantic appeal.

Right from the start, heroic deeds are excluded (Tamino does not even get to kill the serpent— he is the archer without arrows) and the opera ends on an anticlimactic note. The union of Papageno and Papagena upstages Tamino and Pamina's. Ingmar Bergman, whose film version of ***The Magic Flute*** is now considered a classic, inverted the order of the final scenes.

Pamina and Tamino are symbolic participants and their significance must be sought beyond the immediate plot. The magic of the Word depends on a ritual identification between the Name and its priestly carrier. The *hieros gamos* through which Pamina and Tamino are recombined into the philosopher's stone are also the process of *genesis* by which an effective Word is magically re-created.

In alchemical operations the outcome depends on the level of purification by fire achieved during the magical procedure. Much of that is conditioned by the environment in which the operations take place. If the Temple has been corrupted, no union can be achieved in practice. That message is conveyed in pessimistic statements coming from the Lodge:

"In Masonic Lodges the acacia is no longer known, the heart of Hiram has not been preserved in the mystic urn; atheists and ignorant power-seekers say INRI and inscribe YEVE on the fronts of their Temples. They are more to be feared even than the clergy which receive their abuse, for at least the latter have kept the devotion which makes saints, even though they have lost the tradition which makes initiates." [15]

These are harsh words, but purity is never achieved by making compromises. Purity is found in Being; compromise in the process of Becoming. In previous volumes, we have looked at Martin Heidegger's conception of *genesis* (unconcealment) and *phtora* (concealment*)* as ritual forms of birth and death. Heidegger's interest in these words arose in conjunction with his study of the Anaximander Fragment, considered to be the oldest piece of western thinking. A cycle of äÝíåóéò-öèïñÜ frames the process of Becoming, which is, in turn, supported by Being:

"...if Becoming *is*, then we must think Being so essentially that it does not simply include Becoming in some vacuous conceptual manner, but rather in such a way that Being sustains and characterizes Becoming (ãÝíåóéò-öèïñÜ) in an essential appropriate manner." [16]

By studying Homer's use of language in an important place in the *Iliad*, where the concept of Being is related to different aspects of time, Heidegger arrives at the conclusion that knowledge is not science in the modern sense; but a remembrance of Being.[17] The passage in the *Iliad*, on which he bases his conclusions is at the beginning of Book I (68-72). The Greek camp has been ravaged for nine days by the plague and Achilles commands the seer Kalchas to interpret the wrath of Apollo— the god by whom plagues are sent. Kalchas is described by Homer in the following words:

"... and among them stood up Kalchas, Thestor's son, far the best of the bird interpreters, who knew all that is [ôÜ ô' Ýüíôá], is to be [ôÜ ô' Ýóóüìåíá], or once was [ðñü ô' Ýüíôá], who guided into the land of Ilion the ships of the Acheans through that seercraft of his own that Phoibos Apollo gave him." [18]

The ability to 'see', which Phoibos Apollo dispenses, refers to the world of symbols, usually hidden to ordinary senses. The 'triumphant sun' works in ways that ordinary thinking cannot follow and Heidegger explains why as he comments on the above passage from the *Iliad*:

"Only when a man has seen does he truly see. To see is to have seen. What is seen has arrived and remains for him in sight. A seer has always already seen. Having seen in advance, he sees into the future. He sees the future tense out of the perfect.[...] If in the poetic designation of Kalchas what is present is thought in relation to the seer's seeing, this means for Greek thinking that the seer, as the one who has seen, is himself one who makes-present and belongs in an exceptional sense to the totality of what is present. [...]ôÜ Ýüíôá, what is present, whether or not at the present time, is the unobtrusive name of what expressly comes to language in the Anaximander Fragment. This word names that which, while not yet spoken, is the unspoken in thinking which addresses all thinking." [19]

The 'unspoken in thinking which addresses all thinking' is precisely what active creation is all about. Since Apollo is the god of music and poetry, who presides on Mount Parnassus over the activities of the Muses, there is an implicit relationship between inspiration and musical craft.

When the world of magic is entered, the Cabinet of Reflection becomes a place where death is to be faced literally. The process of self-concealment, or ceasing to Become (*phtora*) initiates the proper transition into the crucial state of Being. The sacrificial framework cannot be cheated with last minute escapes:

"Death and facing death [...] are central to eighteenth-century Masonic texts, and involve the idea of a journey, trials, and rebirth. In Architecture and in the design of gardens, the themes of a route, a progression, of allusion, of metaphor, of mnemonics, of conjuring moods, cultures, or exotica, and of passing through to a climactic end are not unusual, and yet the Masonic content of such designs often escapes commentators. Masonic concepts of death, trial, and descent to the depths are clearly described in many books, and are explicit in the text of *Die Zauberflöte*, although obscured in the opera houses of today where productions and designs strive after 'originality' and 'contemporary meaning' only to make nonsense of the work and display an abysmal ignorance of the essence of the piece. *Die Zauberflöte* with no Masonic iconography and no Egyptian Architecture for the sets misses the point entirely and leaves the audience mystified, bored, or irritated by what appears to be a nonsensical story." [20]

In his *The Masters of Truth in Archaic Greece*, Marcel Detienne points out that the musician/poet is a 'master of Truth' because he has the power to see *aletheia*. What this power consists of can further be abstracted from Hesiod's **Works and Days** where, as Detienne notes, there is a double instantiation of this particular word. The first a*letheia* manifests as magico-religious speech and interacts with poetic memory; the second is defined as a non-forgetfulness of the poet's precepts.[21]

Heidegger defines *aletheia* as unconcealment and what he means by that can be inferred from his discussion of Becoming (ãÝíåóéò-öèïñÜ), which he characterizes as a process of luminous disclosure, phasing in and out of the primordial darkness. The power to see *aletheia* (Truth) is thus equivalent to Kalchas' gift, bestowed by Apollo. In short, the ability to see 'Light' is full of prophetic characteristics. Darkness, in turn, can be defined by a failure to 'see' and therefore to connect to this prophetic dimension.

THE GENEALOGIES OF DARKNESS AND LIGHT

The first basic opposition— at a linguistic level— is between *aletheia* (truth about to manifest) and *lethe* (oblivion, or silence). In Greek mythology these are echoed in the genealogies of 'light' and 'darkness' supplied by Hesiod in his **Theogony**. They provide valuable clues to the traditional sources for the Brotherhood of Light, led by Sarastro, and those of the wicked dominion of the Queen of the Night:

> Again, although she slept with none of the gods,
> Dark Night gave birth to Blame and sad Distress,
> And the Hesperides, who, out beyond
> The famous stream of Oceanus, tend
> The lovely golden apples, and their trees.
> She bore the Destinies and ruthless Fates,
> Goddesses who track down the sins of men
> And gods, and never cease from awful rage
> Until they give the sinner punishment.
> Then deadly Night gave birth to Nemesis,
> That pain to gods and men...
> [...]
> And Oath, who brings most grief to men on earth
> When anyone swears falsely, knowing it.
>
> And Pontus' firstborn child was Nereus,
> The honest one, the truthful. The old man
> Is called this name because he never errs,
> And he is gentle and remembers Right,
> And knows the arts of Mercy and the Law.[22]

From a structural point of view, one can thus speak of a Sarastro-Nereus, honest and truthful, who knows the arts of Mercy and the Law; and a Queen of the Night who gives birth to endless calamities, but also to the Hesperides who tend to the golden apples of immortality. The musician/poet needs to be at ease in both worlds because his words of praise or blame impact these unsubstantial realms and activate their powers.

"Through the power of his speech, a poet made an ordinary mortal 'equal in destiny to a king', conferring on him being and reality. His praise was called etumos. However, like the Indian ideal of samsa, the poet's speech was double-edged, both good and bad. As Pindar puts it: 'Praise touches on Blame'. There is a negative aspect: 'bitter speech' has a 'crowding bite' and the face of Momos.[...] While in certain traditions blame is malevolent speech, it can also be defined as a lack of praise. In the most ancient religious thought, Momos, described as 'shadowy', is one of the children of Night and a brother to Lethe, oblivion. Through its affinities with oblivion, blame is the negative aspect of praise; used simply as a doublet to Lethe, its meaning is silence." [23]

This gets quite technical and Marcel Detienne shows how aletheia finds its ultimate meaning in the triple opposition between memory and oblivion, praise and blame, light and night.[24] What is brought into the light, remembered and praised by the poet is what is magically destined to triumph. The power of the poet's word ensures that the symbolic finds its expression in the real— and that is exactly where The Magic Flute evolves into a magic ritual.

Behind the never ending fight between chaos and cosmos, is an implicit understanding that rites created to re-enact the primordial struggle can be effective in managing its outcome. In his study of the Delphic myth, Joseph Fontenrose mentions that one possible interpretation of the combat between Apollo and Python is that it was connected to rituals of community renewal:

"It is not impossible that the entire interpretation of the combatants as chaos and cosmos, death and life, arose through the myth's connection with rituals of community renewal. We noticed that street fighting occurred in the Akitu [Babylonian New-Year] festival and fistic contests in most of the festivals discussed.[...] But it is doubtful whether these fights or contests were instituted to commemorate a mythical combat. More likely they had a purely magical purpose at first [...] The familiar sham fights of rural festivals in Europe and Latin America do not necessarily invoke the combat myth [...] Sometimes the celebrants assert that they are commemorating an historical conflict, such as that of the Crusaders against Saracens or of Spaniards against Moors [...] Here history is being shaped into myth. In some places it was shaped to the combat myth, to the St. George variant, for instance. Long ago the war between Delphians and Phlegyans became a legend that was modelled upon the Apollo-Python combat." [25]

Community renewal rituals are foundation rituals designed to generate new forces so that the equilibrium with chaos may once again be achieved in dynamic rather than static fashion. Forces that are already spent cannot be used to sustain a working social order. A weak power has be overthrown because its original strength has been dissipated.

In the Masonic degrees dealing specifically with the Lost Word, these Hesiodic elements of truthfulness are transcribed into hermetic notions of justice. That is why the Knights Rose-Croix, of the 18th degree, consider Hermes their master and insist on using 'Mercy and the Law' against prevalent forms of injustice revealed by the Enlightenment. These well-intentioned strivings, however, easily get out of hand when the traditional ideas supporting them are poorly understood.

Marcel Detienne shows just how extensive and precise the connections were between poetic speech, as developed by Hesiod, and hermetic speech, as conceived by Homer. The linguistic foundations were, for all intents and purposes, identical:

"Hesiod describes the negative powers of the children of Night, and then lists the descendants of Pontus, beginning with the eldest and most venerable, Nereus [..] the Old Man of the Sea: 'But Pontos, the great Sea, was Father of truthful (*apseudes*) Nereus, who tells no lies (*alethes*), eldest of his sons. They call him the old Gentleman because he is trustworthy (*nemertes*) [...]' Three epithets, *alethes, apseudes,* and *nemertes*, confer exceptional importance on Nereus. The association of these epithets is in all likelihood traditional, since we also find them linked in this way in the description of the highest form of mantic speech, that of Apollo. In the **Homeric Hymn to Hermes**, when Hermes speaks before the gods, he claims in an *ad hominem* argument addressed to Apollo that he has the same virtues as those usually associated with his rival. He declares that he will speak *aletheia* and that he is *nemertes* and *apseudes*. The 'truth' of the Old Man of the Sea thus seems to cover two domains: prophecy and justice." [26]

The Rosicrucian connection is difficult to explore beyond the open references to Hermes found in the rituals of the Scottish Rite's 18th degree. What seems to be missing is a clear indication of the authority standing behind this updated vision of 'truth'. Marcel Detienne notes that in the forms of justice associated with the Old Man of the Sea the function of sovereignty emerges.

The type of justice associated with the Old Man of the Sea is justice by ordeal. Very often the ordeal is by immersion in water:

"The Old Man of the Sea most likely embodies the gravest and most solemn form of justice because he assumed the role in the Greek world that the river gods had played in Anatolia and Mesopotamia. However, justice by ordeal is not unique. There were many other ordeals; among those associated with the Old Man of the Sea, the ordeal by the scales is worth mentioning. This ordeal is doubly interesting in that first, a royal figure presided over it and, second it was placed under the aegis of *aletheia*." [27]

The Old Man of the Sea is a gatekeeper controlling the flow of the primordial waters from which the seer gets his vision. These waters belong to the cosmic ocean and are ritually identified with various existing bodies of water. The relationship between the Egyptian hieroglyph for water, which represents the sound '*n*' (〜〜〜), and divine possession, has already been explored in the first volume of this series. In the same volume we also looked at the Hebrew equivalent of the Old Man of the Sea— that is Melchizedek. The revealing passage must again be quoted here, but in a more extensive context:

"Judeo-Christian tradition," writes René Guénon, "distinguishes between two forms of priesthood, the one 'according to the order of Aaron', the other 'according to the order of Melchizedek'. The latter is superior to the former, just as Melchizedek is superior to Abraham, whose issue composed the tribe of Levi and consequently the family of Aaron.[...] We shall not pursue here the question of the two priesthoods, but these words of Saint Paul are worth quoting: 'Here [in the Levitic priesthood] these are mortal men who receive the tithes but that there is a man who is attested to be living.'[Epistle to the Hebrews 7:8]. This 'living man' who is *Melki-Tsedeq* is also *Manu*, he who 'lives perpetually' (Hebrew *le-olam*), which means for the duration of this cycle (*Manvantara*) or the world he specifically controls. [...] Through the prescription of his own law he is for this world the expression and image of the Divine Word. [...] The references contained in the Hebrew Kabbalah to the *Shekinah* will complete this exposition: the *Shekinah* is represented in the 'inferior' world by *Malkuth*, which means 'Kingdom' and which is the last of the ten *Sephiroth*. This in itself is of relevance, but more so are the synonyms given to *Malkuth* of '*Tsedeq*', or ' the Just'. This convergence of *Malkuth* and *Tsedeq*, or of Royalty (the government of the world) and Justice, reappears in precisely the title '*Melki-Tsedeq*'.[...] *Malkuth* is the 'reservoir where the waters that flow from the river above unite, that is to say all the emanations that are poured out so abundantly'." [28]

A much clearer picture of the relationship between royalty, the Word, 'water' and justice begins to emerge. The generation of Israel from Abraham, for instance, appears as a magical procedure in which *Melki-Tsedeq* acts as the mediator. It starts with the blessing of Abraham, described at **Genesis** 14:19-20. Abraham is called Abram by *Melki-Tsedeq* and from a Kabbalistic standpoint the Name he has been given becomes the root-seed from which Israel will eventually grow. But not before that Name has been empowered with the characteristics of generation.

Philip Beitchman (***Alchemy of the Word***) discusses Abraham's blessing in the light of Pico della Mirandola's (1463-1494) Kabbalistic speculations concerning its meaning. Pico's conclusion was that "unless the letter HÉ had been added to the name of Abram, Abraham would not have begotten.":

"This bit of zoharic arithmetic," says Beitchman, "according to which the 'h', fifth letter of the Hebrew alphabet, is *the* letter of generation, seems to have been one of the most widely disseminated Kabbalistic commonplaces of the Renaissance, turning up, for instance, very prominently 150 years later, in the *fifth* chapter of Sir Thomas Browne's **The Garden of Cyrus**, a book about the number *five*. Here Pico is combining a Platonic theory of correspondences with Kabbalistic numerology in regard to events in the 'lower' world. The realm of scriptural *words* constitutes an ideal realm, of which the earth is a copy. Therefore any alteration above is reflected by a corresponding one below." [29]

René Guénon adds that "the name *Abram* had then not yet changed to *Abraham*; at the same time (**Genesis** 17) the name of his wife *Sarai* was changed to *Sarah*, so that the numerological value of the two names together stayed the same."[30] This generative aspect is what creates 'Chosen People'— their seed 'named' by the King of Justice to be the vehicle for His rule of

Law.

There is no doubt that contemporary Jews would just as soon pass on the privilege and follow the example set by Moses Mendelssohn. But unfortunately things are not that simple. The frenzied search for a working ecumenical arrangement that prizes the secular and discounts past covenants is a highly dangerous pursuit.

This message is not popular with today's generation of freethinkers because they forget that the world did not start when they were born. It is even less popular with contemporary Freemasons, who have no real understanding of their complex heritage.

Occult connections come with their responsibilities and Mozart was well aware of the subversive trade-offs acquired with mastery. A strong desire for mastery must always be treated with suspicion. Many of the characters that haunt Mozart's operas— particularly after he became a Mason— dramatize the hazards of controlling personalities. Don Alfonso, the puppet-master of *Cosi Fan Tutte*, and Don Giovanni, the unstoppable pleasure seeker from yet another opera, are case-studies in initiation gone awry.

"Don Giovanni is half-way to joining the company of Greek heroes whom the Masonic enlightenment adopted as prototypes for its own initiants. He has descended into hell in his lifetime; if he could only achieve the return journey, he would change— at least in enlightened eyes— from outlaw into hero. Just as the legend of King Arthur, by refusing him a physical death, holds out hopes of his second coming and makes him *rex quondam rexque futurus* [once and future king], so the legend of Don Juan makes him *anti-rex quondam* and hints at his being *anti-rex futurus* by suggesting hopes— or fears— of his return." [31]

Today we can speak of darkness and light in abstract terms only. From where we presently stand, the genealogies cannot be traced to existing organizations with any degree of certainty. The element of trust has disappeared from the scene and we must continuously ask ourselves whether organizations offering initiation are qualified, or even legitimate.

Given the inherent difficulties and the openness required to undertake a journey of initiation, it surely comes across as a doomed enterprise under today's conditions. To expect results on a grand scale is naive to the point of disingenuousness.

"A true mastery of the world," writes Daniel Beresniak, "will be possible when the fellowship of free men is realized throughout the entire universe.[...] the 'free' man is he who knows himself, who has traveled the difficult path leading down to his hell and returned. The real revolution is internal and individual. There is nothing good to be expected from men who have not undertaken this journey. These cannot be 'brothers'. They only know how to be accomplices. The limitation of meaning through stereotypes, intellectual laziness, a weak motivation to go further [...] to be content with reaction instead of action, to parrot and yet believe that one is speaking, to be satisfied with a single meaning, all of this constitutes the behavior of the slave, incapable, if he cannot conduct a strenuous reevaluation of himself, of finding the Word." [32]

When superficial meaning is raised to the level of a standard, the desire to curtail alternatives becomes quite strong. What cannot be scrutinized here and now is forcibly rejected. As the man who knows himself emerges from his hell and joins the ranks of those who have survived similar voyages, a group dynamic starts to develop. 'Individualists unite' is a doomed slogan, but the herd instinct cannot be suppressed. Old prejudices are quickly forgotten in favor of new ones and life continues on an accelerating downward slope. The psychotic zone of no return delineates these personal hells and Mozart probes them very well.

Beresniak— and those around him— have kept a vigilant eye on the forces of darkness, which they conveniently identify with neo-Nazism, religious fundamentalism and occult movements in general. In their zealous hunt for transgressors they forget their own admonition against stereotypes. Darkness takes many forms and seldom uses past disguises. It thrives where expectations have already been set and arrives as a confirmation, a validating command performance that quickly captures a mindless following.

The Magic Flute has repeatedly been drawn into political controversies and an interesting little book (*La flute désenchantée* (1991) [the disenchanted flute]) tries to 'rescue' Mozart from the abuse of his work by past totalitarian regimes. The book opens with a quotation from Papageno (Act I Scene 14): "Wasn't I a fool to be frightened? There are black birds in the world, so why not dark people?" Nothing to do with blacks, of course; but everything with those who might be attracted to the dark side, where the enemies of universalism hide. Papageno's words of wisdom are followed by an introduction along the same lines, written by Jean-Robert Ragache, Grand Master of the French Grand Orient.

The genealogies of darkness and light are referred to at various points in the action as *The Magic Flute* unfolds. For Judith Eckelmeyer, Tamino's initiation is strictly within the bounds of a Christian mystical tradition. She lists many similarities between Sarastro's realm and the fictitious setting of Johann Valentin Andreae's *Christianopolis* (1624) and concludes that both were created for the same purpose. "*Christianopolis* is predicated on the grievous tribulation of the true Church of Christ under the oppression wreaked by Antichrist [...] The book contains explicit references to Martin Luther's works and ideas." [33]

THE TWO ARMED MEN

Tamino's initiation takes place in caves where the trials by fire and water are conducted. Two Armored Men escort Tamino to the entrance and Mozart has them sing a devotional hymn to Isis and Osiris to the tune of the Lutheran chorale "*Ach Gott vom Himmel sieh' darein.*" The original text of the chorale, which paraphrases Psalm 12 "is concerned with the tribulation and oppression of the Saints by the godless, who speak and act in falsehood and evil."[34] The text used in the opera is borrowed from Terrasson's ***Sethos***, but for anyone familiar with the chorale there would have been a second meaning.[35] It remains to be seen whether the Christian parallel is intended, or simply borrowed for purely Masonic purposes.

The symbolism of the Armed Men is consistent with the Christian apocalyptic tradition identified by Eckelmeyer. Craig Wright traces it to the construction of labyrinths found in medieval cathedrals and shows how apocalyptic visions evolved with time through theological reinterpretations.

"Erasmus of Rotterdam's ***Trusty Weapon of the Christian Soldier*** (***Enchiridion Militis Christiani***) was the most influential work of pre-Reformation theology. First printed in 1503, it appeared in eight Latin editions between 1514 and 1518 [...] For Erasmus, the labyrinth functions, as it had earlier with the patristic fathers, as a metaphor for the sinful world. The faithful will need a guiding thread, a set of rules, to chart a course through a life of temptation. [...] Steeped in classical literature, Erasmus knew well the myth of Daedalus and the Cretan maze."[36]

The double retrogrades of the maze signify the *descensus* and *ascensus* of Christ. They are further associated with the victorious Redeemer, who in Christian tradition appears in the form of the warrior/lamb of the Apocalypse. There is also a connection to music, which is quite surprising:

"Surely it is not a coincidence that the Christian image of the Armed Man, then nearly fifteen hundred years old, was given musical expression for the first time immediately after the fall of Constantinople. So too it must not be happenstance that the musical tradition of the Armed Man radiated from the lands of

2. Albrecht Dürer's Knight, Death and the Devil

the duke of Burgundy. Dufay, Regis, Josquin, and Busnois, four of the earliest musicians to compose an Armed Man Mass, were Burgundian subjects and, in some cases, court employees. [Duke] Philip's son, Charles the Bold, took special delight in the six Naples Armed Man Masses, as we have seen. Indeed, these Masses may have been created expressly for the Order of the Golden Fleece." [37]

After Charles the Bold's death, sovereignty over the Order of the Golden Fleece passed into the Habsburg line. In 1516, the future Emperor Charles V assumed command of the Order.

"Poets saw the warrior Charles preparing a new Christian Age. Ludovico Ariosto (1474-1533] began his **Orlando Furioso**— as did the creator of the sixth Armed Man Mass in the Naples set— by alluding to the first line of Virgil's **Aeneid**: ' I sing of arms and a man'. Here, however, Ariosto sings not of Aeneas but of Emperor Charles, a new Jason who leads a band of Christian Argonauts." [38]

The appearance of these themes in Mozart may seem accidental, but Craig Wright points out that the composer actually had an interest in mazes. Items in his personal library and subsequent associations suggest that the symbolism of the two Armed Men may not have been casual. Of the books listed as part of his estate, No. 59 is **Labyrinthe, klein harmonisches von Bach**. He also owned a copy of Joseph Haydn's cantata **Ariadne auf Naxos**.

Wright notes the appearance of the two Armed Men in **The Magic Flute** and further mentions that this opera was the inspiration for a subsequent Schikaneder opera, called **The Labyrinth** (1798); but goes on to discount the Christian associations:

"Tamino presses forward through raging fires and rushing waters, shielded only by the sounds of his flute. No thread of Ariadne or lifeline of Christian faith here— now the instrument of salvation is a magical instrument! And though there are Armed Men in this hell, these warriors are not soldiers of Christ. This is no Christian allegory. Rather, *The Magic Flute* mimics key elements in the secret rituals of the Freemasons." [39]

3. Titian's Emperor Charles V as an Armed Man (1548)

THE TRIALS BY FIRE AND WATER

The Armed Men guard the entrance to the caves where the trials take place. The lack of Christian symbolism need not stand in the way of the magical operations performed here. The candidate to initiation, suitably purified, is temporarily transformed into a sacrificial lamb as he enters the premises. Ritually destined for death, he nevertheless emerges as the victorious first fruit of a *genetic* process (again in the Heideggerian sense of the term) by which a new humanity is to be reseeded. In a pre-Christian context, we have the story of Isaac, where the same symbolism is used. It is told at **Genesis** 22:10-13. As Abraham is about to sacrifice his son, a suitable substitute appears:

"And Abraham lifted up his eyes and looked, and behold behind him a ram caught in a thicket by his horns: and Abraham went and took the ram, and offered him up for a burnt offering in the stead of his son."

In this particular trial by fire, the substitution is not without musical implications. The remainder of the sacrifice has been transformed into a musical instrument by which the beginning, or completion of major ritual cycles is announced:

"The story of Abraham and Isaac has special relevance to Jewish religious practices, for the horns of the ram survived the sacrificial burning, becoming the prototype for the *shofar*. With the *shofar* came symbolic music to the people of Israel, and thus it enjoyed a privileged place in Jewish services. In the centuries after the destruction of the Temple, the *shofar* was the only musical instrument allowed in the synagogue, all others being banned until the coming of the Messiah. Even today its sounds announce and terminate all festivals in the Jewish religion as well as commemorations of the state of Israel. Like the sign of the lamb, the *shofar* signals beginnings and endings."[40]

We have already discussed Abraham's role as a magic progenitor, but a few words should still be said about the fire itself. Fire is the vehicle of the sacrifice and it can take many symbolic disguises. In Egyptian religion, the God of Fire was Ptah; in Wagner's *Ring*, he appears as Loge. Fire always originates from the 'tongue of Ptah', which Thoth inherits. It is the corrupting instrument of choice used for tests of ritual purity. In Wagner's *Ring*, Loge uses it on Wotan in preparation for the apocalyptic ending of *Götterdämmerung.*.

The trial by water belongs to the Argonautic tradition, which also addresses ritual considerations surrounding the lamb. The Greek myth of the Golden Fleece has many parallels with the story of Abraham and Isaac. In the legend of the Golden Fleece, King Athamas decides to offer his son Phrixos as a sacrifice to the god of the harvest. As Phrixos awaits his fate, a ram with a golden fleece appears and abducts him to the island of Colchis. Once in Colchis, Phrixos sacrifices the ram and offers its fleece to King Ætes. The spirit of the ram goes up to heaven where it is said to reside in the form of the Aries constellation.

Phrixos is an aerial fugitive; but Jason, his kinsman, appears as a conquering mariner knight tasked with returning the Golden Fleece to its homeland. In his trials, he is assisted by King Ætes's daughter Medea. Pamina standing by Tamino' side is nothing new from the standpoint of esoteric myth. In some accounts Medea is mentioned as a daughter of Hecate, the patroness of magicians. As a priestess of Hecate, she is responsible for putting to death any foreigner entering Colchis.

The trials by fire and water are a re-enactment of the lamb's departure and return. Whoever enters the cave of the trials in the spirit of sacrifice emerges as a magic warrior. The story is not about Christianity, Judaism, or Greek myth— but about ritual action in the eternal battle between darkness and light. False light is easily manufactured, but it always begets its *Doppelgänger*. The ignorant power-seekers who say INRI and inscribe YEVE on the fronts of their Temples need to understand what is at stake and by what means these battles are fought.

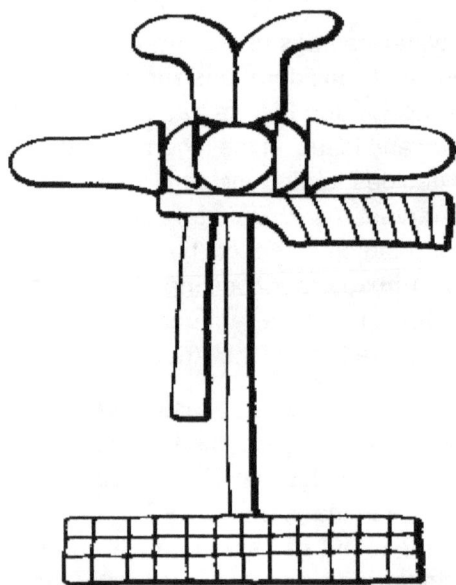

THE THREE TEMPLES

According to pictures we have of Schikaneder's mise-en-scène of 1794, the three Temples are represented on stage by entrances. Nature is to the right, Reason to the left and Wisdom takes center stage.

THE TEMPLE OF NATURE

Nature was not a vague concept for the Masons surrounding Mozart and as a reference it is entirely consistent with the Egyptian setting of the opera. Given the extremely precise connotations within which Nature was understood, it is highly significant that Tamino is not allowed to enter this specific Temple.

"Hermes Trismegistus had a triumphant comeback in the eighteenth century, and this was due to Ralph Cudworth's rehabilitation. In rescuing Hermes Trismegistus from Casaubon's devastating critique [i.e. that the **Corpus Hermeticum** was a late compilation and a Christian forgery], Cudworth inaugurated a new phase of Egyptophilia, which in Germany, coincided with a wave of Spinozism. [...] The object of the esoteric monotheism or the 'mysteries' of the ancient Egyptians came to be identified as 'Nature'. In the idea of Nature as the deity of an original, nonrevealed monotheism, which survived in Egyptian religion under the almost impenetrable cover of symbols and mysteries, the hermetic, hieroglyphic, and Biblical discourses on Egypt merge. This development led to the height of Egyptomania in the late eighteenth century, Mozart's **Zauberflöte** and Napoleon's expedition being two particularly notable examples."[41]

Since Tamino is not allowed into the Temple of Nature, toward which he turns first, there is a message in his explicit rejection. What our hero is looking for is love and virtue; but for the moment, as he stands in front the three Temples, he is in the opposite state. He is seeking death and vengeance. This polarity cannot be inverted by crossing the threshold of the Temple of Nature. It is the seat of the sublime, where terror reigns supreme:

"The association of 'nature' with 'the sublime' goes back to Edmond Burke, who published his ground-breaking essay on the sublime in 1759. The beautiful inspires pleasure, the sublime terror. The inspiration of terror is 'the prerogative of nature only'. Typical terror-inspiring phenomena of the sublime are obscurity, vacuity, darkness, solitude, and silence— experiences which *The Magic Flute* (1791) and other works, such as Abbé Terrasson's *Sethos* (1731) and Ignaz von Born's essay on the Egyptian mysteries, linked with the Egyptian mysteries and initiation. Burke viewed the Egyptian temples as architectural realizations of the sublime and this association soon became commonplace." [42]

THE TEMPLE OF REASON

The Temple of Reason would have been dedicated to the comprehension of nature. This was Ignaz von Born's home and it reflects many of his views on Freemasonry as well.

"Reinhold's contribution to the Moses discourse consisted of the equation of Jehovah and Isis (alias Nature). According to Clement of Alexandria, the last and highest initiation led to a point where all teaching ends, discursive instruction stops, and immediate vision takes over. [...] This is how Ignaz von Born, the Grand Master of True Concord, Vienna's most important Lodge (of which Reinhold was a member in 1783-1784) summarized the ultimate aim of the Egyptian mysteries: 'The knowledge of nature is the ultimate purpose of our application. We worship this progenitor, nourisher, and preserver of all creation in the image of Isis. Only he who knows the whole extent of her power and force will be able to uncover her veil without punishment'." [43]

As a practical chemist and mineralogist, von Born was the archetypal scientist dedicated to the discovery of the rules of Nature. These blueprints would have been kept in the Temple of Reason, where love and virtue are not particularly relevant subjects.

THE TEMPLE OF WISDOM

The Temple of Wisdom is patterned on the 'hermetic cave' used in Egyptian initiations. Jan Assmann points out that in the 1740s there was plenty of accurate information concerning the eastern Mediterranean at the end of the 5th century B.C. The letters of Orsames, from which the quote below is taken come from a compendium of four volumes, published in London between 1741-1743 and titled *Athenian Letters or, the Epistolary Correspondence of an Agent of the King of Persia, Residing at Athens during the Peloponnesian War*. [44]

Here is the section that describes the cave— a description that in many ways matches Ignaz Alberti's illustration, found in the original libretto:

"The strange solemnity of the place must strike everyone, that enters it, with a religious horror; and is the more proper to work you up into that frame of mind, in which you will receive, with the most awful reverence and assent, whatever the priest, who attends you is pleased to reveal [...] Toward the farther end of the cave, or within the innermost recess of some prodigious caverns, that run beyond it, you hear, as if it were a great way off, a noise resembling the distant roarings of the sea, and sometimes like the fall of waters, dashing against rocks with great impetuosity. [...] Surrounded with these pillars of lamps are each of those venerable columns, which I am now to speak of, inscribed with the hieroglyphical letters with the primeval mysteries of the Egyptian learning [...] From these pillars, and the sacred books, they maintain, that all the philosophy and learning of the world has been derived." [45]

4. Frontispiece to The Magic Flute's libretto (1791)

THE FOUR WORLDS

The Magic Flute is constructed on three ternaries which ritually influence the action that is to take place in the world of becoming. That is where the forces of light and darkness confront each other under various disguises. The Masonic arrangement is borrowed from Kabbalistic sources and throughout this section we will refer to Claude Guérillot's recent studies (*A la recontre des premiers Franc-Maçons Ecossais* (1740-1760) and *La Rose Maçonnique*) where the emergence of Scottish Rite Masonry during the eighteenth-century is discussed in very knowledgeable terms.

There have been too many superficial assessments from poorly informed sources concerning what was, or was not known about the Higher Degrees of Freemasonry in Mozart's time. Academic authors outdo each other, claiming that Austrian Freemasonry was based exclusively on the British system and that it never went beyond the three basic Degrees. The fallacy of these claims becomes apparent as soon as one examines the available facts.

Austrian Lodges, as we have seen, were in tight contact with the rest of the German world which had adopted Baron von Hund's Order of Strict Observance, into which Knightly Degrees had already been introduced. Von Hund was allegedly admitted into the Order of the Temple by Lord Kilmarnock, Grand Master of Scottish Masons between 1742 to 1743.[46]

The Strict Observance did not gain much momentum until after the Seven Year War [1756-1763]. During the Seven Year War, von Hund's property was destroyed multiple times and he was forced to flee since he was known as an Austrian sympathizer.[47] After the Seven Year War the Order's growth was explosive and it largely dominated continental Masonry until its claims to a Templar heritage, allegedly received through Unknown Superiors, was publicly challenged. The challenges culminated in 1782 and were resolved at the Masonic Congress of Wilhelmsbad. Following Wilhelmsbad, a complete reform was undertaken. The end result was the Scottish Rite with its Knightly Degrees.

It is important to remember that the Knightly Degrees were not a Masonic 'invention', but a complete system inherited from a much older esoteric tradition. The challenges were not to the tradition itself, but against claims that a Templar succession still existed. There are many correspondences between the Higher Degrees of the Scottish Rite and the Kabbalistic principles on which they are constructed. The notion of 'knighthood' associated with these Degrees is also perfectly consistent with the symbolism of the Armed Man, examined earlier. The Higher Degrees concerned the apocalyptic fight between the forces of light and those of darkness.

Since 'Light' is not that easily identified, we will try to avoid a one-sided terminology, with its implied commitment to light. **The Magic Flute**'s ambivalent introduction of the principal characters (the Queen of the Night and Sarastro) indicates that there is a problem. Sarastro is first depicted as a tyrant and the Queen of the Night as a victim. Then the characterization is reversed and Sarastro is praised for his wisdom while the Queen of the Night is derided as a power hungry terror. The opera ends with the victory of the forces of light— but that victory is, to a certain extent, axiomatic. Light is always destined to triumph; yet as soon as a new cycle begins, the same old darkness reappears in disguise. It is as unstoppable as our own individualistic drives.

In his study of the origins of the Thirty Three Degrees of the Ancient and Accepted Scottish Rite, Claude Guérillot points out that a distinction was always made between the 'complete' degrees into which someone was actually initiated, and those whose secrets were merely communicated at the appointed time. He thus speaks of ten Higher Degrees and three symbolic Degrees that make up the core of the Scottish Rite. The esoteric derivation of this arrangement is as follows: the Zohar opens up with Rabbi Hizkiah's commentary on a verse from the **Song of Songs** ["like a lily in a field of thisles, such is my love among the young women" (S.S. 2-2).

"What does the lily symbolize? It symbolizes the community of Israel. As the lily among thorns is tinged with red and white, so the Community of Israel is visited now with justice and now with mercy; as the lily possesses thirteen leaves, so the Community of Israel is vouchsafed thirteen categories of mercy which surround it on every side." [48]

Having stressed the importance of this passage, Guérillot elaborates on the connections between the 'complete' Degrees and the Kabbalistic Tree of Life. He notes the following correspondence to the Sephiroths:

Keter (the Supreme Crown)
   Souverain Grand Inspecteur General (33⁰)

Hokmah (Wisdom)
   Prince du Royal Secret (32⁰)

Binah (Intelligence)
   Grand Inspecteur Inquisiteur Commandeur (31⁰)

Gevurah or Din (Judgment/Rigor)
   Chevalier Kadosh (30⁰)

Gedullah or Hesed (Love)
   Chevalier du Soleil (28⁰)

Tiferet (Beauty)
   Chevalier Rose✠Croix (18⁰)

Nezah (Endurance)
   Grand Elu de la Voûte Sacrée (14⁰)

Hod (Majesty)
  Maître Elu des Neuf (9⁰), or alternately
  Grand Maître Architecte (12⁰)

Yesod (Foundation)
  Maître Secret (4⁰)

Malkuth (Kingdom)
  the three symbolic Degrees (Blue Lodges)

It is here that we find the basic opposition between the 'light of mercy' and the 'night of judgment', with which **The Magic Flute** is concerned. To the left column of the Sephirotic Tree corresponds the 'way of Justice' *(Hod, Gevurah, Binah)*, while the right column is identified with the 'way of Mercy' (*Nezah, Gedullah, Hokmah*).

The attributes of the way of judgment are majesty, rigor and intelligence. At the level of the *Maître Elu des Neuf* (The Elect of the Nine), the 'way of Justice' introduces the symbolism of the dagger (which the Queen of the Night hands to her daughter) and that of the cavern, or grotto, where the murderers of the Master (Hiram) are hiding. The *Chevalier Kadosh* (Knight Kadosh) is tied to rigorous aspects of the 'way of Justice', administered by the *Grand Inspecteur Inquisiteur Commandeur*. The Kadosh Degree introduces the theme of Revenge, here tied to the Templar legend.

At the other pole, from the 'way of Justice', is the 'way of Mercy'. It begins in the basement of the *Grand Elu de la Voûte Sacrée* (Perfect and Sublime Mason), where we find the symbolism of the 'Secret Vault'— to which the grotto of the *Maître Elu des Neuf* is opposed. Perfect and Sublime Masons are the custodians of the Ineffable Word— the Tetragrammaton— whose

5. The Ancient and Accepted Scottish Rite and the Sephirotic Tree of Life

correct pronunciation they are supposed to learn.

To the Kadosh of the left-hand column corresponds the *Chevalier du Soleil* (Knight of the Sun) of the right-hand column. His task is to help transform chaos into order. The Knights of the Sun are heirs to the hermetic 'Solar Circle' (*den siebenfachen Sonnenkreis*) given by the Queen of the Night's husband to the initiates of Isis. Sarastro, their leader, now bears this powerful emblem on his breast. It is unfortunate that most librettos— not to mention performances of ***The Magic Flute***— cut the dialogue where these revelations are made.

The implication is that Sarastro's legitimacy and power comes from a symbolic token left over from the original marriage of the Sun and the Moon (the Queen of the Night and her husband). That couple is to be recreated with Tamino and Pamina and Sarastro is just the intermediary who waits for the qualified applicant— somewhat like Gurnemanz in ***Parsifal***. The magical lineage is maintained through the maternal line, where the succession is clearly identified.

As the leader of the forces of 'Light', Sarastro ranks at the top of the column of Mercy. He is a 'wise' leader and therefore entitled to be a *Prince du Royal Secret*— a degree which originally corresponded to the last and highest degree of the Rite of Perfection, known as *Trés Illustre Souverain, Prince de la Maçonnerie, Grand Chevalier, Sublime Commandeur du Royal Secret*.

Commenting on particular aspects of this degree, Albert Pike (***Morals and Dogma of the Ancient and Accepted Scottish Rite***) has this to say:

"The Occult Science of the Ancient Magi was concealed under the shadows of the Ancient Mysteries [...] Magism was the Science of Abraham and Orpheus, of Confucius and Zoroaster. It was the dogmas of this Science that were engraven on the tables of stone by Trismegistus. Moses purified and re-*veiled* them [...] He covered them with a new veil, when he made of the Holy Kabbalah the exclusive heritage of the people of Israel, and the inviolable Secret of its priests [..] Magic is the science of the Ancient Magi: and the Christian religion, which has imposed silence on the lying oracles, and put an end to the prestiges of the false Gods, itself reveres those Magi who came from the East, guided by a Star [...] Tradition also gives these Magi the title of '*Kings*'; because initiation into Magism constitutes a genuine royalty." [49]

The legend of the *Prince du Royal Secret* is very interesting. The Masons of this degree are supposedly holding a council within a Templar encampment. The purpose of the meeting is to assemble Masonic armies for a reconquest of Jerusalem. Frederick II (or sometimes Frederick III), King of Prussia, is said to preside over this army. He is given the title of *Souverain des*

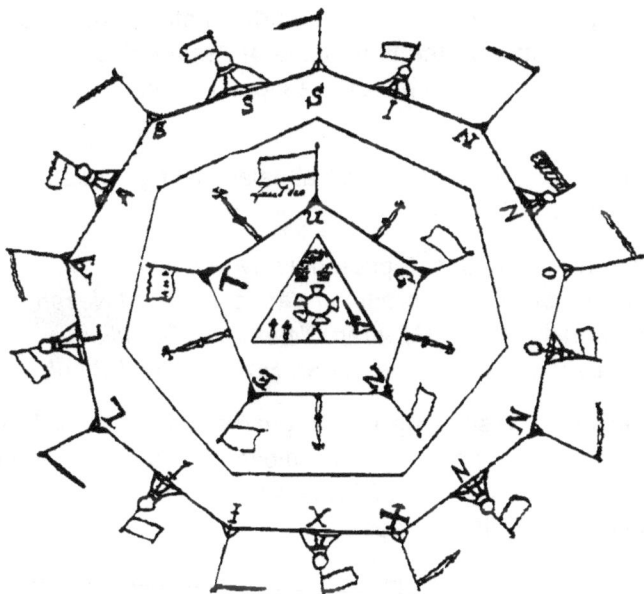

6. Camp du Rendez-Vous after Henry Francken

Souverains, Grand Prince, Illustre Commandeur en Chef.

Claude Guérillot points out that 'Frederick' was a symbol of the conquering Messiah, and as such should be understood as the anticipated future victor of the battle of Armageddon:

"To fight this battle, to win back the Holy Land, and thus *'end history'*, an army was needed. It would be furnished by Masonry, but not exclusively since other volunteers occupy the last tent."[50]

The fighting elements of this army are installed inside a pentagon under the command of five princes. This brings up the interesting question of who the princes actually are? Particularly meaningful, in this respect, is the architectural symbolism of the Pentagon which houses the United States military. The architectural choice of form may be purely coincidental, but it matches a magic plan first outlined in eighteenth-century Masonic notebooks. When that plan suddenly materializes in the real world to harbor nothing less than the forces committed to the final battle of Armageddon, by which history is to end, a number of questions very naturally come to mind.

Guérillot mentions[51] that the Kabbalah distinguishes between four worlds:

- the world of action, represented by *Malkhuth*
- the formative layer, grouping *Yesod, Hod* and *Nezah*
- the creative layer: *Gevurah, Tiferet* and *Gedullah*
- the layer of emanations: *Keter, Hokhmah* and *Binah*

If we keep investigating **The Magic Flute** along these lines, it soon becomes apparent that it exhibits an underlying structure roughly based on groups of three (with *Malkhuth* encapsulating the three Symbolic Degrees).

The **cosmic layer**, where emanations originate, is constructed from the radical STR and the concept of sovereignty, identifiable in Sarastro's name ('Sar' + 'Astro'). Since the Queen of the

Night is referred to explicitly as die *sternflammende Königin* (star-flaming Queen), the astral element is present here as well. The hidden third actor is the Queen of the Night's mysterious husband, who must be identified with *Keter* (the Crown) and the principle of Kingship at its highest. Sarastro belongs to *Hokmah* (wisdom), while the Queen of the Night lives in *Binah* (intelligence). It is through her that things are revealed.

The **creative layer** is hidden behind *Tiferet* and is associated with the *Chevalier Rose✠Croix* (18^0), whose task it is to retrieve the Lost Word of Freemasonry. This layer provides two esoteric name roots for the magic to be exercised by the recombined Word, or third element, which represents the creative power of the 'new couple'.

The **formative layer** is occupied by the new priesthood. This is the world of Tamino and Pamina as symbolic avatars for the creative principles they embody. Their union creates the Philosopher's Stone, through which higher worlds become accessible by means of ritual magic. In the Masonic symbolism of *Yesod*, one finds the ivory key of the Secret Master, equated with the Mysteries of the Egyptian god Ptah.

The **world of action** is shared by Papageno and the two aspects of Papagena. Their names imply common generation, as in *genos* (race) and *papa* (fatherhood). Papageno is representative of Masons who go through the three Symbolic Degrees. They are exposed to the inner world of the Temple, where everything is converted into symbols; but their interest in these things is superficial and easily diverted. They have joined by accident and yet are proud to be members of a secret society. They enjoy gatherings at which spirits are consumed in abundance and draw some satisfaction from charitable work. But none of these activities reach beyond the ordinary.

Papagena is more interesting in her double aspect. She appears as the old repulsive hag that Papageno first encounters and later turns into a sexy young girl that he cannot resist. She represents the essence of action, where desire and repulsion dominate.

In the opera, the cosmic layer supervises the initiation of the new priesthood and then vanishes, leaving Tamino and Pamina at the head of future generations of common men whose status cannot be raised through initiation. The Hebrew Kabbalah refers to the chain of 'celestial intermediaries' in the following terms:

"The 'celestial intermediaries' are *Shekinah* and *Metatron*— *Shekinah* denoting in a general sense the 'real presence' of the Divine. The scriptures that make special mention of this presence are mainly those that are concerned with the establishment of a spiritual center, such as the construction of the Tabernacle and the Temples of Solomon and Zorobabel. Such a center, set up according to rigorously defined conditions, should be in effect a place of divine manifestation, always represented by 'Light'. [...] 'The Kabbalah gives the *Shekinah* a deputy [lesser deity] that bears names identical to its own and that consequently possesses the same characteristics [...] Its name is *Metatron*, a title that is numerically equivalent to *Shaddai* [the number is 314], the 'All-Powerful', said to have been the name of the God of Abraham. The origin of the word *Metatron* is most obscure; one of the most interesting among the many hypotheses that have been advanced is its derivation from the Chaldean *Mitra*, which means 'rain', but relates through its root form to 'light'. Even accepting this proposition, there is still no valid reason for believing that similarity with the Hindu and Zoroastrian *Mitra* represents a borrowing by Judaism from foreign doctrines, as it is not useful to envisage the relationship that exists between the different traditions in such an external manner. For most traditions the symbol of rain signifies the descent of 'spiritual influences' from Heaven to Earth. In this connection Hebraic doctrine describes a 'dew of light' emanating from the 'Tree of Life' and through which there occurs the resurrection of the dead, whilst both Alchemical and Rosicrucian symbolism is recalled by the 'effusion of dew' that represents the celestial influence communicating with all the worlds." [52]

The central and principal node through which that communication takes place is *Tiferet*, identified in Masonic terms with the Degree of *Chevalier Rose✠Croix* (18^0). Guérillot points out that in sexual aspects of the symbolism of the Sephiroth, *Tiferet* stands for the male channel through which the divine seed flows into *Malkuth*. That also explains the special place this degree occupies in **The Magic Flute**:

"Sarastro, the High Priest, first appears in Act I, Scene 18. At the beginning of Act II, Sarastro and his Priests enter: there are (as the libretto of 1791 makes sure to mention) precisely eighteen priests and eighteen chairs, and the first section of the chorus they sing, *O Isis und Osiris*, is eighteen bars long. When Papageno asks the hideous old woman, who will turn out to be Papagena, how old she is, she answers 'eighteen' (whereupon the audience always laughs). And when the three boys appear suspended above the stage in a machine, it (notes the libretto of 1791) 'is covered with roses'." [53]

Not everyone is happy with this particular exegesis of the libretto and people have various reactions to the assumed significance of the number 18 and roses. Jacques Chailley, for one, is highly skeptical:

"'*Eighteen seats made of leaves. Above each seat there are a pyramid and a large black horn encrusted with gold*'. Nettl thought eighteen the mystic number of the Rosy Cross, but that exegesis remains risky because the libretto of **Die Zauberflöte** never touches upon the symbolism of the Higher Degrees; furthermore the number eighteen was not associated with the degree in question until the early nineteenth century." [54]

Chailley was obviously never told that the Rite of Perfection originated in Paris, in or about 1758, and that it consisted of twenty-five Degrees, of which the eighteenth was that of Knight Rose-Croix (*Chevalier Rose✠Croix*). Similar doubts agitate William Stafford (***The Mozart Myths***) who boldly asserts that "there is no good reason whatsoever for accepting [...] that Mozart's death in general and ***Die Zauberflöte*** in particular have to be understood in terms of the symbolism of the eighteenth, Rosicrucian grade. There is no evidence that the Lodge to which Mozart belonged had Higher Grades." [55]

The *Chevalier Rose✠Croix* is essential to ***The Magic Flute***. It is through the sexual symbolism of that degree that one arrives at the esoteric link between the cosmic layer of emanations and the formative layer at which the priesthood starts to assume its visible form.

THE COSMIC LAYER

THE QUEEN OF THE NIGHT

The Queen of the Night has no proper name and is referred to simply as *Königin der Nacht* in the playbill of the first performance of *The Magic Flute* (30 September 1791). Generally speaking, there is not a lot of speculation as to why she was not given a name. Jacques Chailley ventures that she is simply a "lunar symbol of [feminine] rebellion against the supremacy of the 'strong sex'." [56]

For Robert Donnington (*Opera and its Symbols*), she is "the Great Mother of a thousand names". Elsewhere she is recognized as the Austrian Empress Maria-Theresa, who hated Freemasonry with a passion— even though her husband, Francis Stephen was a member of the Craft. For others yet, she represents the 'dangers of nature' to be mastered by the initiate.

The Queen of the Night is cast as a high coloratura soprano, which puts her at one end of the vocal spectrum. Sarastro, as a *basso profundo*, is at the other end. All intermediate layers are bracketed by these two extremes.

To understand the Queen of the Night, we must return to the Greek legend of Demeter, whose daughter was abducted by Hades with Zeus' secret consent. Many authors have invoked eighteenth-century misogyny to explain the negative view of women set forth in *The Magic Flute*. However, if one goes back to the story of Demeter, one quickly realizes that women were not exactly consulted when it came to certain choices. Zeus, Persephone's father, and Hades, Zeus' brother, unilaterally decided that Hades could have Persephone and she was promptly abducted to his subterranean realm.

As Demeter desperately searched for her daughter, the earth became sterile and Zeus had to find a compromise to restore the primordial fecundity. Persephone was allowed to split her time between the Underworld and her mother. She could escape from captivity in the spring, but had to bury herself once again at seed-time. During her absence, the earth would remain sterile.

Superficially, this story can be interpreted as a fertility myth. That is the accepted practice in academic circles where everyone marvels at the 'naive' explanations for natural phenomena developed in ancient tales (we are so much more intelligent now...). The only perplexing legacy is that the legend served as the basis for the Mysteries of Eleusis.

Eleusis is synonymous with 'initiation' and in ancient iconography Demeter is often portrayed seated, holding torches or a serpent.[57] Torches were necessary for any foray into darkness and the serpent was a symbol of renewal through death.

At Eleusis Persephone was the 'bride of death' and her attendant was Hecate— the gatekeeper who kept the keys to the realm of the dead:

"Hecate was commonly portrayed as an attendant of Persephone, particularly in the matter of her yearly journeys to and from the Underworld.[...] Perhaps Hecate was for the initiates in ritual what she was for Persephone in myth: a caring personal guide. This role may also explain why the most common attribute of Hecate in art was her torches, and why she often had the title of *Phosphoros* ('light-bringer')." [58]

In **The Magic Flute**, Sarastro's Temple is a re-creation of the world of the dead. The Masons inhabiting the Temple of Wisdom have renounced the world and their condition is ritually equivalent to being dead. Their actions are non-actions, since they are no longer driven by personal motives, and their inspiration is Truth, to which— as initiates— they are supposedly highly attuned.

The realm of pure spirit, presided over by Hades, is where every form of renewal has its source. Persephone— and Pamina, who in **The Magic Flute** acts as her substitute— represents a special link between the world of spirit and that of the living. A dying world owes its renewal to Persephone's periodic return in a surge of life. In Kabbalistic terms, the Eleusinian triad of Demeter (the Mother Goddess), Persephone (the bride of Hades) and Kore (the Maiden) is functionally equivalent to the *Shekinah*— or divine presence, whose life-giving emanations permeate every aspect of generation. The feminine principle is triadic in nature. In the Kabbalah, that division is into active lover, autonomous being and nurturing being.

In Act I of **The Magic Flute**, all female characters— including the Queen of the Night— have a protective function. They await the potential candidate to initiation: the highly qualified stranger who will agree to undertake the dangerous journey to the world of the dead, to once again rescue the maiden held hostage there, and bring her back to light— back to her mother.

The Three Ladies are patterned on a traditional model:

"There are other protective female figures that bear some interesting similarities to Hecate. The three Horai ('Seasons'), for example, are the Homeric gatekeepers of Olympus. They are *kourotrophoi* for Hera in Olen's **Hymn to Hera**. They also commonly serve as attendants of deities, especially Aphrodite and Hera. One Orphic hymn has Persephone led back from Hades by the Horai and two other triplets, the Morai and the Charites.[...] While the Horai and the Charites are sometimes given individual names, both are generally treated as indistinguishable sets." [59]

Of all the puzzling things about the Queen of the Night, none is as mysterious as her quest for power, which Sarastro derides.

At one point, where Pamina is given the assignment to kill Sarastro and take possession of the magic sun-circle, one is tempted to conclude that the Queen's quest is also Masonic. Most writers have refused to identify the Queen of the Night with Isis, but there are lesser known aspects of that deity that fit the story well.

The Queen must be reconciled with Isis trying to recover what is rightfully hers. In his **Ueber die Mysterien der Aegiptier**, Ignaz von Born mentions the solar circle explicitly[60] and connects the sun with the image of the godhead. A godhead identified with Osiris— certainly— but also with the Apis Bull incarnating his living image. A topic that R.E. Witt throws much light on as he discusses the implications regarding Greece:

"From the aretologies it is clear that in Hellenistic times the Northern Aegean and Thrace had become acquainted with Egyptian Isis. We are told that the Thracians identified her with the Mother of the Gods. At Tenedos she is said to have taken an heliolatrous title 'name of the sun' and at Samothrace to have been 'bull-faced'. [...] Clearly in that part of the Greek world where the traditional *orgia* of Orpheus and Bacchus and of the Kabiri were especially popular Isis and her associates were no strangers." [61]

Tamino, who gets to charm wild animals with the flute given to him by the Queen of the Night, is an updated version of Orpheus about to undertake the classical journey to the Underworld. The Queen supplies him with the magic instrument and Pamina gives a conclusive dissertation about its origins, stating that her father carved it at a magic hour from the deepest heart of a thousand year old oak.

The oak indirectly points back to Indo-European notions of the Law, as embodied in the Sanskrit term *dharma*, which René Guénon traces to the Greek name for the oak (*drus*).[62] At Dodona, the oak-tree represented the 'Tree of the World', which symbolized a fixed axis joining the esoteric Poles. A tree definitely related to the Sephirotic Tree, by which magical operations are informed.

"The oak yields a golden wood and is thus mythologically associated with Zeus and his lightning. That the flute was created in the midst of a great storm, 'amid lightning' suggests not only the effort needed to form the instrument but as well the lightning stroke of intuitive knowledge that attended this momentous event. By invading its 'deepest heart', Pamina's father made of the god's tree a tool by which he could produce a protective, healing sound. In the time of Tamino and Pamina's reign, the healing power of the flute's music would accompany the betterment of a society, the regeneration of humanity." [63]

The Queen of the Night's revenge is directed at a Masonry that no longer recognizes her role as the custodian of all magic. The anti-feminine statements scattered throughout the opera can be traced to von Born's explicit views on the subject. These are found toward the end of his essay on the Egyptian Mysteries, in the pages where he discusses the similarities between the Egyptian priesthood and modern Freemasonry:

"Our wise law-givers also excluded the beautiful sex from our secrets:" says von Born, "they feared the charm of the sisters would interfere with the brothers' work. But instead of dirtying their hands like the Egyptian women, we ask them to tie the ribbons of our ornaments and aprons and reward them with gloves and swear faithfulness and devotion as we advance to each level, as befits true knights." [64]

This spirit of exclusion is in direct opposition to what the two Armored Men have to say in reference to Pamina: "a woman that fears neither night nor death is worthy, and will be initiated." (scene xxviii). But how is Pamina different from her mother? The answer is that the Queen of the Night does not need to be initiated— she already is. She knows all the secrets and just wants to make sure that her daughter is not 'misused'.

The aspect of Isis that the Queen of the Night incarnates is that of the consort of Ptah— the Great Architect of the Universe, whose children were the Kabiri:

"The association of Isis with the Kabiri is a fascinating problem. The Kabiri were originally demi-gods, sons of Hephaestus, who could themselves share in the chtonic rites of Demeter and Kore.[...] Herodotus, identifying the Greek Hephaestus of Lemnos with the Egyptian Ptah of Memphis, was convinced that the great Egyptian fire god and Architect of the Universe had the Kabiri as his sons and that they were natives of Egypt. [..] The bonds between the goddess and the fire god of Memphis grew to be close in the Ptolemaic age. [...] The theology of Memphis during the later dynasties established a family relationship between the Lady traditionally joined to Osiris as sister-wife and the Lord to whom all the epicleses of Osiris could be applied. The link was provided by the Apis Bull. Isis was 'the Mother of the God', the Apis: the Apis could be called 'the living son' of Ptah. In this way the goddess became the consort, *paredros*, of Ptah [...] In the first century BC Cicero can describe Ptah as 'the Guardian of Egypt' and Diodorus ascribes to him the hegemony of this land owing to his having been the first to discover fire." [65]

It must be remembered that the Queen of the Night is referred to by Papageno as the 'star-flaming Queen', which puts her in correspondence with the 'flaming star' of the Freemasons. Ignaz von Born derives the 'flaming star' from the eternal fire burning in Solomon's Temple and mentions that it had another meaning for the Egyptians.[66]

Citing ancient sources for his derivation, von Born says that the Egyptians identified the 'flaming star' with Canopus.[67] In *Hamlet's Mill*, Giorgio de Santillana and Hertha von Dechend, conclude that Canopus was the Pilot star of the Ship of the Dead, with Osiris on board.[68] This points to a guiding role, which the Queen of the Night certainly has in the opera. As the 'consort of Ptah', she is the instigator of renewal. The casting out of the Queen, as evil, indicates an intended break with tradition.

"Freemasonry justly claims to be a system of morality. Within it allegory and symbolism play an indispensable part. The affiliation of Freemasonry with the rites of Isis and Osiris was recognized years ago by the percipient genius of Mozart in *The Magic Flute*. When Tamino and Papageno are led within the Temple for their initiation into the mysteries of Isis they must be thought of from two standpoints. They typify modern Freemasonry. They also follow in the steps of their ancient brethren, the Kabiri, and Isis who went in search of the slain Osiris, or met the same god, no longer a corpse but resurrected as Ptah, the Lord of Life, opening and closing the day, creating with his 'heart and tongue', superintending architects and masons at the building of temples and pyramids, ordaining that the house should be established firmly, and holding the *djed* column as his emblem of stability." [69]

What the Queen of the Night represents cannot be dismissed so easily. Casting her into infinite night is an interesting exercise, but it does not take reality into account. Egypt started out under the emblem of 'Light', but from the standpoint of Judaism— which emphasizes its degenerate state— that 'Light' had to be uprooted. Christianity did the same thing to Judaism, claiming that Christian revelation superseded all earlier doctrines. In modern times, Christianity has been given a rough time by militant rationalists, whose 'Light' is yet of a different composition.

Evil holds 'Light' in captivity with its accommodating notions of Truth. The apocalyptic model requires a complete cleansing and leaves no room for debilitating compromises:

"Just as the *Shekinah* had to descend to Egypt— the symbol

of everything dark and demonic— to gather in the ten fallen sparks, so the Messiah too at the end of the ages starts on his most difficult journey to the empire of darkness, in order to complete his mission. In the urgency and desperation of this escalating process of incorporation of the demonic into the morality of everyday life, the idea of the harmony of evil and good— the way, according to a metaphor in the Kabbalah, our right and left hands work together is *dropped* in favor of a plunge into the extremity of evil, on the other side of which presumably good is waiting." [70]

When the *Shekinah* is kept at bay and forced back into infinite darkness, the Temple of Light in which her demise is celebrated becomes a center of falsehood where counter-initiation is dispensed.

SARASTRO

The identification of Sarastro as *Metatron*'s heir follows from the decomposition of his name into Sar-Astro, 'Prince of the Stars'. The method used here has nothing to do with traditional linguistics, since it is based entirely on multilingual roots to which esoteric meanings can be assigned. Names like Sarastro and Cagliostro, with endings in '-*stro*' and the intent to convey hermetic associations, provide at least one key to the construction of occult names in general. In Greek '*stro*' is used as a compound in words where the notion of whirling, revolving, spinning or turning is to be conveyed. In that sense '*astro*' can be conceived as something that does not revolve (a-*stro*) and would therefore be appropriate when applied to a fixed star. By the same token, '*stro*' as in *strophaios* is an epithet of Hermes that translates into 'standing as porter at the door hinges' and refers indirectly to both the hermetic journey and the guide of soul's twisty and shifty character. Hermes, like Odysseus *polutropos* ('of many turns'), is not be trusted. Odysseus has a way with words, turning them with skillful deceit. Hermes takes people on journeys where they often get lost. Cagliostro, the Grand Cophta of Egyptian Masonry, is likewise characterized as a charlatan and a fake by contemporaries and historians. This gives us something of a hint regarding Sarastro's character.

The title 'Prince of the Stars' applies both to the Chaldean Magi-kings, whose tradition is based on the principles of Zarvanism and Zoroastrianism, and to *Metatron* as *Kohen ha-gadol* ('Great Priest') and *Sar ha-gadol* ('Great Prince'). If one wanted to derive Sarastro's name directly from Zarathustra, one would have to take into account the meaning ascribed to this name by the scholia found in the margins of the **Alcibiades I**, originally attributed to Plato, but now thought to be the work of an Academic philosopher writing shortly after Plato's death.[71] The scholiast claims that 'Zarathustra' translated into Greek means 'Astrothutes', a 'star-worshipper'.[72] At any rate, the connection to the domain of stars is hard to miss.

With respect to Zarathustra, or Zoroaster, some authors remind us of Mozart's fondness for the carnival and his appearance as Zoroaster, in Vienna, during the carnival of 1786:

"Where, beyond official carnival, might one spy in Josephinian Vienna the glints of the truly forbidden, the refusal of politesse and rationality, the reclaiming of the grotesque body and irreconcilable appetite, the endangering of hierarchy, identity, and fixed discursive categories? We may receive a hint in Mozart's [...] carnival performance in Vienna [...] in 1786. He appeared, not in a typically erotic commedia scenario, but in the role of Zoroaster, and he distributed (under the title **Excerpts from Zoroaster's Fragments**) eight riddles and fourteen proverbs. Of this, the former comically mystified the coarse body [...] and the latter bitterly teased class conflict by opposing station against ability and merit." [73]

R.E. Witt points out that the carnival has always been tightly bound to the symbols of Isiac faith and its claims that human life is a voyage over life's ocean under Isis' guidance. Subversive riddles and proverbs handed out by a disguised Magi-King serve to underscore Zoroaster's magic function.

"The carnival of medieval and modern times is the obvious successor of the *navigium Isidis*. The ship-carriage, prominent in carnival-processions of Italy and the Rhineland, has descended from the *tensa* of Isis. The name itself may be derived from the expression *carrus navalis*, the carriage of the ship. This does not specifically feature in the account we owe to Apuleius. On the numismatic evidence, however, we can be sure that it could be included in the pageantry." [74]

It is also interesting to note that the prefix '*sar-*', which means either 'prince' or 'king' in various Middle-Eastern languages, was adopted as a title by a number of modern exponents of Rosicrucianism. Péladan, a principal founder of the Kabbalistic Order of the Rosy-Cross, also known as the 'Rose-Croix de Toulouse' (1888), used the name Sar Mérodack. Emile Dantinne (1884-1969), a leader of the Belgian Rose-Croix, was known as Sar Hiéronymus. Dantinne's disciple, Jean Mallinger, who was himself a member of the Masonic Order of Memphis-Misraïm, claims that 'Sar' derived from a contraction of Egyptian words: *sa* 'son' and *ra* 'sun'." [75]

The occult title of 'Son of the Sun' predates these modern restatements and can, in fact be traced, to Gnostic origins:

"In the **Pistis Sophia** of the Alexandrine Gnostics, Melkizedek is qualified as 'Great Receiver of Eternal Light'; this also fits the function of [the Hindu] Manu, who in effect receives the intelligible light by a ray emanating directly from the Principle to reflect it to the world which is his domain; and, besides, this is why Manu is called 'Son of the Sun'." [76]

Whatever the correct origin, it is pretty clear that the title 'Sar' had great occult significance. This is further confirmed by René Guénon's remark concerning the symbolic significance of the Kabbilistic 'number of the beast'— the apocalyptic 666— which, according to him, is a solar number which corresponds to the dark face of *Metatron*: "This number is formed in particular by the name of *Sorath*, demon of the Sun." [77]

The struggle between the forces of light and darkness was central to Zoroastrian religion. The subject was of interest to the Freemasons assembled around Ignaz von Born. The anonymous article in Born's ***Journal für Freymaurer***, titled '*Über die Magie der alten Perser und die Mitraischen Geheimnisse*', "tells of the light of wisdom believed to have arisen in the Orient before the Greeks. Discussing the two commonly accepted forms of Zoroastrianism, the author notes that the optimistic form of Zoroastrianism [the divine spark in man] was adopted by the Kabbalists, Gnostics and neo-Platonists, in their belief that 'a time will come in which [the divine spark] released through the work of fire, will regain its original freedom, and be united with the general cosmos'. The second, pessimistic form, the Manichean belief that matter is entirely evil, the author dismisses as being not properly Zoroastrian." [78]

In ancient Iran, the solar tradition of *Ahura Mazda* distinguished between the beneficent spirit of *Spenta Mainyu* and the destructive spirit of *Angra Mainyu*. [79] These are, again, the two faces of *Metatron* and the entire subject is tied up with the origins of Alchemy, which some writers trace to Zoroastrianism:

"Our purpose is to draw attention to the general likeness of the alchemic idea to the spirit of the ***Gathas***, and to what plausibly may have been Zarathustra's effect on Magian religion. Whether or not one follows the Greeks in crediting the prophet with an interest in the heavens, his hymns are permeated with an alchemical attitude toward the earth. [...] To describe the alchemist as 'the brotherly savior of nature' is again to identify the prophet's disciple. [...] That molten metal, the basis of much alchemical symbolism interested Zarathustra is also evident in the Gathas (Y.XXX.7, XXXII.7) and whatever its significance in Iranian eschatology, the glowing metal of these early hymns appears to offer the blessings of immortality to the virtuous man, now." [80]

The 'brotherly savior of nature' is the person who maintains the rituals by which the powers of light are continuously renewed. The final victory of 'Light' can only be conceived in an alchemical sense. It is only because the 'savior of nature' must eventually cross the 'sun gate' that he becomes identified with non-dual aspects of the primordial sun, otherwise visible to mortals through the two faces of *Metatron*.

Zarathustra, Sarastro, *Sorath*— these names all have the same connotation and it is now important to make a distinction between 'Zar' and 'Sar'. It comes down to the difference between 'S' and 'Z'. René Terrasson (***Le testament philosophique de Mozart***), in his extensive analysis of Ignaz Alberti's frontispiece to the libretto of ***The Magic Flute***, mentions the letter Z in conjunction with a motif placed to the right of the head of the bull found on the pyramid.[81] At first sight this motif seems to represent the number 2, but Terrasson argues that it is graphically closer to a Z. To this remark he adds that the letter Z is tied to a major event in any Mason's evolution. Like the letter G, it constitutes a notion that can only be met head on. The letter G is first encountered in the Fellow Craft Degree; the letter Z is discovered in the fourth degree of Secret Master. It occurs in two places: first on the jewel of the degree, which is a small ivory key, on the wards of which, in black, is the letter Z; secondly, on the sky blue apron, where a branch of laurel crosses an olive branch— at the crossing of the branches the Z is embroidered in gold.[82] The ivory key gives access to the Higher Degrees, opening the doors to the Temple where the search for the Lost Word is initiated.

As Terrasson points out, the letter Z also occurs in the seventh trump of the pack of Tarot cards, representing a chariot drawn by lions.[83] According to Court de Gébelin (1728-1784), a noted Freemason who gave an Egyptian interpretation to these cards, the seventh trump represents 'Osiris triumphant' and this image may well have inspired Schikaneder's staging of Sarastro's entrance— in a chariot drawn by lions. It must also be remembered that Osiris, in Egyptian, is *Wsir*, which some occultists have rightly or wrongly correlated with the English 'wizard'.

EMBLEME, CHIFFRE OU SCEAU
de Cagliostro

marquant apposé sur cire verte
au commencement et à la fin le manuscrit original
du RITUEL DE LA MAÇONNERIE EGYPTIENNE

7. Cagliostro's seal

Dummett, Decker and Depaulis convincingly argue, that Court de Gébelin had no idea of what he was talking about when he ventured wild guesses in the area of Egyptian symbolism.[84] Nevertheless his work was widely disseminated in Masonic circles, since he was at one time (1778) secretary of the Lodge *Les Neuf Sœurs*, to which Voltaire was admitted shortly before his death and to which Benjamin Franklin also belonged.[85] What is intriguing, of course, is the association of the seventh trump with the letter Z, as well as the Hebrew letter Zain, which in Kabbalistic lore is given the value 7.

8. Symbols found on the column of Ignaz Alberti's illustration

The letter 'S' is tied to the symbolism of the serpent and it just so happens that Cagliostro, a pioneer of feminine Masonry and the earliest documented founder of Egyptian Masonry, used it as his emblem, cipher and seal.

The serpent transfixed by an arrow and still holding the apple of immortality in its mouth refers symbolically to the combat between Apollo and Python— that is to the battle between light and darkness.

One wonders to what extent Mozart himself was conscious of the relationship between his own name and the words 'Sar' and 'Zar'. Maynard Solomon mentions that Mozart engaged in exercises that created many variations on his name:

"The reader of Mozart's letters must soon grow accustomed to the numerous permutations to which the composer, who was baptized Joannes Chrysostomos Wolfgangus Theophilus Mozart, subjected his own name [...] Thus we are not surprised to find such variations on the surname as 'De Mozartini', 'Mozartus, or 'Mozarty', though we may be momentarily startled by such anagrammatical variants as 'Trazom' or 'Romatz'." [86]

These transpositions and alterations are reminiscent of the Kabbalistic practice of *temurah*, so essential for magic purposes. Whether or not Mozart was aware of the formal origins of this activity— which can be traced all the way back to ancient Egyptian wordplay— is, of course, significant; but at the same time unlikely to be resolved

In French, Mozart's name can be read as an anagram for *'Mot Zar'*. The composer would have been fluent enough in that language to produce this particular derivation. It is right in line with his incomprehensible use of the middle-name *Adam*, which shows up on all of his marriage documents, except for one.[87] According to Kabbalistic lore, as outlined in the **Zohar**, Adam's function was to tend to the Garden of Eden. This metaphor describes the mystery of womanhood, which Adam had to cultivate. The Garden was also known as a rose garden and the roses were the children of the *Shekinah* (the Rose of the World), whose symbol the Garden was.[88] The same tradition is echoed in ***The Song of Songs***, where esoteric unions are considered:

> I am the rose of Sharon,
> The wild lily of the valleys"

says the young woman in ***The Song of Songs*** (2.1) as she invokes her lover (4.16):

> Awake, north wind! O south wind, come,
> Breathe upon my garden,
> Let its spices stream out.
> Let my lover come into his garden
> And taste its delicious fruit."

To which the lover immediately replies (5.1):

> I have come into my garden,
> My sister, my bride..."[89]

Mozart's use of the middle-name *Adam* is much too appropriate to the esoteric meaning of marriage to be discounted as coincidental. "We shall see in due course," says A.E. Waite, "that the Holy One does not make His dwelling except where male and female are united [...] This is why Scripture says: And God 'blessed them and called their name Adam, on the day when they were created'. [***Genesis*** v.2] It is recognized by the ***Zohar*** in no uncertain manner that the condition of side to side was one of imperfection, because it was not a true union in the likeness of heaven; the latter is eye to eye [...] When the time came for man and woman to be joined face to face the text which here follows is applied to the intercourse: 'They stand fast for ever and ever, and are done in truth and uprightness'. The reference is to the state of true nuptials, ineffable in the holy transcendence, when between the male and the female, as between the wings of the two cherubim, the glory of *Shekinah* manifests." [90]

If the implications of Mozart's choice of middle-name on his marriage documents are correct, their significance is indeed staggering. They imply that by 1782 Mozart was already familiar with advanced Kabbalistic symbolism and that he was likewise proficient in the ritual use of names. An activity that Maynard Solomon regards as meaningful:

"Naturally, there is no need to quarrel with those who take a commonsense approach to such matters, those for whom Mozart's temporary adoption of the name Adam is merely a mistake or a trivial jest, another example of his penchant for mystification, which often took such literary forms as wordplay, ciphers, codes, and riddles. But they ought in turn to be tolerant of those who want to speculate about the implications of such things in the belief that there is often a serious substratum to such 'errors' [...] and that deeper motives may also have been at work here. At issue is the power of names. As the anthropologists showed long ago, in every pre-modern society the name is considered equivalent to the individual who bears it. Frazer noted how, in such societies, one 'commonly fancies that the link between a name and the person or thing denominated by it is not a mere arbitrary and ideal association, but a real and substantial bond which unites the two'. In early societies the widespread, obsessive concealment of names [...] was intended to offer protection from harm.[...] Frazer notes, 'The custom is intended to protect the person against magic, since a charm only becomes effectual in combination with the real name'." [91]

Maynard Solomon's call for tolerance is not likely to be heeded. Speculation along the lines followed here is too big of a departure from accepted ways of looking at Mozart. For a name to have magical properties, the bond uniting the denominated to the name must be dynamic. It corresponds to the activation of a principle that becomes effective as soon as the assigned form matches its vital characteristics.

A name is a certification of form. In certain exceptional cases, it points to a physical occurrence of the ideal form for which it stands. The mechanism for naming is mantic. A hint of how it works is supplied by Greek epic poetry, where heroes are described as ritual substitutes for the gods whose spirit they carry. In the warrior mythology of the *Iliad*, 'the best' (*aristos*) of the protagonists, is identified with the war god Ares, whose spirit enters anyone sealed inside Achilles' armor.

Gregory Nagy mentions that the epithet *ambrota*— 'immortal' — is applied to the armor (*teukhea*)[92] that the ritual substitute (*therapon*) for the war god Ares has to wear:

"...when Hektor puts on the armor of Achilles which he had despoiled from the body of Patroklos, he is sealed in this armor by Zeus ([*Iliad*] XVII 209-210) and then, quite literally, 'Ares entered him'." [93]

Eckelmeyer suggests that Sarastro was patterned after Frederick V, the Elector Palatine and King of Bohemia (1596-1642). Frederick V was the leader of choice of the Protestants as they attempted to wage war against the counter-Reformation headed by the Habsburgs. Most of Eckelmeyer's argument is based on similarities between Gerhard Honthorst's (1590-1656) portait of Frederick, made during his stay at The Hague, and Sarastro's representation in the engraved illustrations of *The Magic Flute* produced by Josef and Peter Schaffer.[94] These illustrations appeared in 1795 and show Sarastro as a young man with a turned up moustache, a dark pointed beard and shoulder-length hair. The similarities with Honhorst's Frederick are indeed striking, but whether they were intended by

Schikaneder and Mozart remains to be seen.

Frederick V was a central figure in the esoteric iconography of the Reformation. He was driven out of Bohemia by the Habsburgs and it just so happens that the Schaffer illustrations were created in conjunction with *The Magic Flute*'s early productions in Bohemia. The best explanation is, perhaps, that this appropriation was intentional on the part of the Bohemian underground, which simply adapted Mozart's battle between darkness and light to the history of its own struggle.

THE CREATIVE AND FORMATIVE LAYERS

TAMINO AND PAMINA

Tamino and Pamina are the 'new couple' announced by Sarastro to the initiates of the Temple. The 'old couple' is presumably the one comprised by the Queen of the Night and her consort. Sarastro and the initiates have inherited his 'solar circle', but their order is incomplete without the ruling couple.

The relationship between Tamino and Pamina is conditioned by the early action of the opera, where Tamino appears on the scene as a new Orpheus predestined to bring Eurydice back from the dead. For many of the reasons already outlined, the Masonic Temple figuratively corresponds to the land of the dead. The place where Eurydice is kept is impervious to human passion. Eurydice can only be brought back to life through a process of enchantment tied to the power of the Word.

"As a potent mythic symbol, Orpheus spans life and death; order and emotionality; animate and inanimate forms; fertility and sterility; man's control over nature and sympathetic fusion with nature; the power of art over death and its futility before death [...] Located at the fringes of the civilized world, the son of the god of order and light [...], he embodies the marginal, 'liminal' position that art and the artist, and artful language too, have always held. Akin to the trickster who defeats death by his wiles, he crosses the boundaries not only between life and death and between man and nature, but also between truth and illusion, reality and imagination. His descendants are the bearers of Mozart's Magic Flute or the recurring magician figures in Mann's fiction, Hesse's 'Magic Theater'..." [95]

It is this command of poetic— and even prophetic— language that Tamino must demonstrate. His trials lead to the Tetragrammaton, unveiled as an eternal symbol of the recovered magic Word.

Paul Nettl tries to make sense of the names selected for the 'new couple' and muses about a possible connection to 18th century Egyptology:

"Particulars about the connections between *The Magic Flute* and 18th century Egyptology can be found in *Die Zauberflöte, eine Studie zum Lebenszusammenhang Aegypten-Antike-Abendland* by Siegfried Morenz (Köln, 1952). Morenz traces the names Pamina and Tamino to Egyptian origins. Unfortunately, Schikaneder was mistaken in naming them. Their names should have been Pamino and Tamina, since Pa-min indicates the male, and Ta-min the female, belonging to Min, a local god of Coptos and Achmin, the patron of the Eastern desert of Egypt." [96]

This derivation opens up difficult lines of speculation since it assumes that 18th century Egyptology was advanced enough to handle such subtleties. To blame Schikaneder, in 1791, for misinterpreting a language that was not officially deciphered until 1822 makes very little sense.

The decoding of the Rosetta stone, on which both Thomas Young (1773-1829) and Jean-François Champollion (1790-1832) worked tirelessly, eventually provided the missing knowledge:

"The exact circumstances of [the discovery of the Rosetta stone] are obscure, but according to the report published in the '*Courier d'Égypte*', a detachment of the French army was working on some fortifications near the small village of Rashid-Rosetta in the Western Delta, some thirty miles from Alexandria on the left bank of the Nile in antiquity known as the Bolbitinic. During the work, the pick of one of the men struck an irregular slab of black granite, and by some sort of miracle, the finder was conscientious enough to notice that its front was covered by inscriptions in three different characters [...] The stone was cleaned and sent to the commanding officer in Alexandria,

General Menoce, who immediately had it transported to Cairo, and committed to the care of the Institute." [97]

The actual decipherment took many years and the final breakthrough came from the study of cartouche enclosed royal names referring to the Ptolemies. The Ptolemies ruled Egypt for nearly 300 years (from 304 B.C.) and the first members of that dynasty founded the famous library at Alexandria, which became the leading center of literary and scientific endeavor in the Hellenistic world. [98]

Thomas Young was able to prove that the name *Ptolemaios,* found in the Greek and Demotic texts of the Rosetta stone, was also displayed in the hieroglyphic text, where it was enclosed in a cartouche. The hieroglyphical rendering was by means of separate alphabetical letters and this produced the first evidence of a rudimentary Egyptian alphabet. Only five letters were indisputably identified: p, t, j, n and f. [99]

Through sheer coincidence the first two letters, 'p' (represented by a square) and 't' (represented by a loaf), are also the starting letters of the names Pamina and Tamino. Together they spell the name of the Memphite God Ptah, written as ▢𝄐𓀭 — about whom so much has already been said.

It is always dangerous to use the results of modern Egyptology to interpret conceptions of Egypt that predate their existence. Jan Assmann has been taken to task by critics for his views on Moses, formulated in the light of current Egyptian scholarship. His extrapolations, however, are mild transgressions compared to what we are about to suggest.

Ptah was the "Father of the fathers of all the gods [...] He who raised Nut and [extended] Geb. He who began everything on the surface of the earth [...] The Fashioner [...] He who begot all Mankind and created their sustenance of life." [100] In an inscription of the ninth or tenth dynasty mention is made of a

Temple of Upuaut "which Ptah built with his fingers and which Thoth founded."[101] From the Middle-Kingdom onwards Ptah is sometimes referred to as "ruler of the Great Throne"— that is Memphis.[102]

"The most important temple of Ptah was at Memphis, the capital of the Old Kingdom. It seems that it was built as early as in the early dynastic period, and there are signs indicating that it was still a center of the cult of Ptah in the third century after Christ." [103]

Ptah was not unknown in the eighteenth-century. He was written about in 1750 by Jablonski, in his scholarly **Pantheon Aegypthiorum**, to which Ignaz von Born refers in his article on the Mysteries of the Egyptians.[104] Jablonski mentions that many ancient writers regarded Ptah as a spiritual being.[105] In another strange coincidence— if one thinks of the 'new couple' of Pamina and Tamino as somehow related to Ptah— it is said that this god was both male and female. His male aspect begot Ra, and the female complement was the mother of the Sun-God of Heliopolis.[106]

E.A. Wallis-Budge confirms that Jablonski's intuitions regarding the true nature of Ptah were essentially correct:

"Many of [Jablonski's] conclusions and derivations are wholly incorrect, but he arrived at one very important fact, viz. that among the gods of Egypt there were some Beings who were invisible and who possessed spiritual natures. To him belongs the credit of calling the attention of scholars to the fact that the Egyptians believed in a spiritual origin for the universe, and that they associated the Eternal Mind and Spirit with Ptah, the most ancient god of Memphis, and regarded him as the source of all that is and of all that shall come into being. Many of Jablosnki's remarks show that he had arrived at a true conception of the characters of the Egyptian gods, and that the statements of classical writers on these subjects contained more accurate information than Egyptologists generally have admitted." [107]

The Egyptian god Min, with whom Paul Nettl thinks Tamino and Pamina's names are associated enters into the equation through a different door. In Plutarch's **De Iside et Osiride**— which von Born continuously quotes— mention is made of Min in conjunction with Horus. But not just any Horus. It is Horus equated with the number five, or the hypotenuse of a right triangle of sides three and four.

In his comprehensive essay on the Lost Word of Freemasonry (**Parole perdue et mots substitués**), René Guénon shows that the number five plays an essential role in the communication of

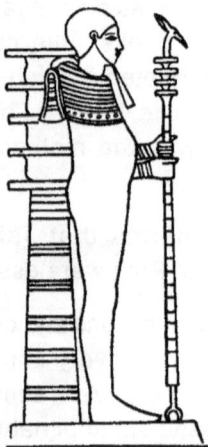

9. Pre-dynastic Ptah

the Word of the Masters, as transmitted in Operative Masonry (by Masters is meant the seventh and last degree of operative Masonry, to which the Hiramic legend originally belonged).

"Why is it that the 'loss of the Word' is [usually] attributed directly to Hiram's death, when legend in fact stipulates that it was known to others? [...] During the construction of the Temple, the 'Word' of the Masters, was according to the legend of the Degree [the 7th of Operative Masonry], in the possession of three individuals who had the power to communicate it: Solomon, Hiram, King of Tyre, and Hiram Abi; this having been said, how is it possible then that the death of the latter, would be sufficient to bring about the loss of the 'Word'? The answer is that in order to communicate it regularly, and in its ritual form, the cooperation of the 'first three Grand-Masters' was required, so that a single absence or vacancy made the transmission impossible— and this as necessarily as it takes three sides to form a triangle. [...] An Operative Lodge can only be opened when three Masters are present, having in their possession three sticks of lengths 3, 4 and 5; it was only when these sticks had been brought together and assembled into a Pythagorean right triangle, that the work of the Lodge was allowed to proceed." [108]

The ritual implications have already been covered, but there are other strong connections with Operative Masonry. Particularly when one considers the activities patronized by the Egyptian Architect of the Universe:

"The god Ptah was considered a patron of craftsmen, perhaps originally of stoneworkers though later also of metalworkers; this creativity of the earth was shared with a falcon-headed deity Sokar, perhaps the original patron of metal crafts, and both gods of earthly creativity had their main cult centers in the area of Memphis, where the Royal residence fostered the greatest concentration of art production in the Old Kingdom." [109]

Ptah was identified as the 'First King'— and an earthly king at that (he was the only Egyptian god represented with a straight royal beard, instead of a bent one).[110] He was also the 'Egyptian Saturn', 'Lord of Maat',[111] who magically provided the other gods with their essential organs.

"Horus, the oldest Sun-god of Egypt, acted as the heart or mind of Ptah, and Thoth, the god of wisdom, as his tongue. What the heart of Ptah thought passed on to Thoth who translated it into words, which were uttered by the one great almighty mouth, from which everything which is has come, and everything which is to be shall come. Though Thoth was the Word-god, his actual creative power was derived from the magical pronouncement by Ptah, who alone knew how to utter the words with the correct intonation." [112]

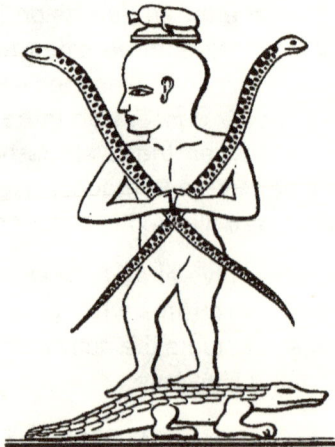

Ptaḥ of the magicians lord of all primal and creative matter, and master of the great serpent gods of Upper and Lower Egypt.

10. Ptah Magician

Translated into Greek notions, the 'mind of Ptah' corresponds to the divine mind (Greek *nous*) and his 'tongue'— inherited by Thoth— is the source of the divine Word (Greek *logos*). The need for correct intonation is even reflected in the hieroglyphic representation of the Egyptian word 'name', or *r* + *n* (mouth +

wavelet), rendered in Coptic as [*Pan*]— which may well be the precursor of the Nordic word 'Rune'. The wavelet corresponding to the letter 'n' comes out of the mouth (letter 'r').

To come back to the earlier analogy of the 'seed', discussed in connection with the Jew's confinement in Egypt, it takes on a special meaning here since Ptah was the source of all seeds. In analyzing this particular aspect, R. A. Schwaller de Lubicz provides a bridge to the god Min, whose name corresponds to the shared radical in Pa[min]a and Ta[min]o:

"As inseminator of all that will vegetate, Ptah is *ithyphallic Min*. There remains the need for a womblike milieu to receive the seed after the living— or animated— water of Isis has delivered it from the prison (coagulation) where Seth keeps it jealously bound to the earth. In this phase of dissolution and vegetation, Nun [the primordial ocean], by the fact of creating Tefnut [one of the Twins whose nature consists in separating Heaven from Earth], makes a living water which the Hebrew Kabbalah calls *Eshmajin*, whence the Arab *Ashmounein*, which designates the ancient city of Hermopolis." [113]

Stephen Quirke mentions that Min is one of the few Egyptians gods whose iconography reaches back before the unification (3000 B.C.).[114] As lord of the deserts Min was the protector of expeditions who went to extract valued minerals from the mountains located to the East of his cult centers of Coptos and Akhmin.

"The typical representation of a sanctuary for Min recalls a desert tent, and New Kingdom temple-wall reliefs depict the ceremony of raising the tent-poles for Min." [115]

In a last aside, we should remind ourselves once again that Herodotus (*Histories*, III.37) identified Ptah with the Greek Hephaestus and that he thought the Kabiri were his sons. They possessed the secrets of fertility and vegetation, and were masters to miners and metalworkers. Their official emblem was a hammer and they were portrayed as dwarves.[116]

"Herodotus identified Hephaestus with Ptah, the Egyptian God of Fire and Architect of the Universe, and the demi-gods, the Kabiri, as his (Hephaestus-Ptah's) sons who were born in Egypt. Late theology of Antiquity established links between the Great Goddess Isis and Memphism, where the temples of the Kabiri and Ptah could be found. [...] Isis was therefore linked to Imhotep, known as a son of Ptah, chief Architect to King Zoser, and builder of the pyramid complex at Sakkara. In due course, Imhotep, who was a real Architect, became the Divine son in the Triad of Memphis, and the subject of worship. Imhotep and Isis had a temple at Epidaurus dedicated to them, which is not surprising, as both were devoted to medicine and the occult. Eventually Imhotep achieved precedence over Ptah, and so the Great Architect of the Universe was none other than Imhotep, Architect and sage, and builder of the Sakkara stepped pyramid: the Master Mason, as Architect, had himself become a God."[117]

11. Ptah standing on hieroglyph for Maat

The common traits shared by Hephaestus and Ptah are best reflected in the iconography of the Egyptian god. In the hieroglyphic image, or ideogram representing Ptah (see above), his corporal quality is emphasized and unlike the other great gods, he is not portrayed wearing a crown. He stands on the hieroglyph for *Maat* and his head is covered by a clinging, blue-cowled beret of the type worn by blacksmiths and artisans depicted in Old Kingdom tombs.[118]

Conceptually, the continuity between Ptah and Min comes from the fact that Min was given a prominent place as a god of fertility in Pharaonic religion.[119] In the esoteric process of genesis, in which Ptah occupies the highest place— representing 'Oneness' as the 'spirit of creation', or 'mind of Osiris'— Min acts as the generic inseminator. In that capacity

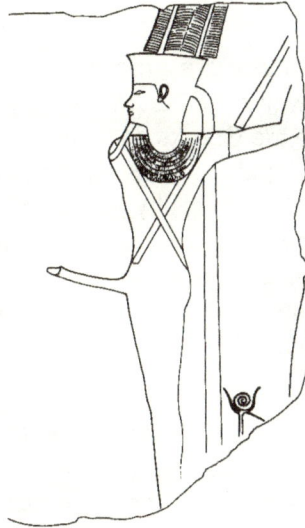

12. Min in front of his tent shrine

he is also the 'founder' of human genealogies manifesting through various civilizations. Ptah is the tongue and heart of Ra, the generator of Thoth and Horus, and the consort of Maat. These esoteric attributes are complemented by Min's function as the essential 'founder'.

We should remember that Min was worshipped at Panopolis.

This creates a connection to the Greek Pan (= 'All') and his pipes. The same pipes that Papageno plays, except that his are made of five reeds, instead of Pan's original seven. The short five note runs heard during his introductory aria, *Der Vogelfänger bin ich ja*, establish the fundamental limitations of his instrument. According to the Orphic Hymn to Pan, the Greek god was a *kosmokrator* and dance-master. Papageno inherits a detuned version of his pipes, but also the dance-master role through the use of the *Glockenspiel*. As the 'All', Min has multiple forms and these are implicitly present in the concept of generation propagated into Papageno's name. The explicit use of the god's name to form the common root of Tamino and Pamina's names serves the same function. Min is everywhere.

These occult notions are preserved in the Apis bull cult, founded by the lawgiver of the 1st Dynasty, at Memphis. That ruler was known to the Greeks as Menes, or Min. At Memphis, the Apis bull was worshipped as an incarnation of Osiris and the second life of Ptah.[120] It is by establishing this 'second life', which could be propagated through a succession of Apis bulls, that Menes was given the symbolic status of 'founder'; and through the identity of name came the fertilizing principle associated with Min.

The function and the name occur in other cultures as well. The Hindu Manu, who acts as progenitor and lawgiver of mankind, and the legendary ruler of Crete, Minos, are two examples that come to mind. These examples cannot easily be generalized, but they offer plenty of food for thought:

"There is, then, a remarkable triple parallel. In Egypt there were bull cults associated with the name *Mn*, which was also the title of the founding pharaoh/lawgiver and a bull associated with a 'winding wall'. All of these date back to the Old Kingdom, that is, before the foundation of the Cretan palaces. In Crete, there was a bull cult associated with a King Minos and a labyrinth. The parallels become even more intricate as traditions reported that King Minos was not always a dignified lawgiver but was sometimes a lecherous satyr. This resembles yet another Egyptian figure, the god Min, distinguished iconographically by his enormous phallus and in later times seen as the original of the Greek god Pan, the patron of satyrs. It would also seem that the god Min was at times confused or syncretized with the founder Min/Menes." [121]

Martin Bernal captures these strange connections and arrives at a most intriguing place. He draws a further parallel between the Egyptian god of fertility [Min] and the modern East African divinity Bʷäzä, who represents the fertilizing power of thunder followed by rain, also worshipped for its sexual appetite.[122] He then points out that the name Bʷäzä comes from the Semitic or Afroasiatic root BZ, usually given two sets of meaning: 'split, divide, distribute' and 'inflate, inseminate, abound'. Bernal also claims that the name Bʷäzä had a Canaanite equivalent in Boʿaz.

"In the **Book of Ruth** Boʿaz was the name of Naomi's kinsman whose association with fertility is shown by his consummation of his marriage to Ruth, on a threshing floor at harvest time in Bethlehem, 'House of Bread'. The thundering aspect of Bʷäzä is paralleled in the Biblical use of the name Boʿaz as the name of one of the pair of pillars placed in front of temple of Yahve."[123]

The pillar acted as a symbolic lightning rod designed to capture the fierce divinity's creative outbursts. Whether one accepts this explanation, or not, one should remember that in the case of the Temple of Solomon, at least, tradition claims that the columns were made of brass. Boaz was the column located to the right of the Temple on the way in. The word means 'in it is strength'. The other column, Jachin, means 'he shall establish'." [124]

The Two Columns played a significant part in early Masonic Legend as captured by the Old Charges. Yet the Two Pillars were not the Two Columns found at the entrance of Solomon's Temple:

"These Two Pillars of Masonic Legend are the medium by which the secret knowledge was saved from destruction by Fire and Water. The story [...] appears to have a Babylonian origin. [...] A Babylonian priest had a vision of a flood and proceeded to write the history of the beginning, procedure, and end of all

13. Min in a stylized bed of tall lettuces, whose white sap was regarded as a symbol of semen

things on clay tablets which were then burned hard in a fiery furnace. These tablets were buried in the City of the Sun at Sippara, and were the basis for knowledge upon which the rebuilding of Babylon was made possible. In Hebraic versions Eve instructed Seth and his siblings to record on tablets of stone and baked clay the words of the Archangel Michael when he ordered them from the Garden of Eden. The tablets would survive whether flood or fire destroyed the world. [...] Later versions [...] grant Adam the credit for prophecy and the tablets become 'pillars'. [...] Zoroaster (Zarathustra) was said by Petrus Comestor to have inscribed all seven Liberal Arts on fourteen columns (seven on brass and seven on brick) to preserve them against destruction by a vengeful god." [125]

The theme of the 'lightning rod' designed to somehow preserve a knowledge acquired in the 'vegetative state', which corresponds to life in the Garden of Eden, leads back to both Min and Ptah as complementary gods of creation and procreation.

In these highly symbolic representations of fertility, the characterization of Min as the original model for the Greek god Pan leads again to the impregnating power of the sun, for which Pan stood. Like Ptah, Pan was tied to Saturn and thus acted as a controlling spirit for the lower world.[126] He was represented as a 'horned' god and his sacred dances were used to mimic the revolutions of the heavenly bodies over which he presided as 'world-mover'. Associations of Pan with the animal figure of the goat, create correspondences with the constellation of Capricorn— Saturn's home— which opens the year.

If Ptah was the god of artisans and blacksmiths, who transformed raw metals into ritual objects, it was Min who patronized the laborers extracting the basic ores. Min could be older than Ptah and mineral riches were the fruit of his insemination of the earth:

"Min is one of the few deities whose iconography reaches back before the unification *c.*3000 BC. Damaged colossal statues of the late fourth millennium BC from his temple at Coptos show a male figure with his left hand grasped around a space in which a stone phallus would once have been.[...] As lord of the deserts Min gave protection to expeditions extracting valued materials from the mountainous and waterless wastes East of his cult centers Coptos and Akhmim." [127]

It is tempting to suggest that two modern words: 'mine' (as in 'mining') and '*minne*' (as in the German word for courtly love) are somehow derived from the name of this god. The marriage of metals— or chemical marriage— addresses the ritual operations of alchemy through which a fertility grounded in *Maat* is exalted and maintained. The Masonic interest in alchemy was therefore not necessarily grounded in superstition. The ritual significance of alchemical operations extended to foundation issues and these may well have been understood by eighteenth-century Masons.

"From the detritus of a half-understood miscellany of magical symbolism later eighteenth-century German writers divined a spiritual programme. In Lessing's Masonic dialogues **Ernst und Falk** the older and wiser interlocutor Falk restrains his younger, earnestly rational colleague's fulminations against the alchemical pursuits of mystical Masons, making it clear that there is more to Freemasonry than utilitarian social programmes and charitable deeds. We know that Goethe had immersed himself in alchemical tomes as a young man, and that alchemical symbolism permeates his work.[...] Schiller's unfinished novel **Die Geisterseher** contains clear evidence that he too had studied the spiritual implications of Alchemy, traces of which recur in his **Aesthetic Education**. In England, Blake's extensive knowledge of Gnostic, alchemical, neo-Platonic and mystical writings is well established. Among the mystics who influenced Blake most strongly was the mineralogist Emmanuel Swedenborg. It can be no coincidence that the greatest of the German Romantic mystical symbolists, Novalis, was also a mineralogist, for it seems clear that during the eighteenth-century the apparently prosaic study of mineralogy and metallurgy entailed careful perusal of alchemical texts. Both mineralogy and alchemy flourished in seventeenth and eighteenth-century Vienna [...] and the most prominent mineralogist in eighteenth-century Vienna was Ignaz von Born, who had an extensive knowledge of Alchemy as a quasi-scientific discipline. Born's study of Alchemy was most certainly not directed towards the occult, but precisely because scientists like Born had failed to penetrate the secrets of nature, others were ready to revisit Born's alchemical texts for different purposes." [128]

The secrets of nature can be restated as physical laws, but their manipulation formed only part of what interested people like von Born. Magic correspondences between the Kabiri and the subterranean world of minerals would have been even more fascinating. The Kabiri were master miners who used smelting furnaces to melt down minerals. The molten metals where then turned into ritual objects suitable for magic. In those days, any activity taking place underground was considered 'womb like' and interpreted as an aspect of fertility. Metals were part of the earth's mineral fecundity and the caverns in which they were extracted were privileged locations for initiation and rebirth. They were direct points of contact with creative powers tied to the spiritual world of Ptah.

In 1782, in his influential journal **Der Teutsche Merkur** Wieland published a piece (*"Das Land der Seelen, Ein Fragment"*) which claimed that all cultures evolved the concept of a life beyond earthly existence.[129] Together with Herder, he looked upon descents underground as Orphic exercises through which a young man, during initiation, could come in contact with his feminine complement.

Ignaz von Born's rationalist group, which maintained close contact with Wieland, would have been aware of this line of investigation:

"The Born circle worked hard to establish links with the Northern German Enlightenment. Aloys Blumauer maintained a regular correspondence with Wieland, and in 1784 the poet Johann Baptiste von Alxinger made a tour of northern Germany, visiting Lessing's colleague Friedrich Nicolai in Berlin and

Wieland in Weimar. Even closer contacts were established with Weimar by another former member of Born's group, Karl Leonhard Reinhold, who settled in Weimar and married Wieland's daughter. From Weimar he continued to contribute to the **Realzeitung** [a literary journal closely associated with Born's lodge '*Zur wahren Eintracht*'] and Gemmingen's **Magazin für Wissenschaften**, and maintained a prolific correspondence with Born, Alxinger, and the poets Ratschsy and Gottlieb Leon. He was a close friend of Schiller and immersed himself in Kant [...] In 1789 he dedicated a book to '*seinen vaterlichen Freunden Ignaz von Born in Wien, Immanuel Kant in Königsberg und Christoph Martin Wieland in Weimar*', A telling constellation of names linking Mozart's Vienna, Königsberg, and the Weimar of Wieland, Goethe and Schiller." [130]

Giesecke's **Oberon der Elfenkönig**, commissioned by Schikaneder in 1789, can be seen as an extension of this tremendous activity. Wieland was the 'literary hero' of Mozart's household. He was also one of the principal supporters of the German *singspiel*, to which both Schikaneder and Mozart were very much committed. In his **Versuch über das deutsche Singspiel** (published as the preface to **Alceste**), he tried to make a case for simplicity in German opera.[131]

One can, of course, question their collective knowledge of ancient Egypt, but their approach to ritual was fairly solid. The articles in von Born's **Journal für Freymaurer** give a good overview of the source materials used to arrive at this knowledge— much of it still authoritative. Von Born refers to Ptah as Vulcan in his writings, but he was familiar with Jablonski's work. His considerable knowledge of Plutarch extended, no doubt, to the Pythian Dialogues where the death of the Great Pan was announced (**The Obsolescence of Oracles**).

The **Journal für Freymaurer** gives only a superficial glimpse at what was undoubtedly a much more comprehensive investigation into ritual. Certain things would have never been published, but the direction of investigation can still be deduced from the subjects under consideration. The use of names would have been part of the Kabbilistic framework already associated with the Higher Degrees of Freemasonry.

Pamina and Tamino, as 'Ptah-Min', represent the summation of all insights. 'Ptah-Min' is literally the 'One-and-All', or '*Hen kai Pan*' around which eighteenth-century Masonic searches revolved. In spite of the historical obstacles, and the apparent lack of connectivity between eighteenth-century Vienna and ancient Egypt, the pattern is well in line with ancient Egyptian practices concerning names:

"The radiant power of speech made the divine realm, in all its otherworldliness, capable of being approached, conceptualized and represented, and speech was thus a dimension of divine presence. Because the Egyptians had the concept of the sacred word, the sacred was not ineffable to them, although the utterance of the sacred word, the use of the radiant power of speech [*akhu*], was bound up with the strictest of requirements. Only the deities could make use of the 'radiant power of words', along with the king, insofar as the latter acted as a god, and the priests to whom the king delegated his priestly function." [132]

THE WORLD OF ACTION

PAPAGENO AND PAPAGENA

Based on what has been said so far, it would be absurd to argue that Papageno and Papagena's names are not meaningful. If the entire opera is constructed around occult names, that pattern must be maintained throughout.

Papageno and Papagena are simple characters identified with 'ordinary' humanity, as many authors have pointed out.[133] But that does not mean that they are of lesser symbolic importance. We have already noted the utopian nature of Papageno's character. When Tamino asks him who he is, he shoots back: "Silly question! A man like you."

There is a sort of New World innocence woven into Papageno's personality and the Jesuit experiment in the Guaraní Republic may well be the source for some of Papageno's more exotic attributes. There is indirect support for this interpretation from rather unexpected quarters. Karl Marx, who knew a thing or two about social utopias, provides the indispensable insight:

"The idea of the 'noble savage', which occurs in two of Mozart's early operas, ***Zaide*** and ***Die Entführung***, was afterwards commented on by Marx. 'According to a fiction current in the eighteenth century, the natural state was considered the true state of human nature. People wanted to see the idea of man through the eyes of the body and created *men of nature*, *Papagenos*, the naivety of which idea extended even to covering the skin with feathers. During the last decades of the eighteenth century, it was supposed that *peoples in a state of nature* possessed primeval wisdom and everywhere one could hear bird-catchers imitating the twittering method of singing of the Iroquois, the Indians, etc..., in the belief that by these arts the birds themselves could be enticed into a trap. All these eccentricities were based on the correct idea that the *primitive* state was a naive Dutch picture of the *true* state'." [134]

The idea was perhaps naive by North-American standards, but it had been converted into reality in South America. Here was a functioning communal state, subdivided into smaller communities of anywhere from 2,000 to 7,000 people for a total population of about 50,000 before the forced migrations began.

"You cannot examine the case of the Guaraní Republic without referring to the Golden Legend that enveloped it from the start, sometimes the work of sworn enemies of the Company like Voltaire or d'Alembert.[...] The Italian philosopher Antonio

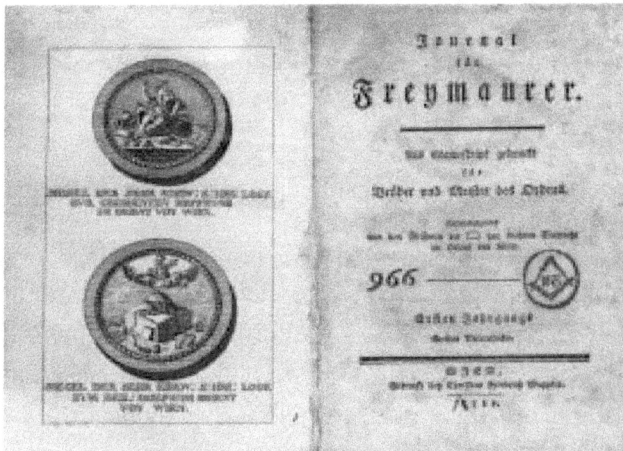

14. *Journal für Freymaurer*

Muratori [...] saw the missions as a reincarnation of the Early Church. Comparing their Jesuit lawmakers to Lycurgus and Plato, Montesquieu saluted them as founders of the ideal city, where they had managed to 'govern men by making them happy' and glimpsed in this 'model republic' a finally realized Utopia.[...] In **Candide**, Voltaire was pleased to convey his hero through Paraguay, where he saw Jesuits eating 'a luncheon in golden bowls... in a verdant room adorned with parrots, hummingbirds, and flycatchers', while Indians ate 'maize in wooden gourds in their fields by the heat of the sun'. [...] But in his ***Essai sur les moeurs***, the same Voltaire almost fervently hails this Society, in which everything undertaken was in the name of 'reason' and by the paths of 'persuasion' and which on many counts was a 'triumph of mankind'. [...] Auguste Comte, so admired [the Jesuits] that he proposed to forge an alliance with the Company to found the Positivist State he dreamed of." [135]

The Jesuits were not ignorant monks eager to propagate religious superstitions. As an ex-Jesuit Ignaz von Born would have been aware of this, yet if we trust the language used in his resignation from the Bavarian Academy of Sciences, to protest the persecution of the *Illuminati* in 1785, we are forced into a confusing position:

"I declare myself to be an open enemy of ignorant monks..., who ought never to be entrusted with the education of youth: I declare that the words Jesuitry and Fanaticism can be equated with roguery and ignorance, superstition and stupidity; in short, my opinion is completely opposed to what seems to be the official opinion in Bavaria." [136]

This is overdoing it a little bit. Fanaticism would have never gotten the Jesuits— as refugees— into the Protestant enclave of Frederick the Great, or the Orthodox dominions of Catherine II of Russia, where they thrived. Ignorance is just as unlikely a charge. A complete lack of tolerance, perhaps, but that was well documented and even satirized all across Europe. Voltaire, who liked to keep track of slants against the Jesuits, excitedly wrote to d'Alembert that "*Un fils du comte Romanzof vient de faire des vers français dont quelques-uns sont encore plus étonnants que ceux du comte Chouvalof. C'est un dialogue entre Dieu et le Révérend Père Hayer [a Jesuit], auteur du **Journal Chrétien**. Dieu lui recommende la tolérance; Hayer lui répond:*

> *Ciel! que viens-je d'entendre? Ah! Ah! je le vois bien,*
> *Que vous-même, Seigneur, vous ne valez rien.*"

[A son of count Romanzof has just produced French verses some of which are even more astonishing than those of count Chouvalof. It is a dialogue between God and father Hayer (a Jesuit), author of the **Christian Journal**. God preaches tolerance to him and Hayer answers:

> Heavens! what have I heard? Ha! Ha! I see it well,
> You Lord are worthless, I can tell.] [137]

Von Born's diatribe against the Jesuits was most likely an exageration purposefully generated to better conceal associations that could have been made between the new utopians— the *Illuminati*— and their predecessors. The fact that many of the *Illuminati* were ex-Jesuits is already more than suspicious. When Voltaire and d'Alembert approached the subject with humor, why did von Born have to take it on with such a hard edge.

The three occult couples (the Queen of the Night and her husband, Tamino and Pamina, Papageno and Papagena) form a hermetic triad matching the triad of alchemical pairs that condition solar birth (Saturn and the Moon, Jupiter and Mercury, Mars and Venus). The process has been described in the first two volumes of this series and will not be covered again here.

The legend of Isis and Osiris specifies exactly under what circumstances the new solar hero comes to life. The procedure refers to a necromantic union between Isis and the dead Osiris, revived only for one ultimate copulation from which Horus/ Harpocrates is born.

"Important details about Harpocrates are to be found in Plutarch. In telling the Osirian legend Plutarch uses the name Horus for Isis' son until he has almost finished when he states: 'Isis when Osiris had mated with her after his death became by him the mother of one untimely born and weak in his nether limbs, Harpocrates'. Later on the divine nativity is alluded to again when Plutarch is urging his readers to give the story a cosmological interpretation instead of tiresomely alleging that theology can be summed up in the seasonal changes of Egypt."[138]

The ritual union requires an otherworldly insemination and Isis plays a key role in this complex cycle. Because an inexplicable pregnancy can be challenged, it is important that the carrier of the solar child be able to defend herself against critics. Papagena displays her suitability for divine-child bearing by exhibiting transformations usually associated with Isis and her trial:

"Whenever we look we find that it is the goddess who is the magic life-giver, the indefatigable sorceress who secures for her son Horus the final victory in his perpetual struggles with the archenemy Seth. Thus when the question of the son's paternity is challenged by Seth she transforms herself first into an old hag, then into a beautiful damsel, and lastly into a bird. In this form she almost wins the votes of the tribunal who are trying the case." [139]

Before we get any deeper into the subject of birds, we should point out that the battle between light and darkness is here redefined by the struggle between Horus and Seth. The symbolism of the armed man, investigated earlier, is already present in this context and archeological evidence from Pompei shows that the model was well established even at that time:

"A story related by Plutarch about the conflict between Horus and Seth is that the latter escaped capture by turning himself into a crocodile, represented as the type of what is base and harmful. From Plutarch, too, we learn that Horus was supposed to have replied to his father's question, what he thought the most suitable animal for a man going out to battle, with the surprising answer 'a horse', and not 'a lion'. Whereas the representation of Horus as a cavalier is not characteristic of his native Egypt, he becomes so in the art of imperial times, Harpocrates-Helios appearing at Pompei on horseback. A work in the Louvre known as the 'Horus St Georges', perhaps of the fourth century, depicts a man with the head of a hawk running his spear through a crocodile, on which the horse he rides is trampling [...] Two of Christendom's most celebrated military saints, George and Michael, had to win the fight against a dragon. Michael's was waged at the time when 'a woman... travailing in birth' fled into the wilderness, and was caused by her serpent persecutor 'to be carried away of the flood' (*potamophoretos*, an epithet appropriate to Isis). For the great dragon, 'that old serpent called the Devil, and Satan', and for Michael the battlefield was heaven. But the same dragon, when he 'was cast out into the earth' turned his attack from the celestial hero to 'the woman' who had previously been encompassed with the Sun and the Moon but was now a terrestrial mother with her baby boy. Moreover the dragon was *pyrrhous* in color: and Plutarch thrice applies the same epithet to the complexion of Seth-Typhon." [140]

There is plenty of food for thought is these early apocalyptic representations. The bird theme, whose significance is brought up by the last transformation of Isis, completes the mystery. Papageno and Papagena are of that species and we have to look at the mythical origin of bird unions to arrive at a fruitful statement concerning the couple's esoteric function.

In cosmic terms, Papageno and Papagena represent the stars of Vega and Altair in the constellation of Cygnus— the original home of the birds:

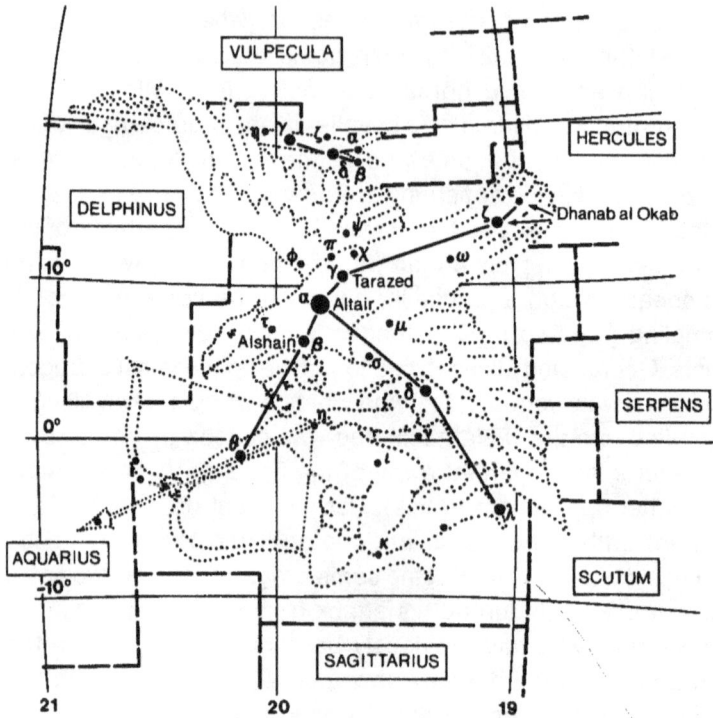

15. The eagle (the bird of kings)

"In ancient Greece the constellation we now know as Cygnus was known as the Bird (*'Ïñïéò*). The Romans gave it the more specific title of the Swan. There are other variants of the name of this constellation, such as the duck and the hen. The Swan was Venus' personal bird.[...] In the Oriental stories of the Swan the first stars of Aquila [the Eagle] and Lyra, called Altair and Vega, were considered two gods in love. These gods were separated by the Milky Way because they thought more about their own love-making than taking care of their divine duties. Only once a year were they allowed to meet each other, this when the Swan— who in the Far East is called the Magpie— formed a bridge by which the lovers could cross the stream of the Milky Way." [141]

Altair is the brightest star at the center of the constellation of the Eagle [Aquila]. The three central stars (á, â, ã) were considered by the Hindus as the footprints left over from Vishnu's cosmic walk.[142] Vishnu's vehicle was another well-known bird.

16. Vishnu's footprints

"The demigod, Garuda, who is part man and part eagle, is best known as the creature which carries Vishnu. He is the king of the birds, a symbol of the wind and the sun, and equally fast. The unimaginable speed with which he travels from one world to another effortlessly, means that he is also a symbol of the esoteric wisdom of the **Vedas**. The power of the magical words of these writings can give man symbolic wings with which he too can move from one world to the next with the speed of light or of Garuda." [143]

Esoteric traditions are seldom disconnected and as Julius Staal acknowledges, the trio of stars found in the constellation of the Eagle reminds the observer of the belt stars in Orion.[144]

The connections of both of these triplets with birds remains as enigmatic as it is widespread and puzzling:

"In our sky, the name of the celestial Samson is Orion, the

mighty hunter, alias Nimrod. He remains such even in China as 'War Lord Tsan', the huntmaster of the autumn hunt, but the Hyades are changed there into a net for catching birds [...] and in Polynesia, deprived of every kind of big game, Orion is found in the shape of a huge snare for birds. It is this snare that Maui, creator-hero and trickster, used to catch the Sunbird; but having captured it, he proceeded to beat it up, and with what?— the jawbone of Muri Ranga Whenua, his own respected grandmother." [145]

Orion and Papageno are both 'bird-catchers'. Orion has access to Sirius, or Pan— the operative symbol of the Great Goddess, or Queen of the Night, whose daughter incarnates her feminine spirit. This brings us back to the relationship between Ptah [the Egyptian Saturn-Hephaistos] and Apis— the ritual repetition of Ptah. **Hamlet's Mill**'s take on the subject through a somewhat convoluted argument, but it is well worth following for the additional insights it offers into the Papageno/ Papagena question:

"This is a long way from Great Pan, and it is not clear yet who or what was supposed to have passed away in the time of Tiberius, that is, which 'Pan'. Creuzer claimed right away that it was Sirius— and any suggestion from Creuzer still carries great weight— the first star of heaven and the kingpin of archaic astronomy. And Aristotle says [**Rhet**. 2.24, 1401 a 15] that, wishing to circumscribe a 'dog', one was permitted to use 'Dog-star' (Sirius) or Pan, because Pindar states him to be the 'shape-shifting dog of the Great-Goddess' (*O makar, honte megalas theou kyna pantodapon kaleousin Olympioi*).[...] The amazing significance of Sirius as leader of the planets, as the eighth planet, so to speak, and of Pan, the dance-master (*choreutes*) as well as the real *kosmokrator*, ruling over the 'three-worlds', would take a whole volume." [146]

These obscure references to a long forgotten tradition in which the 'horned one' stands for the rule of witchcraft cannot be decoded without a great deal of effort. A certain amount of help is available from mythological tales involving constellations; but even here the footing is tenuous. The relationship between Altair and Vega is somehow tied to Orion's hunting quest:

"A Babylonian cuneiform tablet states: 'The Goat-Star is also called the witch-star; the divine function of Tiamat [the Milky Way] it holds in its hands'. The Goat-Star (*enzu*), apart from representing Venus, 'rises together with Scorpius' and has been identified with Vega. If one can rely on this identification, it seems to describe the situation as seen from across the sky: the shifting from Sagittarius to Scorpius, and Vega taking over the Northern part of the 'function' of the Galaxy." [147]

Vega brings Papageno to life. As Papagena, she represents the Harp of Orpheus that was once used to launch the Argo. The necromantic urgency of rescuing the maiden abducted by Hades is what will someday induce Papageno to bring a real solar avatar into the world. Papagena is the bright star of Lyra through which this esoteric renewal occurs. Her miraculous transformation from old hag to a beautiful maiden is in line with the ritual manipulations of witchcraft. These transformations use alchemical procedures in which the god of fire plays a major role.

Pamina and Tamino— as 'Ptah-Min'— point to the Eye of Horus, which stands for the healing and nearly forgotten principle of cosmic reunion. The key to this reunion is Osiris' phallus, which Seth transforms into a magic talisman through a second dismemberment.

"The last time one saw it in historic action, Seth's charm was still in the hands of Attila, King of the Huns and 'Scourge of God', from whom it was audaciously stolen by a secret agent from Byzantium, on a diplomatic mission to his court. Thus Attila lost his 'almighty black relic' in 451, one the eve of the great continental battle during which Aetius would defeat him for good, and cut his great 'army of the steppes' to pieces." [148]

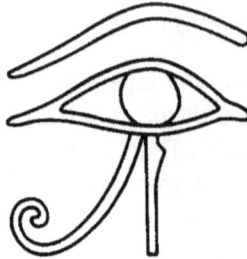

Whether one ascribes to such occult explanations of history, or not, there is ample evidence of a continuous tradition at work and this warrants a great deal of caution when it comes to dismissive statements. Chailley attempts to derive Papageno's name from *Papagei* (Old French *Papageai*), which means 'parrot'. There are indeed parrots shown in Papageno's cage in early illustrations of the opera. Annie Paradis points out that there is very little distance between the parrot and the falcon— Horus' bird. Training a falcon for the hunt is not that different from teaching a parrot to speak.

"The specific language of falconry develops an entire metaphor for initiation: from the 'foolish falcon', taken in infancy from its nest, to the adult 'brought out of the savage state', the journey of the bird in the mastery of its art is marked by 'trials' imposed by its trainer: it must learn to handle darkness, silence, lack of sleep and food before it can streak toward the light, toward the open sky." [149]

The underlying assumption is that the bird-man catches birds— that is creatures like Isis in the last stages of her transformation. As he waits for that rare bird Papageno appears as a cosmic 'sufferer' identified with the human race at large. His pain is our pain and his joys are our little joys. The Greek ðáðáé ãÝíïò (*papai genos*) is applied to such people by

Aristophanes. The word ãÝίϊὸ (*genos*) means 'race, stock, family, offspring' and ðáðǽ (*papai*) is an exclamation of suffering, from which Aristophanes once created comic material. The exclamation ðáðáé has repetitive forms, some as long as ðáðáðáðòáðáðàðáðàðàðáðàðàðáðàé.[150]

But the race of sufferers must at some point produce a magic offspring. In Goethe's sequel to *The Magic Flute* that child is 'Genius' and one is not exactly overwhelmed with the concept.

Goethe's child belongs to Tamino and Pamina— which is already an error from an esoteric perspective. Tamino and Pamina's union is not meant to be a childbearing affair. The only reference to children comes in the context of Papageno and Papagena, who indicate their intention of producing as many little Papagenos and Papagenas as possible. Since they represent the future, they also get to close out the opera, with Tamino and Pamina already in the background.

Many authors have insisted on the folk-theater aspect of *The Magic Flute*, which they consider to be in line with Schikaneder's taste for popular fare. From this they conclude that there is nothing unusual about *The Magic Flute* and that it perfectly fits the pattern of earlier works from other sources— right down to couples with cute names.

"*Der Stein der Weisen oder Die Zauberinsel* (The Wise Men's Stone or The Magic Isle), one of the greatest successes of Schikaneder's first season, vanished quickly, but it is important as a forerunner of *The Magic Flute*. Composed a year earlier, this magic opera probably also drew upon Wieland's collection of fairy tales, *Dschinnistan*. In both, the theme is the testing of a noble pair; there is even a trial by fire and water, and the hero is accompanied by a droll servant, a nature boy called Lubano who in the end wins his Lubanara. They too have a duet '*Wo Lubanara nur miauen kann*' (Lubanara can only miaow). Who isn't reminded of the 'Pa-Pa-Papageno-Papagena' duet?" [151]

Another way of looking at it is to note that Mozart and Schikaneder had a well established genre to work with. A harmless genre that someone cleverly adapted to more subversive needs. If anyone wanted to question **The Magic Flute**, this trivial legacy could be invoked to disarm further scrutiny.

MONOSTATOS

Monostatos is an indicator of darkness and his animal is the classic plague rat. In antiquity plague rats were major disease carriers. They were Apollo's way of spreading punishment. Monostatos' presence in Sarastro's Temple, in Act I, is an indication that something is seriously wrong with Sarastro's brand of Masonry.

The Queen of the Night had already accused Sarastro of being a tyrant and there is nothing at the beginning of the opera that contradicts this statement. Tamino volunteers to retrieve the Queen's daughter, abducted by the tyrant, but only manages to get subverted to Sarastro's cause. He is the archer without arrows who cannot even slay the serpent that is pursuing him. What he lacks at this point are not Masonic secrets; but Pamina, who represents his power of attainment.

In Act I Monostatos is introduced as Pamina's tormentor. Since Sarastro is supposed to be her mentor, there is an implied complicity between the two characters. The mentor and the tormentor take turns in trying to break her down, but she holds up well until Tamino's arrival. Monostatos is thwarted by Papageno's magic bells and Sarastro soon realizes that he has been defeated by love. The self-appointed mentor orders a beating for the tormentor and Monostatos' exclusion creates the right conditions for Tamino's acceptance.

As Monostatos is cast out of the Temple ("I know that your

soul is just as black as your face. Go!"), active darkness shifts to the realm of the Queen of the Night where he takes refuge. Monostatos cannot experience love— only desire. In this he is reminiscent of Wagner's Alberich, from **Das Rheingold**. Monostatos' Act II aria contains a very moving confession:

> All the world is full of lovers,
> Man and maiden, bird and bee.
> Why am I not like the others?
> No one ever looks at me! [tr. Ruth and Thomas Martin]

Jacques Chailley points out that Monostatos, in Greek, means he who 'stands alone'. A very appropriate designation. Monostatos and the Queen of the Night eventually become entangled through their need for revenge. The same need that drives Alberich's descendants insane in **Götterdämmerung**.

Apollo's plagues appear out of nowhere, but in Mozart's opera they are unable to defeat the powers of Sarastro's Temple. Their eleventh hour assault results in self destruction and the final scene brings to mind the ending of Albert Camus' **The Plague**, written under the spell of the Nazi phenomenon:

"And, indeed, as he listened to the cries of joy rising from the town, Rieux remembered that such joy is always imperiled. He knew what those jubilant crowds did not know but could have learned from books: that the plague bacillus never dies or disappears for good; that it can lie dormant for years and years in furniture and linen-chests; that it bides its time in bedrooms, cellars, trunks, and bookshelves; and that perhaps the day would come when, for the bane and the enlightening of men, it would rouse up its rats again and send them forth to die in a happy city." [152]

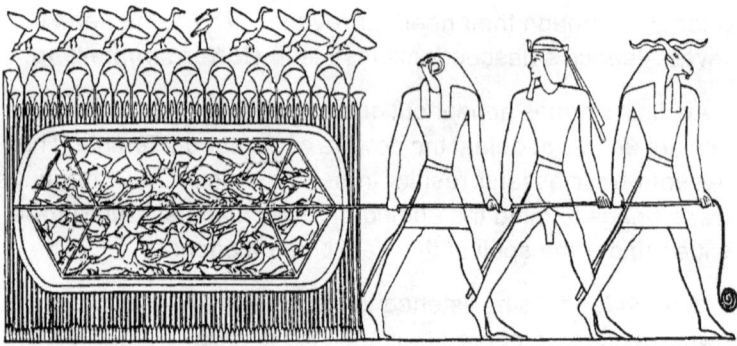

ILLUSTRATIONS

Chapter 1 • The Modern Egyptian Priesthood

1. *Ignaz Alberti's frontispiece to the first edition of the libretto,* p. 8
2. *Illustration from Ignaz von Born's Monachologie,* p.10

Chapter 2 • Mozart and the Enlightenment

1. *Dürer's Feast of the Rose Garlands,* p. 58
   Rudolf II's magic ring, p. 97
   Rudolf II's magic bell showing the Moon and Saturn, p. 98

Chapter 3 • Ritual Action

...

Chapter 4 • Toward Egyptian Masonry

...

Chapter 5 • The Magic Flute and its Symbolic Structure

1. *Triumph of Joseph II's liberal idea*, p. 167
2. *Dürer's Knight, Death and the Devil*, p. 189
3. *Titian's Emperor Charles V.*, p. 191
    Min's symbol, p. 194
4. *Alberti's frontispiece and title page*, p. 198
5. *Scottish Rite and Sephirotic Tree of Life*, p. 203
6. *Camp du Rendez-Vous*, p. 205
7. *Cagliostro's seal*, p. 223
8. *Symbols on column of Alberti's illustration*, p. 224
9. *Pre-dynastic Ptah*, p. 234
10. *Ptah magician*, p. 236
11. *Ptah standing on hieroglyph for Maat*, p. 238
12. *Min in front of his tent shrine*, p. 239
13. *Min in stylized bed of lettuces*, p. 242
14. *Journal für Freumaurer*, p. 249
15. *Constellation of the Eagle*, p. 254
16. *Vishnu's footprints*, p. 255

NOTES

Chapter 1 • The Modern Egyptian Priesthood

1. *Mozart's Last Year*, H.C. Robbins Landon, p. 124
2. Vertrauliche Akten des Haus-, Hof-, und Staatsarchivs, Vienna (41) from *Mozart in Vienna*, Volkmar Braunbehrens, p. 254
3. *The Pied Piper of Hamelin*, Drahos Zak
4. *Mozart in Revolt*, David Schroeder, p. 15-16
5. *Mozart*, Maynard Solomon, p. 331
6. *Rites et Symboles de la Franc-maçonnerie*, "les hauts grades", Daniel   Beresniak, p. 371
7. *Mozart*, Maynard Solomon, p. 334
8. *Republic*, Collected Works, Plato, p. 1132
9. *Rites et Symboles*, Daniel Beresniak, p. 92
10. *Mozart*, Maynard Solomon, p. 334
11. *Mozart and his Circle*, Peter Clive, p. 28
12. *The Mozart Compendium*, H.C. Robbins Landon, p. 134
13. *Mozart*, Maynard Solomon, p. 328
14. *Le testament philosophique de Mozart*, René Terrasson, p. 113
15. *The Jesuits*, Malachi Martin, p. 31-32
16. *Mozart and the Enlightenment*, Nicholas Till, p. 15
17. *Mozart and his Circle*, Peter Clive, p. 58-59
18. Ibid., p. 58
19. *The Magic Flute Masonic Opera*, Jacques Chailley, p. 35
20. *The Jesuits*, Malachi Martin, p. 213
21. *The Cultural Context of Mozart's Magic Flute*, Judith A.

Eckelmeyer,   vol. 1, p. 194
22. Ibid. , p. 195
23. Ibid., p. 210
24. *The Mozart Compendium*, H.C. Robbins Landon, p. 132
25. *Mozart and his Circle*, Peter Clive, p. 27
26. *The Jesuits*, Malachi Martin, p. 216
27. *Hiram Sans-Culotte?*
    Franc-maçonnerie, Lumières et Révolution
    Trente ans d'études et de recherches, Charles Porset, p. 179
28. *The History of Freemasonry*, Albert Mackey, p. 291
29. *The Religious Roles of the Papacy*: ideals and realities,
    Christopher Ryan, p. 10-11
30. Ibid., p. 41-42
31. *The History of Freemasonry*, Albert Mackey, p. 290-291
32. *The Story of Decipherment*, Morris Pope, p. 28
33. *The Elixir and the Stone*, Michael Baigent and Richard Leigh, p. 236
34. *Jesuits*, Jean Lacouture, p. 232
35. *The Holy Roman Empire*, Friedrich Heer, p. 171
36. Ibid., p. 171
37. *Jesuits*, Jean Lacouture, p. 233
38. Ibid., p. 255
39. Ibid., p. 255
40. Ibid., p. 250
41. *The Man of Light*, Henry Corbin, p. 53
42. Ibid., p. 54
43. *Jesuits*, Jean Lacouture, p. 300-304
44. Ibid., p. 311
45. *Aesthetic Theory*, Theodor Adorno, p. 118-119
46. *Mozart and the Enlightenment*, Nicholas Till, p. 226-227
47. *Mozart*, Marcel Brion, p.80
48. *Mozart*, Maynard Solomon, p. 344-345
49. *The Art and Architecture of Freemasonry*, James Curl, p. 141-142
50. *Maçonnerie Egyptienne, Rose-Croix et Néo-Chevalerie*,
    Gérard Galtier, p. 5
51. *Joseph Balsamo alias Cagliostro*, Raymond Silva, p. 38-39
52. *Cagliostro*, W.R.H. Trowbridge, p. 111-113
53. *The Business of Alchemy*, Pamela Smith, p. 173
54. Ibid., p. 181
55. Ibid., p. 182
56. *Maçonnerie Egyptienne*, Gérard Galtier, p. 26-27
57. *The Egyptian Hermes*, Garth Fowden, p. 20-21
58. Ibid., p. 203
59. Ibid., p. 36
60. *Le testament philosophique de Mozart*, René Terrasson, p. 57
61. *The History of Freemasonry*, Albert Mackey, 409-410
62. *La Rose Maçonnique*, Claude Guérillot, vol. 1, p. 46
63. *En Islam Iranien*, Henry Corbin, vol.1, p. 142
64. *The Harmony of the Spheres*, Joscelyn Godwin, p. 346-347

65. *En Islam Iranien*, Henry Corbin, vol. 1, p. 92
66. *The Hebraic Tongue Restored*, Fabre d'Olivet, p. 284
67. Ibid., p. 392
68. Ibid., p.92
69. *The Hebrew Scriptures*, Samuel Sandmel, p. 172
70. *Python*, Joseph Fontenrose, p. 188
71. *Winterreise*, Michael Besack, p. 225
72. *Tales for Transformation*, J.W. Goethe, p. 133
73. *Cosima Wagner's Diaries*, Vol. 2, p. 29
74. *Sacred Science*, Schwaller de Lubicz, p. 226
75. *The House of Rothschild*, Nial Ferguson, p. 41
76. *Les mystères de l'Art Royal*, Oswald Wirth, p. 86
77. *Jews in Germany*, Nachum T. Gidal, p. 122
78. *Jews and Freemasons in Europe*, Jacob Katz, p. 49
79. Ibid. p. 49
80. *Eros and Magic*, Ioan Couliano, p. 102-103
81. *Judaism in Music*, Richard Wagner, p. 81
82. *The Darker Side of Genius*, Jacob Katz, p. 33
83. *Pro and Contra Wagner*, Thomas Mann, p. 117-118

Chapter 2 • Mozart and the Enlightenment

1. *Letters of Mozart and his Family*, Emily Anderson ed., p. 43
2. *The Masonic Thread in Mozart*, Katharine Thomson, p. 35
3. *Mozart in Revolt*, David Schroeder, p. 3
4. *Living the Enlightenment*, Margaret Jacob, p. 121
5. Ibid., p. 158
6. *Mozart and the Enlightenment*, Nicholas Till, p. 294
7. *Shamanism and the Eighteenth Century*, Gloria Flaherty, p. 118
8. Ibid., p. 121
9. Ibid., p. 125
10. *Oeuvres philosophiques*, Diderot, p. xii
11. *Shamanism and the Eighteenth Century*, Gloria Flaherty, p. 157-158
12. *The Masonic Thread in Mozart*, Katharine Thomson, p. 20
13. *Mozart and the Enlightenment*, Nicholas Till, p.296
14. *The Holy Roman Empire*, Friedrich Heer, p. 192, 194-195
15. *Rudolf II and his world*, Robert Evans, p. 14
16. Ibid., p. 182
17. *Giordano Bruno and the Hermetic Tradition*, Frances A. Yates, p. 315
18. Ibid., p. 308
19. Ibid., p. 308
20. *Eros and Magic in the Renaissance*, Ioan P. Couliano, p. 87
21. Ibid., p. 89
22. *Giordano Bruno and the Hermetic Tradition*, Frances A. Yates, p. 312-313

23. Ibid., p. 408-409
24. *The Man of Light*, Henry Corbin, p. 57
25. Ibid., p. 58-59
26. *Alchemy of the Word*, Philip Beitchman, p. 168
27. Ibid., p. 168
28. *Eros and Magic in the Renaissance*, Ioan P. Couliano, p. 87
29. *Mozart and the Enlightenment*, Nicholas Till, p. 12-13
30. Ibid., p. 81
31. Ibid., p. 39
32. *Private Lives and Public Affairs*, Sarah Maza, p. 29
33. Ibid., p. 28
34. Ibid., p. 168
35. *Mozart*, Maynard Solomon, p. 41
36. Ibid., p. 49
37. *Letters of Mozart and his Family*, Emily Anderson, (62) p. 89
38. Ibid., (296), p. 506
39. *Private Lives and Public Affairs*, Sarah Maza, p. 177
40. Ibid., p. 178
41. Ibid., p. 182
42. Ibid., p. 207-208
43. Ibid., p. 205
44. *Cagliostro*, W.R.H Trowbridge, p. 171-173
45. *Private Lives and Public Affairs*, Sarah Maza, p. 184
46. Ibid., p. 187
47. Ibid., p. 187
48. Ibid. p. 192-193
49. *Cagliostro*, W.R.H Trowbridge, p. 173
50. *The Ancient and Accepted Scottish Rite of Freemasonry*, Charles Sumner Lobingier, p. 81
51. *Cagliostro*, Raymond Silva, p. 82
52. *Cagliostro*, W.R.H Trowbridge, p. 175
53. Ibid., p. 177
54. *Private Lives and Public Affairs*, Sarah Maza, p. 200
55. Ibid., p. 202
56. *Mozart and his Circle*, Peter Clive, p. 58
57. Ibid., p. 58
58. *Plato - Complete Works*, John M Cooper ed., p. 551-552
59. *The Art of Memory*, Frances A. Yates, p. 39
60. Ibid., p. 266 footnote 2
61. Ibid., p. 269
62. Ibid., p. 285
63. Ibid., p. 285-286
64. *Mozart and the Enlightenment*, Nicholas Till, p. 95
65. *Papageno*, Kurt Honolka, p.49
66. Ibid., p. 50
67. Ibid., p. 24
68. *Moses the Egyptian*, Jan Assmann, p. 117
69. Ibid., p. 56

70. Ibid., p. 56
71. Ibid., p. 57
72. *Mozart in Revolt*, David Schroeder, p. 26
73. *Moses the Egyptian*, Jan Assmann, p. 115-116
74. *Autonomy and Mercy*, Ivan Nagel, p. 69-70
75. *Hiram Sans-Cullotte?*, Charles Porset, p. 177-178
76. *Letters of Mozart and his Family*, Emily Anderson, (267) p. 435
77. Ibid. (270), p. 442
78. *Mozart and the Enlightenment*, Nicholas Till, p. 276
79. Ibid., p. 276
80. *1791, Mozart's Last Year*, H.C. Robbins Landon, p. 129-130
81. *Mozart and the Enlightenment*, Nicholas Till, p. 299
82. *Moses the Egyptian*, Jan Assmann, p. 118
83. Ibid., p. 117
84. Ibid., p. 115
85. *Eternal Egypt*, Pierre Montet, p. 146-147
86. *Moses the Egyptian*, Jan Assmann, p, 74
87. *Moses Mendelssohn*, Alexander Altmann, p. 10
88. Ibid., p. 10-11
89. Ibid., p. 37
90. *Moses the Egyptian*, Jan Assmann, p. 125
91. *The Serpent Power*, Arthur Avalon, p. 97
92. *Moses the Egyptian*, Jan Assmann, p. 139
93. Ibid., p. 139
94. Ibid, p. 80
95. Ibid., p. 82
96. Ibid.,p. 141
97. Ibid., p. 141
98. Ibid., p. 141
99. Ibid., p. 142

Chapter 3 • Ritual Action

1. *The Search for God in Ancient Egypt*, Jan Assmann, p. 3-4
2. *Homo Necans*, Walter Burkert, p. 35-36
3. *The Search for God in Ancient Egypt*, Jan Assmann, p. 25
4. *Homo Necans*, Walter Burkert, p. 46
5. *Greek mythology and Poetics*, Gregory Nagy, p. 144
6. *Apollon le couteau à la main*, Marcel Detienne, p. 138
7. Ibid., p. 115-116
8. *Le testament philosophique de Mozart*, René Terrasson, p. 209
9. *Greek Mythology and Poetics*, Gregory Nagy, p. 173-174
10. *Veda and Torah*, Barbara A. Holdredge, p. 190
11. Ibid., p. 190-191
12. *The Jews in the Greek Age*, Elias Bickerman, p. 177
13. Ibid., p. 177-178

14. *Heavenly Powers - Unraveling the Secret History of the Kabbalah*, Neil Silberman, p. 11-12
15. *The White Goddess*, Robert Graves, p. 414
16. *Hölderlin's Hymn 'The Ister'*, Martin Heidegger, p. 54
17. *Apollon le couteau à la main*, Marcel Detienne, p. 27
18. *Autonomy and Mercy — Reflections on Mozart's Operas*, Ivan Nagel, p. 29
19. *Apollon le couteau à la main*, Marcel Detienne, p. 202
20. *Homo Necans*, Walter Burkert, p. 178
21. *La Grande Triade*, René Guénon, p. 62-63]
22. Ibid., p. 55
23. Ibid., p. 63
24. *Etudes sur la franc-maçonnerie et le compagnonnage*, René Guénon, vol. 2, p. 45
25. *The Philosophy of Magic*, Arthur Versluis, p. 55-56
26. *Apollon le couteau à la main*, Marcel Detienne, p. 87-89
27. Ibid., p. 89-90
28. *Joseph de Maistre*, Emile Demerghem, p. 63
29. Ibid., p. 64
30. Ibid., p. 182
31. Ibid., p. 63
32. *Parole Perdue et Art Royal*, Daniel Beresniak, p. 33
33. *Wagner's Hitler*, Joachim Köhler, p. 75-76
34. *Symbolisme et Franc-Maçonnerie dans la Tétralogie Wagnérienne*, Paul Legardien, p. 22
35. *Parsifal opéra initiatique*, p. 41
36. Ibid., p. 43
37. *Wagner's Hitler*, Joachim Köhler, p. 76
38. *The Ideas of Richard Wagner*, Alan David Aberbach, p. 302
39. *Richard Wagner*, Robert W. Gutman, p. 411
40. Ibid., p. 443-444
41. *The Search for God in Ancient Egypt*, Jan Assmann, p. 73

Chapter 4 • Toward Egyptian Masonry

1. *Mozart*, Maynard Solomon, p. 327
2. *Mozart and the Enlightenment*, Nicholas Till, p. 295-298
3. *The Magic Flute Masonic Opera*, Jacques Chailley, p. 77
4. *Hiram Sans-Culotte?*, Charles Porset, p. 15
5. Ibid., p. 15
6. *What is Enlightenment?*, James Schmidt, p. 6
7. Ibid., p. 8-9
8. Ibid., p. 9
9. *Mozart and the Enlightenment*, Nicholas Till, p. 297
10. *The Mozart Essays*, H.R. Robbins Landon, p. 213
11. Ibid., p. 215-222

12. *Mozart and the Enlightenment*, Nicholas Till, p. 297
13. Ibid., p. 297-298

14. *Maçonnerie Egyptienne, Rose-Croix et Néo-Chevalerie*, Gérard Galtier, p. 169
15. *Juifs et franc-maçons en Europe*, Jacob Katz, p. 50-51
16. Ibid., p. 52
17. Ibid., p. 52-53
18. Ibid., p. 54
19. Ibid., p. 54-55
20. Ibid., p. 55
21. Ibid., p. 56-57
22. Ibid., p. 57
23. Ibid., p. 58
24. *Jews and Freemasons*, Jacob Katz, p. 65-66
25. *Juifs et franc-maçons en Europe*, Jacob Katz, p. 59-60
26. *Mozart and his Circle*, Peter Clive, p. 59
27. *Mozart and the Enlightenment*, Nicholas Till, p. 296
28. *Moses Mendelssohn*, Alexander Altmann, p. 310
29. *What is Enlightenment?*, James Schmidt, p. 3
30. *The Jewish Philosophy Reader*, D.H. Frank, O. Leaman and C. Manekin Eds., p. 309
31. *Moses Mendelssohn*, Alexander Altmann, p. 5
32. quoted from *German Question/Jewish Question*, Paul Laurence Rose, p. 9
33. Ibid., p. 46-47
34. *Letters of Mozart and his Family*, Emily Anderson, p. 558
35. *Mozart*, Wolfgang Hildesheimer, p. 76
36. Ibid., 81-82
37. *Le merveilleux au XVIIIème siècle*, D'Hauterive Ernest, p. 113-114
38. *Franc-Maçonnerie et Romantisme*, Daniel Beresniak, p. 131
39. *The Masonic Thread in Mozart*, Katharine Thomson, p. 14-15
40. Ibid., p. 16-17
41. *What is Enlightenment?*, James Schmidt, p. 81
42. *Moses the Egyptian*, Jan Assmann, p. 140
43. Ibid., p. 140
44. *Mozart and Masonry*, Paul Nettl, p. 4
45. *Juifs et franc-maçons en Europe*, Jacob Katz, p. 65
46. *Mozart*, Maynard Solomon, p. 322-323
47. *Maçonnerie Egyptienne, Rose-Croix et Néo-Chevalerie*, Gérard Galtier, p. 24-25
48. *Vocal Arts: the Hermeneutic Dimension*, Michael Besack, p. 113
49. *The Hebraic Tongue Restored*, Fabre d'Olivet, p. 279
50. *Maçonnerie Egyptienne, Rose-Croix et Néo-Chevalerie*, Gérard Galtier, p. 66-67 and p. 83
51. *Jews and Freemasons*, Jacob Katz, p. 171
52. *Mozart in Vienna*, Volkmar Braunbehrens, p. 67
53. *The Jewish Response to German Culture*,

Reinhartz and Schatzberg Eds., Walter Roll, p. 32-34

54. *Mozart in Vienna*, Volkmar Braunbehrens, p. 65
55. Ibid., p. 66
56. Ibid., p. 67
57. *Papageno* — Emanuel Schikaneder, Man of the Theater in Mozart's Time, Kurt Honolka, p. 86-87
58. *Juifs et franc-maçons en Europe*, Jacob Katz, p. 67-68
59. *Maçonnerie Egyptienne, Rose-Croix et Néo-Chevalerie*, Gérard Galtier, p. 172
60. *Juifs et franc-maçons en Europe*, Jacob Katz, p. 65
61. *Mozart in Vienna*, Volkmar Braunbehrens, p. 185-186
62. *Autour d'un trône-- Catherine II de Russie*, K. Waliszewski, p. 267
63. Ibid., p. 267
64. Ibid., p. 271
65. Ibid., p. 269
66. *Autonomy and Mercy* — Reflections on Mozart's Operas, Ivan Nagel, p. 70
67. *The Jewish Philosophy Reader*, D.H. Frank, O. Leaman and C. Manekin Eds., p. 344
68. Ibid., p. 314
69. *The Voyage and the Messenger*, Henry Corbin, p. 141-142
70. *The Search for God in Ancient Egypt*, Jan Assmann, p. 88
71. Ibid., p. 3
72. Ibid., p. 87
73. *The Jewish Philosophy Reader*, D.H. Frank, O. Leaman and C. Manekin Eds., p. 40
74. *Maçonnerie Egyptienne, Rose-Croix et Néo-Chevalerie*, Gérard Galtier, p. 69
75. Ibid., p. 70
76. Ibid., p. 82
77. Ibid., p. 80-81
78. *The Jewish Alchemists*, Rafael Patai, p. 340
79. Ibid., p. 341
80. *Maçonnerie Egyptienne, Rose-Croix et Néo-Chevalerie*, Gérard Galtier, p. 55
81. Ibid., p. 56
82. Ibid., p. 56-57
83. *Heavenly Powers*, Neil Silberman, p. 138

Chapter 5 • THE MAGIC FLUTE AND ITS SYMBOLIC STRUCTURE

1. *The Cultural Context of Mozart's Magic Flute*, Judith Eckelmeyer, vol. 1, p. 54
2. Ibid., p. 52-53
3. *Moses The Egyptian*, Jan Assmann, p. 13-14

4. *Hermetica*, p. 279-281
5. *Isis in the Ancient World*, R.E. Witt, p. 154
6. *Moses The Egyptian*, Jan Assmann, p. 116
7. *The Qabalah*, Papus, p. 126
8. *Moses The Egyptian*, Jan Assmann, p. 117
9. *Mozart*, W. Hildesheimer, p. 324
10. *Mozart and Masonry*, Paul Nettl, p.143
11. *Moses The Egyptian*, Jan Assmann, p. 116
12. Ibid., p. 103
13. *The Cultural Context of Mozart's Magic Flute*, Judith Eckelmeyer, vol. 1, p. 208
14. *Moses The Egyptian*, Jan Assmann, p. 114
15. *The Qabalah*, Papus, p. 127
16. *Early Greek Thinking*, Martin Heidegger, p. 31
17. Ibid., p. 36
18. Ibid., p. 33
19. Ibid,. p. 34-38
20. **The Art and Architecture of Freemasonry**, James Curl, p. 9
21. *The Masters of Truth in Ancient Greece*, Marcel Detienne, p. 49-50
22. *Theogony*, Hesiod, p. 30
23. *The Masters of Truth in Ancient Greece*, Marcel Detienne, p. 47
24. Ibid., p. 49
25. *Python*, Joseph Fontenrose, p. 462-463
26. *The Masters of Truth in Ancient Greece*, Marcel Detienne, p. 53
27. Ibid., p. 57-58
28. *Lord of the World*, René Guénon, p. 36-37
29. *Alchemy of the Word*, Philip Beitchman, p. 67
30. *Lord of the World*, René Guénon, note 6, p. 32
31. *Mozart the Dramatist*, Brigid Brophy, p. 251-252
32. *La Parole Perdue et l'Art Royal*, Daniel Beresniak, p. 67
33. *The Cultural Context of Mozart's Magic Flute*, Judith Eckelmeyer, vol. 1, p. 89
34. Ibid., vol. 1, p. 89
35. Ibid., vol. 1, p. 90
36. *The Maze and the Warrior*, Craig Wright, p. 86
37. Ibid., p. 199
38. Ibid., p. 201
39. Ibid., p. 266
40. Ibid., p. 116
41. *Moses The Egyptian*, Jan Assmann, p. 20-21
42. Ibid., p. 134-135
43. Ibid., p. 125
44. Ibid., p. 248
45. Ibid., p. 133-134
46. *Les hauts grades chevalresques de Stricte Observance Templière du XVIIIe siècle*, Jean-Marie Auzanneau, p. 25
47. Ibid., p. 26

48. *Zohar*, vol. 1 p. 3
49. *Morals & Dogma*, Albert Pike, p. 839-842
50. *La Rose Maçonnique*, Claude Guérillot, vol. 2, p. 293
51. Ibid., vol. 2, p. 311
52. *Lord of the World*, René Guénon, p. 11 & p. 15
53. *1791 — Mozart's Last Year*, H.C. Robbins Landon, p. 130
54. *The Magic Flute Masonic Opera*, Jacques Chailley, p. 234
55. *The Mozart Myths*, William Stafford, p. 49
56. *The Magic Flute Masonic Opera*, Jacques Chailley, p. 102
57. *The Dictionary of Classical Mythology*, Pierre Grimal, p. 133
58. *Hekate in Ancient Greek Religion*, Robert von Rudloff, Hekate, p. 64
59. Ibid., p. 96
60. *The Cultural Context of Mozart's Magic Flute*, Judith Eckelmeyer, vol. 2, p. 449-453
61. *Isis in the Ancient World*, R.E. Witt, p. 154
62. *Lord of the World*, René Guénon, p. 10, note 17
63. *The Cultural Context of Mozart's Magic Flute*, Judith Eckelmeyer, vol. 1 p. 50
64. Ibid., vol.2 , p 397-399
65. *Isis in the Ancient World*, R.E. Witt, p. 156
66. *The Cultural Context of Mozart's Magic Flute*, Judith Eckelmeyer, vol. 2, p. 431
67. Ibid. p, 433
68. *Hamlet's Mill*, De Santillana & von Dechend, p. 281
69. *Isis in the Ancient World*, R.E. Witt, p. 157
70. *Alchemy of the Word*, Philip Beitchman, p. 111
71. *Plato — Complete Works*, John M. Cooper, p. 558
72. *Plato Prehistorian*, Mary Settegast, p. 211
73. *Silence and Selfhood*, Michael Evenden, p. 81-82
74. *Isis in the Ancient World*, R.E. Witt, p. 183
75. *Maçonnerie Egyptienne*, Gérard Galtier, p. 320
76. *Lord of the World*, René Guénon, p. 34, note 17
77. Ibid., p. 17, note 17
78. *Mozart and the Enlightenment*, Nicholas Till, p.303
79. *Plato Prehistorian*, Mary Settegast, p. 211
80. Ibid., p. 271
81. *Le testament philosophique de Mozart*, René Terrassson, p. 197
82. *Liturgy of the Ancient and Accepted Scottish Rite of Freemasonry*, Albert Pike, p. 12
83. *Le testament philosophique de Mozart*, René Terrassson, p. 200-201
84. *A Wicked Pack of Cards*, Dummett, Decker and Depaulis, p. 57
85. Ibid., p. 55
86. *Mozart*, Maynard Solomon, p. 277
87. Ibid., 277-283
88. *The Holy Kabbalah*, A.E. Waite, p. 264
89. *The Song of Songs*, Ariel and Chana Bloch, p. 55 & p. 81

90. *The Holy Kabbalah*, A.E. Waite, p. 266
91. *Mozart*, Maynard Solomon, p. 278-279
92. *The Best of the Acheans*, Gregory Nagy, p. 173
93. Ibid., p. 294
94. *The Cultural Context of Mozart's Magic Flute*, Judith Eckelmeyer, vol. 1, p. 260 & p. 273
95. *Orpheus*, Charles Segal, p.34
96. *Mozart and Masonry*, Paul Nettl, p. 72-73
97. *The Myth of Egypt and its Hieroglyphs*, Erik Iversen, p. 127
98. *Historical Atlas of Ancient Greece*, Robert Morkot, p. 116
99. *The Myth of Egypt and its Hieroglyphs*, Erik Iversen, p. 135
100. *The God Ptah*, Maj Sandman Holmberg, p. 33
101. Ibid., p. 27
102. Ibid., p. 29
103. Ibid., p. 204
104. *The Cultural Context of Mozart's Magic Flute*, Judith Eckelmeyer, vol. 2, p. 315
105. *From Fetish to God in Ancient Egypt*, E.A. Wallis Budge, p. 13
106. Ibid., p. 13-14
107. Ibid., p. 261
108. *Etudes sur la Franc-Maçonnerie*, René Guénon, vol. 2, p. 44-45
109. *Ancient Egyption Religion*, Stephen Quirke, p. 45
110. *Hamlet's Mill*, De Santillana & von Dechend, p. 222
111. Ibid., p. 129 & 135
112. *From Fetish to God in Ancient Egypt*, E.A. Wallis Budge, p. 14
113. *Sacred Science*, Schwaller De Lubicz, p. 193
114. *Ancient Egyption Religion*, Stephen Quirke, p, 46
115. Ibid., p. 46
116. *Initiations et sociétes secrètes*, Yves Dacosta, p. 43
117. *The Art and Architecture of Freemasonry*, James Curl, p. 35
118. *Hieroglyphics*, Maria Carmela Betro, p. 81
119. *Ancient Egypt*, Barry J. Kemp, p. 85
120. *From Fetish to God in Ancient Egypt*, E.A. Wallis Budge, p. 73
121. *Black Athena*, Martin Bernal, vol.2, p. 23
122. Ibid., vol. 2, p. 167
123. Ibid., p. 168
124. *The Art and Architecture of Freemasonry*, James Curl, p. 29
125. Ibid., p. 29
126. *Secret Teachings of all Ages*, Manly Hall, p. XXXV
127. *Ancient Egyption Religion*, Stephen Quirke, p, 46
128. *Mozart and the Enlightenment*, Nicholas Till, p. 293-294
129. *Shamanism and the Eighteenth Century*, Gloria Flaherty, p.144
130. *Mozart and the Enlightenment*, Nicholas Till, p. 122
131. Ibid., p. 55
132. *The Search for God in Ancient Egypt*, Jan Assmann, p. 92
133. *The Magic Flute Masonic Opera*, Jacques Chailley, p. 104
134. *The Masonic Thread in Mozart*, Katharine Thomson, p. 156
135. *Jesuits*, Jean Lacouture, p. 231

136. **The Masonic Thread in Mozart**, Katharine Thomson, p. 78
137. **Autour d'un Trône— Catherine II de Russie**, K. Waliszewski, p. 252
138. **Isis in the Ancient World**, R.E. Witt, p. 212
139. Ibid., p. 41
140. Ibid., p. 215-216
141. **Patterns in the Sky**, Julius Staal, p. 176-177
142. Ibid., p. 180
143. **The Book of Hindu Imagery**, Eva Jensen, p. 58
144. **Patterns in the Sky**, Julius Staal, p. 181
145. **Hamlet's Mill**, De Santillana & von Dechend, p. 166
146. Ibid., p. 285-286
147. Ibid., p. 261-262
148. **La spirale prophetique**, Jean Parvulesco, p. 246-247
149. **L'opéra réenchanté**, Annie Paradis, p. 352
150. **Greek-English Lexicon**, Liddell and Scott, p. 392
151. **Papageno**, Kurt Honolka, p. 85-86
152. **The Plague**, Albert Camus [Stuart Gilbert Tr.], p.308

BIBLIOGRAPHY

Aberbach, Alan David. *The Ideas of Richard Wagner*. Lanham, 1984.
University Press of America.

Adorno, Theodor. *Aesthetic Theory*. Minneapolis, 1997.
University of Minnesota Press.

Adorno, Theodor. *Critical Models*. New-York, 1998.
Columbia University Press.

Altmann, Alexander. *Moses Mendelssohn—* A biographical study.
Philadelphia, 1973. The Jewish Publication Society of America.

Amadou, Robert. *La Tradition Maçonnique*. Paris, 1986.
Cariscript.

Anderson, Emily Ed. *The Letters of Mozart and his Family*.
New-York, 1985. W.W. Norton & Company.

Assmann, Jan. *Moses the Egyptian* — The Memory of Egypt in Western
Monotheism. Cambridge, 1997. Harvard University Press.

Assmann, Jan. *The Search for God in Ancient Egypt*. Ithaca, 2001.
Cornell University Press.

Beauvert, Thierry. *La flûte enchantée*. 1998. Editions Plume.

Béhar, Pierre. *Les langues occultes de la Renaissance*. Paris, 1996.
Edition Desjonquères.

Beitchmann, Philip. *Alchemy of the Word— Cabala of the
Renaissance*. New-York, 1998. State University of New-York Press.

Béresniak, Daniel. *Franc-Maçconnerie et Romantisme*. Paris, 1987.
Editions Chiron.

Béresniak, Daniel. *La Parole Perdue et L'Art Royal*. Athens, 1997.
Editions Detrad.

Béresniak, Daniel. *Rites et Symboles de la Franc-Maçonnerie—*

les loges bleues. Vol. 1. Athens, 1997.
Editions Detrad.

Béresniak, Daniel. *Rites et Symboles de la Franc-Maçonnerie— les hauts grades*. Vol. 2. Athens, 1997.
Editions Detrad.

Béresniak, Daniel. *Symboles des Franc-Maçons*. Paris, 1997.
Editions Assouline.

Bernal, Martin. *Black Athena*. Vols. 1 - 2. Rutgers University Press, Austin, 1991.

Besack, Michael. *Vocal Arts: the Hermeneutic Dimension*.
Oakland, 1997. Regent Press.

Besack, Michael. *Winterreise— Reflections on a Winter Journey*.
Oakland, 1998. Regent Press.

Betro, Maria Carmela. *Hieroglyphics*. New-York, 1996.
Abbeville Publishers.

Bickerman, Elias J. *The Jews in the Greek Age*. Cambridge, 1988.
Harvard University Press.

Boyle, Nicholas. *Goethe - the poet and the age*. Oxford, 1992.
Oxford University Press.

Branscombe, Peter. *Die Zauberflöte*. Cambridge University Press. 1991

Braunbehrens, Volkmar. *Mozart in Vienna— 1781-1791*.
New-York, 1991. HarperPerennial.

Brion, Marcel. *Daily Life in the Vienna of Mozart and Schubert*.
London, 1961. Widenfeld & Nicholson.

Brion Marcel. *Mozart*. 1955. Perrin.

Brophy, Brigid. *Mozart the Dramatist*. New-York, 1988. Da Capo.

Bruno, Giordano. *Cause, Principle and Unity— and Essays on Magic*.
Cambridge, 1998. Cambridge University Press.

Bruno, Giordano. *The Expulsion of the Triumphant Beast*.
Lincoln, 1992. University of Nebraska Press.

Budge, E.A. Wallis. *From Fetish to God in Ancient Egypt*.
New-York. Dover Publications.

Burkert, Walter. *Ancient Mystery Cults*. Cambridge, 1987.
Harvard University Press.

Burkert, Walter. *Creation of the Sacred*. Cambridge, 1996.
Harvard University Press

Burkert, Walter. *Homo Necans*. Berkeley, 1983.
University of California Press.

Burkert, Walter. *Greek Religion*. Cambridge, 1985.
Harvard University Press.

Camus, Albert. *The Plague*. New-York, 1991. Vintage International.

Chailley, Jacques. *Parsifal— Opéra initiatique*. Paris, 1986.
Editions Buchet/Chastel.

Chailley, Jacques. *The Magic Flute, Masonic Opera*. New-York, 1971.
Alfred A. Knopf.

Clive, Peter. *Mozart and his Circle*. New Haven 1993.
Yale University Press.
Coil, Henry. *Conversations on Freemasonry*. 1976. Macoy Publishing.
Corbin, Henry. *Alchimie comme art hiératique*. Paris, 1986. L'Herne.
Corbin, Henry. *Corps spirituel et terre céleste— de l'Iran Mazdéen à l'Iran Shi'ite*. Paris, 1979. Buchet/Castel.
Corbin, Henry. *En Islam iranien*. vols. 1-4. 1991. Gallimard.
Corbin, Henry. *L'imagination créatrice dans le soufisme d'Ibn' Arabi*. Paris, 1958. Flammarion.
Corbin, Henry. *The Man of Light in Iranian Sufism*.
New Lebanon, 1994. Omega Publications.
Corbin, Henry. *The Voyage and the Messenger— Iran and Philosophy*. Berkeley, 1998. North Atlantic Books.
Corbin, Henry. *Temps cyclique et gnose ismaélienne*. Paris, 1982.
Berg International. Couliano,
Corbin, Henry. *Trilogie ismaélienne*. 1994. Verdier.
Couliano, Ioan P. *Eros and Magic in the Renaissance*. Chicago, 1987.
The University of the Chicago Press.
Craig, Gordon. *The Germans*. Meridian, 1983.
Crapanzano, Vincent. *Hermes' Dilemma & Hamlet's Desire— on the Epistemology of Interpretation*. 1992. Harvard University Press.
Curl, James Stevens. *The Art and Architecture of Freemasonry*.
New-York, 1993. The Overlook Press.
Dacosta, Yves. *Initiations et sociétés secrètes*. Paris, 1991.
Berg International.
Darnton, Robert. *The Forbidden Best-Sellers of Pre-Revolutionary France*. New-York. Norton.
De Curzon, Henri. *Lettres de W.A. Mozart, 1769-1781*. Paris, 1956. Plon.
De Curzon, Henri. *Lettres de W.A. Mozart, 1781-1791*. Paris, 1956. Plon.
De Pascalis, Andrea. *Alchemy— the Golden Art*. Rome, 1995.
Gremese International.
De Santillana & Von Dechend. *Hamlet's Mill*. Boston, 1977.
David R. Godine.
Decker, Ronald & DePaulis Thierry & Dummet Michael.
A Wicked Pack of Cards. New-York, 1996.
St Martin's Press.
Degris, Alain. *L'Ordre des Templiers*. Paris, 1994. Editions Dervy.
Dermenghem, Emile. *Joseph de Maistre*. Paris, 1946. La Colombe.
Detienne, Marcel. *Apollon le couteau à la main*. 1998.
Editions Gallimard.
Detienne, Marcel. *The Masters of Truth in Archaic Greece*.
New-York, 1996. Zone Books.
Donington, Robert. *Opera and its Symbols*. New Haven, 1990.
Yale University Press.
Dufrenoy, Marie-Louise. *L'Orient Romanesque en France— 1701-1789*.

Montreal, 1946. Editions Beauchemin.

D'Hauterive, Ernest. *Le Merveilleux au XVIIIᵉᵐᵉ Siècle*. Paris, 1902.
Félix Juven, Editeur.

D'Olivet, Fabre. *The Hebraic Tongue Restored*.
French Original, 1815. English Tr. 1918, Nayan Louise Redfield.
Kessinger Publishing.

Eckelmeyer, Judith A. *The Cultural Context of Mozart's Magic Flute*,
vols. 1 and 2. Lampeter, 1991. The Edwin Mellen Press.

Eliade, Mircea. *Forgerons et alchimistes*. Paris, 1956. Flammarion.

Evans, R.J.W. *Rudolf II and his World— a Study in Intellectual
History1576-1612*. Oxford, 1973. Clarendon Press

Evenden, Michael. *Silence and Selfhood — The Desire of Order in
Mozart's Magic Flute*. Peter Lang.New-York, 1999

Evola, Julius. *Écrits sur la franc-maçonnerie*. Puiseaux, 1987. Pardès.

Evola, Julius. *La tradition hermétique*. Paris, 1988.
Éditions Traditionnelles.

Evola, Julius. *Symboles et "mythes" de la tradition occidentale*.
Milan, 1980. Archè.

Fabricius, Johannes. *Alchemy*. London, 1994. Diamond Books.

Faivre, Antoine. *Accès de l'ésotérisme occidental*. Gallimard, 1986.

Ferguson, Niall. The House of Rothschild. New-York, 1999. Penguin Books.

Flaherty, Gloria. *Shamanism and the Eighteenth Century*.
Princeton, 1992. Princeton University Press.

Fontenrose, Joseph. *Python— A Study of the Delphic Myth
and Its Origin*. Berkely, 1959. University of California Press.

Fowden, Garth. *The Egyptian Hermes*. Princeton, 1986.
Princeton University Press.

Gefen, Gérard. *Les musiciens et la franc-maçonnerie*. 1993. Fayard.

Girard-Augry, Pierre. *Les hauts grades chevaleresques de la Stricte
Observance Templière du XVIIIᵉᵐᵉ siècle*. Paris, 1995.
Editions Dervy.

Godwin, Joscelyn. *The Harmony of the Spheres*. Rochester, 1993.
Inner Traditions International.

Goethe, J.W. *Märchen (Le Serpent Vert)*. Oswald Wirth, tr. Paris, 1999.
Editions Dervy.

Goethe, J.W. *Wilhelm Meister's Apprenticeship*.
Collected Works, Vol. 9. Princeton, 1995. Princeton University Press

Goethe, J.W. *Wilhelm Meister's Journeyman Years*.
Collected Works, Vol. 10. Princeton, 1995. Princeton University

Graves, Robert. *The White Goddess - A Historical Grammar of
Poetic Myth*. New-York, 1966. The Noonday Press.

Greiner Frank, Ed. *Aspects de la tradition alchimique au XVIIᵉ siècle*.
Milan, 1998. Archè.

Grimal, Pierre. *The Dictionary of Classical Mythology*. 1996.
Blackwell Publishers.

Guénon, René. *Études sur la franc-maçonnerie et le compagnonnage*. Vols. 1-2. Clamecy, 1991. Éditions Traditionnelles.

Guénon, René. *Symboles de la science sacrée*. Paris, 1962. Gallimard.

Guénon, René. *The Lord of the World*. Coombe Springs Press, 1983.

Guérillot, Claude. *A la rencontre des premiers Franc-Maçons Ecossais*. Paris, 1996. Guy Trédaniel Editeur.

Guérillot, Claude. *De la porte basse à la Porte Étroite*. Paris, 1998. Editions Dervy.

Guérillot, Claude. *La Rose Maçonnique*. Vols. 1 and 2. Paris, 1995. Guy Trédaniel Editeur.

Guillot, Pierre. *Les Jésuites et la Musique*. Liège, 1991. Mardaga.

Guthrie, W.K.C. *Orpheus and Greek Religion*.

Hall, Manly. *Freemasonry of the Ancient Egyptians*. Los Angeles, 1965. The Philosophical Research Society.

Hall, Manly. *The Secret Teachings of all Ages*. The Philosophical Research Society. 1987.

Hare, Tom. *Remembering Osiris— Number, Gender and the Word in Ancient Egyptian Representational Systems*. Stanford, 1999. Stanford University Press.

Heer, Friedrich. *The Holy Roman Empire*. New-York, 1968. Frederick A. Praeger.

Heidegger, Martin. *Early Greek Thinking - The Anaximander Fragment, Logos, Moira and Aletheia*. New-York, 1984. HarperCollins, Publishers.

Heidegger, Martin. *Erleuterungen zu Hölderlin's Dichtung*. Frankfurt, 1971. Vittorio Klostermann.

Heidegger, Martin. *Hölderlin's Hymn "The Ister"*. Indianapolis, 1996. Indiana University Press.

Heidegger, Martin. *On the Way to Language*. New-York, 1982. Harper Collins.

Heidegger, Martin. *Poetry, Language, Thought*. 1975. Harper Colophon Edition.

Henry, Jacques. *Mozart frère maçon— La symbolique maçonnique dans l'oeuvre de Mozart*. 1997. Editions du Rocher.

Hermetica, Walter Scott Ed. Boston, 1993. Shambala.

Hildesheimer, Wolfgang. *Mozart*. New-York, 1983. Vintage Books.

Hocquard, Jean-Victor. *Mozart, de l'ombre à la lumière*. 1993. Editions Lattès.

Holmberg, Maj Sandman. *The God Ptah*. Lund, 1946. C.W.K. Gleerup

Holredge, Barbara. *Veda and Torah*. New-York, 1996. State University of New-York Press.

Honolka, Kurt. *Papageno* — Emanuel Schikaneder, Man of the Theater in Mozart's Time. Portland 1984. Amadeus Press.

Horne, Alexander. *King Solomon's Temple in the Masonic Tradition*.

The Aquarian Press, 1988.
Jacob, Margaret C. *Living the Enlightenment— Freemasonry and Politics in Eighteenth-Cnetury Europe*. Oxford, 1991. Oxford University Press.
Jam, Jean-Louis, *Mozart* — Origines et transformations d'un mythe, Peter Lang, Paris, 1994
Jansen, Eva Rudy. *The Book of Hindu Imagery*. Diver, 1993. Binkey Kok Publications.
Johnson, Paul. *A History of the Jews*. Harper Perennial, 1987.
Kahn, Didier & Matton, Sylvain Eds. *Alchimie— art, histoire et mythes*. Milan, 1996. Arché.
Katz, Jacob. *Jews and Freemasons in Europe, 1723-1939*. Cambridge, 1970. Harvard University Press.
Katz, Jacob. *Juifs et francs-maçons en Europe, 1723-1939*. Paris, 1995.Les éditions du cerf.
Katz, Jacob. *The Darker Side of Genius*. University Press of New England. London, 1986.
Kemp, Barry J. *Ancient Egypt*. New-York, 1991. Routledge.
Kerényi, Karl. *Apollo*. Spring Publications, 1988.
Kerényi, Karl. *Hermes*. Spring Publications, 1986.
Kingsley, Peter. *Ancient Philosophy, Mystery, And Magic*. Oxford, 1996. ClarendonPress.
Klein, Eliahu. *Kabbalah of Creation* — Isaac Luria's Earlier Mysticism. Jerusalem, 2000. Jason Aronson.
Köhler, Joachim. *Wagner's Hitler*. Cambridge, 2000. Polity Press.
Krieger, Leonard. *Kings and Philosophers, 1689-1789*. New-York, 1970. Norton.
Lacouture, Jean. *Jesuits* — a Multibiography. Washington D.C., 1995. Counterpoint.
Legardien, Paul. *Symbolisme et Franc-Maçconnerie dans la Tétralogie Wagnérienne*. 1995. Editions Zurfluh.
MacBride, A.S. *Speculative Masonry*. Richmond, 1971. Macoy Publishing.
Mackey, Albert. *The History of Freemasonry*. 1996. Gramercy Books. Random House.
Martin, Malachi. *The Jesuits*. New-York, 1987. Simon & Schuster.
Maza, Sarah. *Private Lives and Public Affairs*. Berkeley, 1993. University of California Press.
Mitford, Nancy. *Frederick the Great*. New-York, 1970. E.P. Dutton.
Montet, Pierre. *Eternal Egypt*. London, 2000. Phoenix Press.
Nagel, Ivan. *Autonomy and Mercy* — Reflections on Mozart's Operas. Cambridge, 1991. Harvard University Press.
Nagy, Gregory. *Greek Mythology and Poetics*. 1992. Cornell University Press.
Nagy, Gregory. *Homeric Questions*. Austin, 1996.

University of Texas Press.

Nagy, Gregory. *Pindar's Homer— the Lyric Possession of an Epic Past*. 1990. The John Hopkins University Press.

Nagy, Gregory. *Poetry as Performance*. 1996.
Cambridge University Press.

Nagy, Gregory. *The Best of the Achaeans— Concepts of the Hero in Archaic Greek Poetry*. Baltimore, 1979.
The John Hopkins University Press.

Naydler, Jeremy. *Temple of the Cosmos*. Rochester, 1996.
Inner Traditions International.

Nettl, Paul. *Mozart and Masonry*. New-York, 1987. Dorset Press.

Papus, *The Qabalah*. York Beach, 2000. Samuel Weiser.

Parvulesco, Jean. *La spirale prophétique*. Paris, 1986.
Guy Trédaniel Editeur.

Pike, Albert. *Liturgy of the Ancient and Accepted Scottish Rite of Freemasonry*.
Reprint by Kessinger Publishing Company.

Pike, Albert. *Morals and Dogma of the Ancient and Accepted Scottish Rite of Freemasonry*.
Reprint by Kessinger Publishing Company.

Pope, Maurice. *The Story of Decipherment*. London, 1999.
Thames and Hudson.

Paradis, Annie. *Mozart — l'opéra réenchanté*. Fayard. 1999.

Plato. *Complete Works*. John M. Cooper Ed. Indianapolis, 1997.
Hackett Publishing Company.

Plutarch. *Moralia*. vol. 5. *Isis and Osiris / The Obsolescence of Oracles*. Cambridge, 1993. Harvard University Press.

Porset, Charles. *Hiram Sans-Culotte?* Franc-maçonnerie, Lumières et Révolution. Trentes ans d'études et de recherches.
Paris, 1998. Honoré Champion.

Pushkin, Alexander. *Works*. Avrahm Yarmolinsky Tr. New-York, 1936.
Random House.

Quirke, Stephen. *Ancient Egyptian Religion*. New-York, 1992.
Dover Publications.

Ribaudeau-Dumas, François. *La magie chez les Jésuites*. 1989.
Soleil Natal.

Robbins Landon, H.C. *1791— Mozart's Last Year*.
New-York, 1988. Schirmer.

Robbins Landon, H.C. *Mozart and the Masons*.
New-York, 1991. Thames and Hudson.

Robbins Landon, H.C. Ed. *The Mozart Compendium*. Ann Arbor, 1990.
Borders Press.

Robbins Landon, H.C. *The Mozart Essays*. New-York, 1995.
Thames and Hudson.

Rose, Paul Lawrence. *German Question / Jewish Question—*

Revolutionary Antisemitism from kant to Wagner. Princeton, 1990.
Princeton University Press.

Ryan, Christopher. *The Religious Roles of the Papacy: Ideals and Realities 1150-1300*. Toronto, 1989.
Pontifical Institute of Medieval Studies.

Said, Edward. *Orientalism*. New-York, 1979. Vintage Books.

Schmidt, James. *What is Enlightenment?* Berkeley, 1996.
University of California Press.

Scholem, Gershom. *Kabbalah*. Meridian. New-York, 1978.

Schroeder, David. *Mozart in Revolt* — Strategies of Resistance, Mischief and Deception. New Havem, 1999. Yale University Press.

Schwaller de Lubicz, R.A. *Sacred Science*. Rochester, 1998.
Inner Traditions International.

Schwaller de Lubicz, R.A. *The Temple of Man*. Vols. 1-2.
Rochester, 1998. Inner Traditions International.

Segal, Charles. *Orpheus*. The Johns Hopkins University Press.
Baltimore, 1989.

Settegast, Mary. *Plato Prehistorian*. Lindisfarne Press, 1990.

Silberer, Herbert. *Hidden Symbolism of Alchemy and the Occult Arts*.
New-York, 1971. Dover Publications.

Silberman, Neil Asher. *Heavenly Powers— Unraveling the Secret History of the Kabbalah*. New-York, 1998. Grosset/Putnam.

Silva, Raymond. *Joseph Balsamo alias Cagliostro*. Montreal, 1975.
Editions Québec-Amérique.

Smith, Pamela H. *The Business of Alchemy— science and culture in the Holy Roman Empire*. Princeton, 1994. Princeton University Press.

Solomon, Maynard. *Mozart*. HarperPerennial. New-York, 1996.

Spinoza, Baruch. *Theological-Political Treatise*. Indianapolis, 1998.
Hackett Publishing Company.

Staal, Julius D. *The New Patterns in the Sky*. Blacksburg, 1988.
The McDonald and Woodward Publishing Co.

Stafford, William. *The Mozart Myths*. Stanford, 1991.
Stanford University Press.

Steiner, Rudolf. The Secret Stream — Christian Rosenkreutz and Rosicrucianism. Great Barrington, 2000. Anthroposophic Press.

Stevenson, David. *The Origins of Freemasonry— Scotland's century 1590-1710*. New-York, 1988. Cambridge University Press.

Strebel, Harald. *Der Freimaurer Wolfgang Amadé Mozart*.
Rothenhäusler Verlag Stäfa. Wien, 1991.

Terrasson, René. *Le Testament Philosophique de Mozart*.
Paris, 1996. Editions Dervy.

The Magic Flute. G. Schirmer Collection of Opera Librettos. New-York.

The Magic Flute. Vocal Score. G. Schirmer. New-York.

The Magic Flute. Full Score. New-York, 1985. Dover Publications.

The Jewish Philosophy Reader. D. Frank, O. Leaman, C. Manekin Eds.
New-York, 2000. Routledge.
Thomson, Katharine, *The Masonic Thread in Mozart*.
Lawrence and Wishart. London, 1977.
Till, Nicholas. *Mozart and the Enlightenment*. Norton. New-York, 1995.
Trowbridge, W.R.H. *Cagliostro*. London, 1910.
Reprint by Kessinger Publishing Company. Norton. New-York, 1995.
Tourniac, Jean. *Paradoxes, énigmes et curiosités maçonniques*. Paris,
1993. Editions Dervy.
Vermeil, Jean, *La Flûte Désenchantée*. Editions Ombres. Toulouse, 1991
Versluis, Arthur, *The Egyptian Mysteries*. New-York, 1988. Arkana.
Versluis, Arthur, *The Philosophy of Magic*. Boston, 1986. Arkana.
Von Rudloff, Robert. *Hekate in Ancient Greek Religion*. Victoria, 1999.
Horned Owl Publishing.
Wagner, Cosima. *Diaries*. Vols. 1 & 2. New-York, 1978. Harcourt Brace.
Wagner, Richard. *Judaism in Music*. Lincoln, 1995.
University of Nebraska Press.
Waite, A.E. *A New Encyclopaedia of Freemasonry*. 1970.
University Books.
Waite, A.E. *The Holy Kabbalah*. Citadel Press. New-York, 1995.
Waliszewski, K. *Autour d'un trône — Catherine II de Russie*.
Paris, 1913. Librarie Plon.
Wirth, Oswald. *Le symbolisme hermétique dans ses rapports avec la
Franc-Maçonnerie*. Paris, 1995. Editions Dervy.
Wirth, Oswald. *Le symbolisme occulte de la Franc-Maçonnerie*.
Paris, 1997. Editions Dervy.
Wirth, Oswald. *Les Mystères de l'Art Royal*. Paris, 1998. Editions Dervy.
Witt, R.E. *Isis in the Ancient World*. Baltimore, 1971.
The John Hopkins University Press.
Wright, Craig. *The Maze and the Warrior*. London, 2001.
Harvard University Press.
Yates, Frances A. *Giordano Bruno and the Hermetic Tradition*.
The University of Chicago Press. Chicago, 1964
Yates, Frances A. *The Art of Memory*. The University of Chicago Press.
Chicago, 1966
Yates, Frances A. *The Rosicrucian Enlightenment*. London, 1972.
Routledge.
Zak, Drahos & Holden, Robert. *The Pied Piper of Hamelin*.
Boston, 1997. Houghton Mifflin Company.

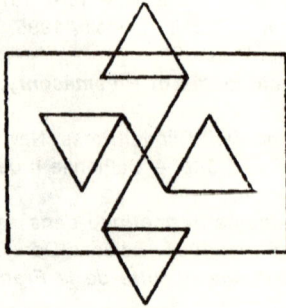

Index

Symbols

18th degree 181-182

A

Abraham 116, 121, 183-184,
    192-193, 204, 208
acacia 104
Académie Française 75
Achilles 176, 228
Acta Latomorum 148
Adam 165, 225-227, 242
Adorno, Theodor 25, 27
Aegyptus 39
Age of Disguise 4
Age of Reason 4
aggadot 104
Agni 102
Ahura Mazda 221
Akhmin 237, 243
akhu 157, 247
Alberich 261
Alberti 7, 8, 104, 197, 222
Alcala de Hénarès 22
alchemical
    164-165, 175, 209,
    221-222, 244-245,
    251, 257
alchemical King 164
alchemical transmutation
    29, 31
alchemy 22, 24, 29-31,
    37, 75, 77, 91, 111,

127, 160, 168-169, 184,
    221, 244
Alembert (d') 52, 68-69, 72
aletheia 106, 108-109,
    177-180, 182
alethes, 182
Alexandria 232
Altair 253-255, 257
Amadeus 70
amber 107
America 2, 14, 19, 249
Amsterdam 53, 154
Anatolia 182
Anaximander Fragment
    175, 177
Ancient and Accepted Scottish
    Rite 200
Anderson 35
Andreae, Johann Valentin 187
angelology 62
Angra Mainyu 221
anthropos 104
Antichrist 20, 187
Antidote 54
Apis Bull 214, 240, 256
Apocalypse 188
apocalyptic
    174, 193, 200, 221
apocalyptic tradition 188
Apollo 35, 40, 102,
    105-118, 121, 165,
    176-178, 180-182, 225,
    260-261
Apollo-Python combat 181
apseudes 182
Apuleius 164, 220
Aquila 254
Arab 62
Aragon 162

Arcana Arcanorum 161
Archangel Michael 242
archer 174
archi-tekton 168
architectural symbolism 206
architecture 103
Arenda, (Count) de 12
Argo 257
Argonauts 190, 193
Ariadne auf Naxos 190
Ariosto, Ludovico 190
Aristophanes 258
Aristotelians 59, 66
Aristotle 102-103, 256
Ark 104
arkhan 36, 111
arkhé 103
arkhon 102
Armageddon 206
Armed Man 189, 190, 200
Armed Men 188-190,
        191-192, 200, 215, 252
Armenian 152
Armored Men 215
Arnstein 135, 148-150,
        153-154
Ars magna sciendi 19
art 48-49,
Art of Memory 80
art of persuasion 80
Articuli adversus mathematicos
        59
Asclepius 60
Asiatic 54
Asiatic Brethren 7, 47, 125,
        127-132, 134-136,
        145-146, 151-155, 157
Assmann 143, 169-
        170, 197, 232

Athamas 111
atheists 175
Athena 119
Athenian Letters 167
Aufklärung 130
Austria 2, 10-13,
        47, 133, 135, 141, 155,
        159-160, 166-167, 199,
        211
Austrian 2, 10-13,
        73, 75, 86, 89
Autexier, Philippe 9
Avignon 159
Awliya 23
Azariah 132
azkarah 105
Azoulai, Hayyim Joseph David
        160

B

Babylon
        46, 106, 181, 242, 257
Bacchus 214
Bacon, Francis 55
bankers 148
Barrington, Daines 71
Bassange 76
Basson, Thomas 82
Bastien and Bastienne 56
Bauer, Bruno 48
Bavaria 250
Bayreuth 120, 121, 122
Beaumarchais 73
Becher, J.J. 29, 31
Becoming 175
Bédarride 147, 159
Being 175
Beitchman 184

Belgium 159
belles-lettres 13
Beresniak 117, 141-142,
    186-187
Bergman, Ingmar 119, 174
Berkeley 96
Berlin 11, 13, 46-47,
    128-129, 130-131,
    133-136, 148-151, 154
Berlinische Monatsschrift, 149
Bernal 241
Bernard of Clairvaux 17
Bethmann 45
Bible 84, 89
Biblical 195, 241
Biblical monotheism 170
bird 176, 187, 248, 250,
    252-256, 258, 261
Bischoff 132
Bischofswerder 151
blame 180
Blue Lodges 202
Blumauer, Aloys 13
Bo<az 241
Boccalini, Traiano 61
Böcklin 118
Bode 15
Boehmer 76
Bohemia 31, 229
Bohemian 56, 79
Bonneville 15
Book of Constitutions 35
Book of Ruth 241
Bordeaux 3
Bossuet 166
Bourbon 11-12, 14
bourgeois 64, 66-67
Brahae, Tycho 57
Braunbehrens 150, 153, 155

bride of death 212
British 199
Brotherhood of Light 34, 179
Browne, Sir Thomas 184
Brünnhilde 119
Bruno Giordano 55, 57, 59-
    61, 79-80, 82
Buddha 48
Bulletin du Grand-Orient de
    Belgique 119
Burgundy 190
Burke, Edmond 196
Burkert, Walter 100
Busnois 190
Byzantine traditions 147

C

Cabinet of Reflection 177
Cagliostro 28-30, 32, 77-80,
    127-128, 143, 161,
    218-219, 225
Calabria 160
Calas affair 67
Calas campaign 66
Cambridge 82, 95
Camillo, Giulio 80
Camus, Albert 261
Candide 250
Cano, Melchor 20
Canopus 216
Capella, Martianus 37
capitulary Degrees 117
Capricorn 243
Carburi 147
carnival 5, 219, 220
Casanova 128-129
Casaubon 195
Cassel 61

Cathar 162
Catherine the Great 23,
    54-55, 65, 154-155, 250
Catholic 11-12, 15-16,
    23-24, 47, 59, 67-68
    89, 126, 169
Caussin, Nicolas 18
Cavaillon 159
cavern 142
caves 192, 197
celestial intermediaries 208
Chailley, Jacques 119,
    209, 211, 258, 261
Chaldean 208, 219
Champollion 173, 231
Charites 213
Charles III. 160
Charles the Bold 190
Charles V 20, 190
Charleston 78
Chateaubriand 21
chemical marriage 244
Cherubim 107, 227
Chevalier Rose-Croix 207,
    209-210
children of Night 180-181
Choiseul, (Duc) de 12
Chosen People
    105, 116, 137, 184
chosen seed 39
Chouvaloff, André 156, 251
Christ 13, 16-17, 20-21, 24,
    33, 46-47,155, 165,
    183, 187-193,
    195, 205, 217, 233,
    246, 251, 253
Christian 115-116, 126-127,
    129, 133-134,
    146-147, 152-153

Christianity 53
Cicero 216
ciphers 26, 227
City of the Sun 242
Clement of Alexandria 196
Clement XIV 11
clergy 175
coagula 111, 118
codes 26
Colchis 193
Collège de France 12
community renewal 180
Comte, Auguste 250
Congress of Wilhelmsbad
    200
Constantinople 189
Coptic 19
Coptos 231, 237, 243
Corbin, Henry 24, 37
Corfu 159
Corpus Hermeticum
    34, 96, 143-144,
    164, 168, 195
Correspondence littéraire
    52, 54-55, 65
Cosi Fan Tutte 1, 56, 185
cosmic pole 62
cosmotheism 96
Council of Trent 20
Counter-Reformation 19, 228
Court de Gébelin 223
Court Library 13, 173
Cratylus 5
creative Word 44
Cretan maze 188
Crete 240
Creuzer 256
criminal 26
Critical theory 25

Croll, Oswald 57
Crusaders 181
Crusades 161
Cudworth, Ralph 95-96,
    143-144, 195
Curl, James 27
Cygne 5
Cygnus 253

D

Daedalus 188
d'Alembert. 249
d'Alfonseca, Don Manuel Pinto
    29
Damascus 160
Danaids 39
dance-master 240, 256
Dantinne, Emile 220
d'Aquino, (Prince) 160
Darkness 172
darkness
        158, 164, 166, 171,
        174, 178-179, 187,
        193, 199-200, 218
Das Rheingold 4, 261
d'Auteroche, Abbé Jean
    Chappe 54
De Indis 20
De Iside et Osiride 234
de la Motte 74, 76, 78-79
De l'Ordre maçonnique de
    Misraïm 159
de Loyola, Ignatius 22, 24
de Lubicz, Schwaller 166, 237
De Magia 60, 62
de Maistre 115, 116, 137
de Pompadour 72
de Prades, abbé 53

de Rohan 74, 76-79
de Saint-Rémi, Jeanne 74
de Santillana, Giorgio 216
de Tillot, (Minister) 12
De umbra rationis 82
De umbris idearum 82
de Valois, Jeanne 74
de Villette, Rétaux 76
De vinculis in genere 60
de Vitoria, Francisco 20
death 177, 212, 230
deception 4-5, 24, 31
Dee, John 57
Del Rio, Martin 82
delosis 106
Delphi 40, 102, 104, 114
Delphians 181
Demeter 169, 211-213, 216
demonology 62
demons 55, 60, 67, 69-71,
        84, 87, 91
Denmark 161
d'Épinay, Louise 52
Der deutsche Hausvater 66
Der Freischütz 25
Der Stein der Weisen oder Die
    Zauberinsel 259
Der Teufel in Wien 150
Der Teutsche Merkur
    142, 245
dervish 62
Dessau 138
Detienne, Marcel 102, 109-
    110, 114, 177, 180-182
Deus Pharaonis 17, 44, 166
deus sive natura 170
di Caramanico, (Prince) 160
Dialogues for Freemasons
    136

Diamond Necklace Affair
  73, 77-78
Dicson, Alexander 82
Diderot 25, 51-53, 55,
  65-66, 69
Die Entführung 248
Die Geheimnisse 142
Die Grotte 6
Die kabirischen Mysterien
  168-169
Die Maurerfreude 22
Die Sieger 48
Die Walküre 41, 43
Dietrich, Otto 118
Dietrichstein, Count 56, 125
Diodorus Siculus 12, 164, 216
Dionysus 39, 107, 110-111
disguise 2, 4-5, 14, 29
Disquisitionum Magicarum 82
divine possession 183
djed 217
d'Oberkirch, Baroness 75, 78
Dodona 214
d'Olivet, Fabre 38, 148
Dominicans 20
Don Alfonso 1, 47, 185
Don Giovanni 1, 47, 185
Don Juan 185
Donnington, Robert 211
Doppelgänger 193
double axe 111-112
dragon 253
drigu 62
Dschinnistan 259
du Barry 72, 76
Dufay 190
Duke of Brunswick 116
Dürer 57, 59

E

Eckelmeyer, Judith
  163-164, 173,
  187-188, 228
Ecker-und-Eckhoffen 132-133,
  146
Écossais vert 141
Edict of Toleration 133
education 12-13, 18, 23, 25
Egypt 11, 12, 17-19, 22,
  28-29, 32-35,
  37-39, 41, 44, 60, 62,
  79-82, 84-85, 87, 89,
  90-92, 94-96, 99, 101,
  106-107,
  125, 127, 135, 141,
  143-144, 146-148,
  157-161,164-174,
  177, 183, 193,
  195-198, 207, 214-217,
  219-220, 223, 225,
  231-238, 240-241,
  246-247, 252-253, 256
Egyptian Architecture 177
Egyptian Masonry
  161, 219, 225
Egyptian priesthood 169
Egyptian Rite 161
Egyptian Temple 158
eighteen, (number) significance of 209
Eleusis 212
emanation 174
Emerald Tablet 35
Encyclopédie 53, 69
Encyclopedie der Freimaurerei
  151
Encyclopedists 52, 54-

55, 61, 65-66
England 82, 152
English 2, 15
enlightened rule 166
Enlightenment 2, 11, 24, 34
    51-56, 63, 66,
    67-69, 84, 86, 89,
    92-93, 95, 127,
    129-130, 135-136,
    138-139, 140, 142, 149,
    156-157, 166-167, 172,
    181, 185, 245
Entretiens sur 'Le Fils Naturel'
    53, 69
Erasmus of Rotterdam 188
Ernst und Falk 244
Eros 47
erotic magic 48
Eshmajin 237
Eskeles 153-155
Esperance Lodge 29
Essai sur la secte des
    Illuminés 151
etumos 180
European 54, 77, 91, 96
Eurydice 230
Evans, Robert 59
Eve 165
Excerpts from Zoroaster's
    Fragments 219
Exodus Rabbah II 104
Eye of Horus 257
Ezekiel 106, 107

F

fairy tale 163, 171
falcon training 258
Falkenstein, Monsieur de 155

family values 66
fanaticism 250
Fastnacht 26
Feast of the Rose Garlands
    57
Feliciani, Lorenza 127
feminine Masonry 225
feminism 57
Ferdinand III 31
Ferdinand IV 160
Ferguson, Niall 45
fertility myth 212
Ficino, Marcilio 60, 65
filial piety 66
Fire 193
fire in earth 44
fire-god 169
First King 235
first time 102, 115
flaming star 27, 216
Fliess, Moises 154
flute 215
Fontenrose, Joseph 180
foundation 99, 102-104,
    106, 108, 111-112, 115-
    116, 240
France 2-3, 11-12,
    15, 55, 61, 65,
    72-74, 76-78,
    80, 82, 128, 139,
    148, 159
Francis Stephen (Maria-
    Therasa's husband) 211
Franciscan 19, 132
Frankfurt 151
Franklin, Benjamin 140, 224
fraternity 101
Frederick II 129, 205
Frederick III 205

Frederick the Great
13, 23, 155, 250
Frederick V 228
Frederick William II 129, 130-
131, 151, 155
Freemasonry 2, 6-7, 9-
10, 13-16,
19, 22, 24, 27, 29,
34-35, 53, 54, 59, 68,
86, 88, 90, 95, 97,
115-117, 126-127,
135-136, 141, 144-148,
151-152, 161,
165-166, 170-174, 196,
199, 207, 211, 215, 217,
234, 244, 247
Freemasons
166-167, 185, 191,
216, 221
Freimaurerpatent 7, 145
French 2, 3, 5, 27-28,
31-32, 51, 55, 69,
72-74, 77, 78
French Revolution 2, 31, 142
Friedländer, David 46, 134
Friedrich, (Margrave) Karl 133

G

Gabriel (Angel) 62
Galilee, (sea of) 162
Galileo 61
Galliani 52
Galtier, Gérard
146-147, 151, 159
Ganganelli, Cardinal Lorenzo
14
Garden of Eden 242
Garuda 255

Gazette de Leyde 77
Gebler, Tobias
11, 79, 80, 82, 163
Gefen, Gérard 15
Gellert, Fürchtegott 52
Gemmingen, Otto von
66-67, 246
Genesis
34, 38, 40, 147, 184,
192, 226,
genesis 175, 239
Geneva 69, 73
'Genius' 42, 43, 259
genius 1, 5, 25
German 6, 11, 15, 30, 42,
46-47, 52, 55, 61,
65-67, 80, 83, 88-
89, 92, 93, 109-110,
118, 120-121, 128, 131,
133, 136, 138-139, 141,
143, 149, 161, 195, 199,
244-246
Germany 110
Giesecke, Karl 163, 164, 246
Gilowsky, (Count) 141
Giordanisti 61
Glockenspiel 240
Gnostic 221
goat 243
Goat-Star 257
God of Fire 45, 193, 238
God-King 17, 44, 45
Goethe 1, 6, 42-43, 52, 68,
133, 141-143, 166,
244, 246, 259
Golden Age 168
golden apples 180
Golden Ass 164
golden calf 107

Golden Fleece 59, 193
Gontard, Jakob Friedrich 45
Götterdämmerung 45,
    193, 261
Gottshed, Hans Christian 52,
    66, 84
government of the world 183
Graben 148
Grades of Revenge 7
Grand Lodge of Perfection 78
Grand Orient 27, 187
Graves, Robert 107, 121
Great Architect of the Universe
    169, 216
Great Pan 246, 256
Greece 100, 102, 104, 108-
    109, 112, 147, 214, 254
Greek
    3, 12, 13, 22, 28, 33,
    34, 36, 38-40, 43-44,
    62, 81, 84, 89, 91,
    95-96, 99, 101-108,
    110, 112, 116, 119,
    141, 144, 147, 149,
    168-169,
    176, 179, 182, 185, 193,
    211, 214, 216, 218-219,
    221, 228, 232, 236,
    237, 239, 240-241, 243,
    258, 261
Greek Tragedy 99
Grimm, (Baron) Melchior
    51, 52, 54-55, 65, 88,
    155
Grimm, Jakob 118
Grotto 7
Guaraní Republic 20-22, 248
Guénon, René
    111-113, 116, 183-184,

214, 221, 234
guér-tsèdèq, 36
Guérillot, Claude
    36, 199-201, 206, 209
Guilds 126
Günther, Johann Valentin 153
Gurnemanz 119, 204

H

Ha-Meassef 149
Habsburg 9, 12, 29, 31, 56,
    58, 125, 145, 154, 190,
    228, 229
Hades 211, 213, 257
Haggadah 105, 108
Hamadani, Ali-e 63
Hamann 143
Hamburg 66, 67, 151
Hamlet's Mill 216, 256
Handel 66
Hanfstaengl, Ernst 118
Harams 148
Harpocrates 252
Harpocrates-Helios 253
Härtel 6
hashmal 107
Haskalah 134, 135, 149, 157
Haydn, Joseph 165, 190
Hayer, (Reverend) 251
Hebrew 33-34, 38-40,
    99-100, 104-105, 107,
    112, 116, 138, 147,
    149, 183-184, 208, 224,
    237
Hecate
    41, 43, 164, 193, 212, 213
Hecateus 164, 167
Hegel 165

Heidegger, Martin
 108-110, 139, 175-
 176, 192
Heliopolis 101
Helvétius 25, 65, 140
Hen kai Pan 95-96, 143-144,
 165, 247
Hephaestus 44-45,
 118-119, 169, 216, 237
Hera 111, 213
Heracleitus 96
Heracles 114, 116
Heraclids 114-116
Hercules 66
Herder 6, 143, 171, 245
Hermes 5, 34-35, 78,
 143, 161, 181-182, 195,
 218-219
hermetic 29-31, 33-35,
 41, 44, 63, 82, 91, 95,
 164-165, 168-170, 181,
 195, 197, 204, 218, 251
Hermetica 34-35
Hermogenes 5
Herodotus
 164, 168, 216, 237
Hesiod 179, 181
Hesperides 179
hestia 102
Hieroglyph 19
hieroglyph 5, 19,
 90-91, 164,
 172-174, 183, 195, 198,
 232, 236, 238, 239
hieros gamos 175
Higher Degrees
 117, 165, 170, 200,
 209, 222
Higher Grades 152

Hildesheimer 140
Hipponicus 5
Hiram 7, 26, 104, 112-113,
 175, 202
Hiramic legend 234
Hirschfeld 132-135, 146
Histories 164
History of Freemasonry 15
Hitler, Adolf
 110-111, 113, 118,
 120-121, 139
Holbach 52
Hölderlin 108, 143
Holland 152
Holy Land 162, 206
Holy Roman Empire 30, 131
Homer 176, 181, 213
Homeric Hymn to Hermes 182
homosexuals 54
Horapollo 18, 164
Horian Logos 44
horned one 256
Horus 165, 234, 236, 239,
 251-253, 257-258
House of Peter 16
Hübner, Lorenz 141
Hugin 118
humanism 156
humanists 59
humanitarian 6
Hunding 40
Hyades 256
Hylas 66
Hyperborean Apollo 107

I

Iah 112
Ibn Hayyan, Jabir 37

Ibn'Arabi 22, 24
Idomeneo 66
ight 166
Iliad 176, 228
Illuminaten-Höhle 141
Illuminati 10, 15, 128,
    141-143, 250-251
illumination 102, 105
Illuminism 29
Illuminist 125-126, 141, 171
image-making 174
image-symbol 24, 29-30
imagination 60
Imhotep 238
Indians 20-22, 250
individualism 186
initiates 175
initiation
    62, 63, 88, 89, 94, 101,
    112, 115,-117, 126-128,
    141, 146, 152, 185,
    186-188, 192, 196-197,
    205, 208, 212-213, 217,
    218, 245, 258
Innocent III 17
Ino 111
Inquisition 61
Inssbruck 151
international law 20
Ionian islands 159
Iran 221
Iranian 34, 37, 62, 63
Isaac 192
Ish Zaddik 132
Ishtar 46
Isiac religion 28
Isis 28, 32, 41, 57, 90,
    94, 96-97, 125, 164,
    165, 168,

    174, 188, 196, 204, 209,
    214, 216-217, 220, 237-
    238, 251-253, 258
Israel 38-40, 100, 104,
    106-108, 116, 121,
    122, 160, 184, 192,
    201, 205
Italic king 104
Italy 14, 29, 160
Itzig 46, 135, 149, 151
ivory key 207

J

Jablonski 233, 246
Jachin 241
Jacob (Biblical) 40
Jacobi 95
James II 15
James III 15
Jansenism 72, 173
Jason 190, 193
Jehovah 107, 196
Jeremiah (prophet) 107
Jerusalem
    17, 44, 45, 96, 107,
    132, 134,
    137, 157, 160, 205
Jesuit 9-21, 23,
    24, 47, 82, 86, 126,
    141, 169, 171, 173,
    248-251
Jewish 13, 28, 34-36, 39,
    44-47, 105,
    106, 112, 116, 121,
    132-135, 138-
    139, 146, 148,
    149-152, 154-155, 157,
    159-160, 162

Jewish bankers 45-46
Jews 13, 34, 38, 39, 45,
    4648, 106, 107, 114,
    127-128, 130,
    132-133, 135, 137-139,
    147, 149-150, 152-
    153, 185
Joseph (Biblical) 38
Joseph II
    2, 10, 13, 22, 59, 80,
    82, 84, 87, 146, 153,
    155, 166-167, 173
Josquin 190
Journal Chrétien 251
Journal für Freymäurer 9,
    168, 170, 221, 246
journey 177, 212
Judaism 48, 134-
    135, 137, 153,
    193, 208, 217
Judeo-Christian tradition 183
justice 181-182, 201-202
Justus 132

K

Kabbalah
    117, 160, 162, 169,
    170, 183, 205, 206, 208,
    213, 218, 237
Kabbalistic
    106, 116, 132, 134,
    135, 153, 165, 169,
    170, 173-174, 184,
    199-201, 213, 220,
    224-225, 227
Kabbalists 162, 221
Kabiri 168-169, 214,
    216-217, 237, 238, 245

Kalchas 176, 178
Kant 246
Karneios 114
Katz 132, 134-135, 151,
    152-153
Kaunitz 156
Kelley, Edward 57
Kepler, Johannes 57
Keter 170, 174, 206, 207
Kilmarnock (Lord) 199
King Ætes 193
King Arthur 185
King Jeroboam 107
King Josiah 106
King of Justice 184
King of the Universe 112, 168
Kingdom 183
Kingdom of Back 9, 26
Kingdom of Judah 106
Kircher, Athanasius 18-19
Knightly Degrees 199, 200
Knights of the Sun 204
Knights Templar 162
Köhler, Joachim 120
Kore 169, 213, 216
kourotrophoi 213
Kronauer, Johann Georg
    47, 135
ktizein 103
Küfstein, (Count) 56

L

La clemenza di Tito 131
La flute désenchantée 187
La Sagesse Triomphante 161
labyrinth 188
Labyrinthe, klein harmonisches
    von Bach 190

Lacombe, Roger 21
Lacouture, Jean 21
lamb 39, 192-193
Lampas triginta statuarum 60
language
    101, 103, 140, 149, 157,
    158, 172-173, 176, 179,
    181, 218, 230, 258
Languedoc 159
Latin 12, 18, 34, 135, 157,
    149, 188
Latin America 181
Law 99-101, 105, 116,
    119-120, 133, 135,
    137, 138, 150, 152
    179, 185, 214
Law of Moses
    36, 105, 137, 166
Law of Sevens 37
Le Clerc, Jean-François 73
Le devin du village 56
Le Guay, Nicole 76
Le père de famille 66
Legardien, Paul 119
Légendes maçonniques autour
    de Mozart 15
Leibniz 55
Leiden 82
Lemnos 169, 216
Leopold I 30
Lessing, Gotthold Ephraim
    11, 66, 92, 93, 95, 135,
    136-137, 143-144, 184,
    222, 244, 245
Lethe 180
Letter G (Masonic) 112
Levi 121-123
Lichnowsky, Karl 130

light
    1, 2, 3, 6, 7, 9, 10, 11, 21,
    26-27, 34, 36-39
    41, 44, 51-57, 60, 62,
    69, 71, 76, 86-89,
    93, 95, 158, 164,
    171, 174, 178-180,
    193, 199, 200, 208, 217,
    220
light-bringer 212
Lodge 2-3, 10,
    12-13, 15, 26-29,
    46-47, 51, 56, 67,
    78, 86-88, 94, 113, 115,
    125-128, 130-131,
    133, 135, 140-141, 145,
    147, 151-152, 160-161,
    170-171, 175, 196, 199,
    210, 224, 235, 246
Lodge Amalia 141
Lodge of adoption 160
Lodge of the Nine Sisters 140
Loge 43, 45, 46, 193
logos 45, 166, 236
London 71, 77, 197
Lord of Maat 235
Lost Word
    104, 112, 113, 165, 172,
    181, 186, 207, 222, 234
Louis the XVI 73
Louis XV 72, 76
love 4, 21, 26, 31, 145, 244
Lubanara 259
Lubano 259
Luchet, Marquis de 151
Lucifer 26, 44
Ludwig II 120
Luria, Isaac 160
Luther, Martin 187

Lutheran 61
Lutheran chorale 188
Lycurgus 249
Lykaon 111
Lykurgus 111
Lyra 254

M

Ma'aseh Merkabah 106, 108
Maat 99, 100, 123, 138,
    158, 239, 244
Mackey, Albert 15, 18, 35
Macrobius 36
magic 1-7, 17, 21, 22,
    24, 25, 27,
    31, 33, 37, 40, 42-48,
    52, 57-60, 64, 69,
    71, 79, 82, 90-91, 93-
    95, 144, 160, 169, 175,
    177, 180, 184, 192-193,
    204, 206-207, 215, 220,
    235, 245
magic flute 21
magic tradition 113
magical incantations 118
Magism 204
Maier, Michael 57
Maimonides 158
Maitre Elu des Neuf 7
malevolent speech 180
Malkuth
    153, 170, 174, 183, 206,
    209
mallet 112
Mallinger, Jean 220
Malta 29, 78, 161
manipulation 64, 60, 72, 91
Mannheim 66, 67

mantic 228
mantike 102
Manu 183, 220, 240
Marburg 151
Maria-Theresa (Empress)
    12, 75, 211
Marie-Antoinette 73, 75, 76
marriage 226
Marriage of Figaro 73
Marx, Karl 48, 61, 248
mask 4, 5
Mason
    2-16, 19, 22, 24, 26,
    35, 46, 51, 53-54,
    54, 56, 59, 62, 66-68,
    78-80, 82, 83, 85-91, 95,
    97
Masonic 2-16, 19, 22,
    26-28, 32, 38, 43,
    46-47, 104
    111-112, 117, 119-120,
    125-133, 135-136, 142,
    144-148, 151-152,
    155, 159-160, 163,
    164-166, 169,
    172, 175, 177,
    181, 185, 188, 199,
    200, 205-207, 209,
    214, 220, 224, 230, 241,
    244, 247, 260
Masonic Square 28
Masonic work 46
Masonry 10, 15-16, 28, 32-
    33, 38, 112-113, 125-
    129, 143-144, 146-147,
    157, 159, 161, 199, 206,
    215, 219, 225, 234,
    235, 260
master of Truth 177

Masters of Truth 108-109
mastery 185-186
Maui 256
Mauvillon 15
Maximilian I 58, 59
Mazdean chivalry 38
Medea 193
Mediterranean 147
Megiddo 106
Melchizedek
    152-153, 183, 220
Mélissino, (Count) 147
Mémoire à Brunswick
    115, 116
Mémoire contre le Procureur
    général 32
Memphis 18, 169, 216, 220,
    233, 235, 238, 240
Memphis-Misraïm 220
Mendelssohn 46-47, 67,
    92-93, 95, 134-139,
    149-150, 157-158, 185
Menes 240
Mephistopheles 1
Mercurius 82
mercy 201
Mesmer, Anton 56
Mesopotamia 182
Messiah 192, 206, 217
Metatron
    208, 218-219, 221, 222
microcosm 138
Middle-Ages 18
Midrash 105
Milky Way 254, 257
Min 231, 233, 234, 237,
    239, 240-241, 243,
    247, 257
mind of Osiris 239

mind of Ptah 236
mineralogists 197
mineralogy 244
mining 244
Minos 240
Mirabeau 15
Mishnah 108
Misraïm 147, 161
Mitra 208
Mittwochsgesellschaft 136
Mitzeraïm 38
mitzvah 105
Molitor, Franz 132, 135
Momos 180
Mönchsnaturkunde 9
Money 46, 47
Monostatos
    3, 4, 42, 156, 260, 261
Montesquieu 250
Moor 4
Moors 181
moral high ground 63
moral institution 67
Moral Law 84
Moray, Sir Robert 19
Morenz, Siegfried 231
Morin Patent 78
Mosaic Law 84
Moses 67, 84, 85, 90, 92,
    94-96, 105, 116,
    170, 196
Mount Canaan 162
Mount Parnassus 177
Mozart 1-9, 11, 13, 15,
    18-19, 22, 24-25,
    26-27, 31-32, 34, 42,
    48-49, 51, 52, 55-56,
    64-73, 79-80, 83-88, 93,
    94, 120-121, 123, 125,

126-131, 135, 140-
141, 143-145, 148-
154, 163, 165,
170, 172-173, 185-190,
195, 199, 210, 217,
219, 225, 226-230,
246, 248, 259, 261
Mozart, Leopold 26,
51, 52, 66, 69, 71
Mozart, Constanze
6, 131, 173
Mozart in Revolt 4
mundus imaginalis 62, 63
Munich 118, 121
Munin 118
Muratori 21
Muratori, Antonio 249
Muses 177
music 1, 4,,
6, 11, 21, 25, 27, 31, 36,
49, 52, 55-56, 69,
70-71, 85,
128-129, 168, 173,
177, 180, 188-190,
192, 215
mystic urn 175

N

Nagel, Ivan 156
Nagy, Gregory 102, 104, 228
name formulas 158
Naples 11, 159-161, 190
National Socialism 109
Naturae et Scripturae
Concordia 172
natural knowledge 157
Nature 195
nature 172

Naumann 163
Nazi
109, 111, 128, 139, 187,
261
Neapolitan Masonry 161
Necker, Jacques 65
necromancy 43
necromantic aspects 123
nemertes 182
neo-Platonic 144, 244
neo-Platonist 221
neologisms 26
Nereus 182
Neter 44
Nettl, Paul 144,
171, 209, 231, 234
New Testament 16
New World 19-21
Newman 120
Nibelheim 46
Nibelungenlied 118, 121
Nicolai, Friedrich
11, 80, 92, 130, 245
Niemetschek, Franz 69
Nietzsche, Friedrich 64
Nilus 148
Noachite 35
Noah 35
noble savage 248
noble traveler 128
Novalis 244

O

oak 215
Oberon der Elfenkönig
164, 246
oblivion 180
Occident 63

occult
125-126, 133, 146, 148,
153, 161
occult couples 251
Odysseus 218
Old Charges 241
Old Man of the Sea 182
Old Testament 16, 121
Olympus 213
One-and-All 95, 170, 247
Operative Masonry
112, 126, 147, 235
oracular word 103
Oragna figata 26, 27
Order of Light 156
Order of Malta 78
Order of Mopses 127
Order of the Golden Fleece
190
Orient 62, 63, 78, 140
Orion 255, 256, 257
Orlando Furioso 190
Orpheus
21, 96, 204, 214, 230, 257
Orphic 245
Orphic Hymn to Pan 240
Osiris 32, 39, 96, 97, 111,
125, 163-165, 174,
188, 209, 214, 216-
217, 223, 239,
240, 251-252, 257
Oxulos 115

P

Padua 61, 147
Paï-Sumé 21
Palais-Royal 76
Palestine 36, 160, 161

Pamina
37, 42, 45, 96, 128, 158,
164-166, 174, 175,
193, 204, 207, 208,
213-215, 230-234,
240, 247, 251, 257,
259, 260
Pan
37, 95-96, 239, 241,
243, 256
Panopolis 239
Pantheon Aegypthiorum 233
Papacy 12, 16, 17, 20, 23
Papagena
28, 165, 174, 207, 209,
248, 251-253, 256,
257, 259
Papageno 21, 85, 120, 165,
174, 187, 207, 209, 216,
217, 240, 248, 251, 253,
256-260
papyri Gracae Magicae 96
papyri Graecae Magicae 144
Paradis, Annie 258
Paraguay 250
Parenti 159
Paris 51, 53, 55, 65-
66, 72, 76-78,
80, 140, 147, 159
Parmenides 96
parrot 186, 250, 258
Parsifal 44, 119-123, 204
Péladan 220
Peloponnese 115
pentagon 206
Pergen, Count Johann Anton
2
Persephone 211-213
Persian 62, 152

Peter 17
Phaedon 135, 150
Phaedrus 81
philosopher 138
philosophers
    52, 53, 55, 63, 67-68
Philosopher's Stone 164, 207
philosopher's stone 44, 175
philosophes
    52, 54, 55, 61, 63, 66,
    72, 78
Philosophical Scottish Rite of
    Avignon 161
philosophy 3, 12, 31, 34
Phlegyans 181
Phosphoros 212
Phrixos 111, 193
phtora 175, 177
Pico della Mirandola 184
Pied Piper 3, 109
Pike, Albert 204
Pindar 180, 256
plague 109, 176, 261
Plato 5, 7, 80, 84, 96, 219,
    250
Plato's Cave 7
Plotinus 144
Plutarch
    164, 234, 246, 252, 253
poet 177, 180
Poimandres 34
Pole star 112
polein 109
police 101
polis 101
political
    52, 54, 57, 58, 63, 72, 76,
    82, 84, 85
Politics 102, 109, 166, 167

Pombal, (Marquis) de
    12, 14, 22
Pompei 252
Pontus 182
Pope 11, 14, 17, 20, 23
Porset, Charles 128
Portugal 14, 152
Portuguese 20, 21, 22
power behind the throne 45
power of names 38
power of speech 180, 247
power-seekers 175, 193
Prague 22, 31, 56, 57,
    59-60, 151
praise 180
prima 103
prokathegemon 113
Promethean promise 64
prophecy 157, 176, 182
Prophet 38
prophetic 157, 178, 230
prophetic powers 43
prophetic tradition 37
Protestant
    13, 15, 23, 47, 67, 68, 86,
    130, 171, 250
Protocols of the Elders of Zion
    148
Provence 159, 162
Prussia
    13, 23, 136, 149, 151,
    154-155, 205
Psalm 12 188
Psellus 34
Psenptais 33
Ptah 33, 44-45, 90-91, 118,
    168, 169, 174, 193, 207,
    216, 217, 232, 233,
    235-237, 238-240, 243,

245-247, 256, 257
Ptah-Min 247, 257
Ptolemaic age 216
Ptolemies 232
puns 26
purification by fire 175
Pushkin, Alexander 26
Pythagoras 96
Pythagorean triangle 113, 235
Pythian Dialogues 246
Python 180, 225

Q

Queen Marie-Caroline of
     Austria 160
Queen of Sheeba 127
Queen of the Night
     4, 35, 42, 43, 45, 120,
     156, 165, 179, 200, 202,
     204, 206-207, 211, 213,
     214-217, 230,
     251, 256, 260-261
Quirke, Stephen 237

R

radiant power 157
Ragache, Jean-Robert 187
Ragguagli di Parnaso 61
rationalist 9
rationalists 53, 54
rats 260
raven 118
reason 169, 195
rebirth 177
Reformation 188
Regis 190
Reinhold 86-90, 93, 94,
     168-171, 196, 246

Renaissance 80, 90, 184
renovation 172
Republic 7, 20, 21
Requiem 7
revolutionary innovator 7
Rheingold 121
rhymes 26
Richter 121
riddle 219, 220, 227
Ring 25, 43, 44, 45,
     119-121, 193
Rite of Misraïm 148, 159, 161
Rite of Perfection 204, 209
ritual 4, 6, 7, 16, 17, 21-24,
     29, 30, 32, 33, 35,
     36-40, 42-44, 100-103,
     105, 106, 109, 111, 113, 115,
     116, 118-123
     126-127, 137-138,
     143-144,
     153, 158, 180, 191,
     207, 256
ritual magic 173
ritual purity 193
Röll, Walter 149
Roman 103, 118
Romanzof 250
Rome 100
roses 28, 58, 209
Rosetta stone 231
Rosicrucian
     7, 10, 53, 56, 61, 62,
     125, 126,
     130, 132, 145-146,
     182, 209, 210, 220
Rothschilds 45
Rousseau
     51, 52, 56, 68, 69,
     72-73

Royal Art 111, 168
Royal Power 120
Rudolf II 31, 56, 59
Russia 23, 250
Russian 54
Russian court 154

S

Sabbatian 134, 153
Sabbatian movement 132
sacrifice 100, 101, 115,
    192, 193
sacrificial fire 102
sacrificial fireplace 104
sacrificial lamb 192
sacrificial ritual 105
Safed 160, 161, 162
Sagittarius 257
Saint John 152
Saint Paul 183
Saint-Petersburg 147
Sakkara 238
Salieri 1, 70
Salman the Persian 38
Salzburg 70, 71
Samothrace 169
San Demetrio, Duke de 160
Sanhedrin 151
Saracens 181
Sarah, 184
Sarapis cult 33
Sarastro
    4, 32, 34, 35, 37, 45, 96,
    119, 120, 156, 174, 179,
    187, 200, 204, 206, 207,
    209,
    211-214, 218, 219, 222-
    223, 228, 230, 260-261

Saturn
    30, 235, 243, 251, 256
Saturnalia 36
Savaron 115
Saverne 75, 78
Savitri 49
Scepsius, Heius 82
Schachtner, Andreas 25
Schaffer, Peter 70
Schelling, Friedrich Wilhelm
    143
Schikaneder, Emmanuel
    83, 85, 89, 150,
    163-164, 190,
    195, 223, 229, 231,
    246, 259, 260
Schiller, Johann 244, 246
Schleswig 146
Schlichtegroll, Friedrich 9
Schlosser, Johann Georg 133
Schnorr, Malvina 120
Schoenfeld, Thomas
    132, 133, 134
Scholem, Gershom 134, 152
Schönbrunn 69
Schroeder, David 4, 52
Schwaller de Lubicz, R.A. 44
science 64
Scorpius 257
Scotland 82
Scottish Masons 199
Scottish Rite
    111-117, 182, 199, 200
Scripture
    105, 106, 117, 170, 172,
    226
secret societies 2-3, 6-7, 26,
    207
secret tongues 26

Seiler, Wenceslas 31
Semiramis 24
Sephardic Jew 159
Sepher Yetzirah 112
Sephiroth 183, 201, 209
Sephirotic Tree
    117, 170, 202, 215
Septuagint 34, 106
serpent 174, 212, 225, 253
Servius 104
Seth
    237, 242, 252, 253, 257
Sethos 12, 163, 188, 196
Seven Year War 72, 199
seven-holed flute 37
sexual images 65
Shaddai 208
Shekinah
    183, 208, 213, 217, 218,
    226-227
Ship of the Dead 216
shofar 192
Sicilian 160
Sicily 11
Siegfried 117, 121
Sieglinde 42, 43, 44
Siegmund 40, 41, 42, 43, 44
sign language 26
signe 5
singspiel 246
Sirius 256
Society of Jesus 11
Socrates 81
solar child 252
Solar Circle 35-36, 204
Solomon (King) 16, 24,
    107, 112, 113
Solomon, Maynard
    6, 7, 125, 225, 227

solve 111, 118
Son of the Sun 220
Song of Songs 201, 226
Sorbonne 53
sovereignty 206
Spain
    11, 12, 14, 20, 152, 160
Spaniards 181
Spanish 14, 20-22
Speculative Masonry
    126, 147, 157
spells 158
Spencer
    84, 85, 86, 91, 92, 100
Spenta Mainyu 221
Spinoza
    55, 93, 95, 96, 137,
    143, 157, 169-170, 195
Spiritual Exercises 22
Spiritual Power 120
Sraosha 62
St. Georges 59, 181, 253
St. Waast, Abbey of 74
Staal, Julius 255
Stafford, William 210
Standler, Anton 6
star-flaming Queen 216
Stoics 96
Strabo 164
Strasbourg
    74, 75, 77, 78, 134
Strict Observance
    6, 29, 141, 161, 199
Stuart 15
sublime 196
sufi 37, 62-63
summa 103
summus angularis lapis 16
superior Degrees 117

superstition 9, 10, 169, 172
Swan 254
swastika 111-112
Swedenborg, Emmanuel 244
symbol
　　9, 18, 19, 24, 27, 29, 30,
　　35-36, 38, 41, 44, 47
Symbolic Degrees 117, 200,
　　206-207

T

Tabernacle 104, 208
Tabernacle in the Wilderness
　　40
Tamino 4, 35-
　　37, 40, 42, 45,
　　85, 89, 93, 96,
　　119, 120, 125, 127,
　　158, 164-166, 172,
　　174, 175, 187, 188, 190,
　　193, 195, 204,
　　207-208, 214, 215,
　　217, 230-234, 240,
　　247-248, 251, 257,
　　259-260
Tanucci, (Marquis) of 161
Taoism 62
tapping of mallets 27, 43
Tarot cards 223
Tavistock, (Marquis) of 65
Templar 6, 11, 17, 162
Templar encampment 205
Templar succession 200
Temple
　　4, 7, 16, 17, 35, 36,
　　44-45, 48, 106, 107,
　　112-113, 117, 123,
　　165, 172, 175, 192,

194-197,
199, 207, 208, 212,
216-217, 218, 222, 230,
233, 235, 241, 260-261
Temple of Light 165
Temple of Nature 195-196
Temple of Reason 196
Temple of Solomon
　　208, 216, 241
Temple of Wisdom 96, 128,
　　197, 212
Temple of Zorobabel 208
Temple's priesthood 48
temurah 225
Terrasson, (Abbé) Jean 12,
　　163, 188, 196
Terrasson, René 85, 222
terror 156, 196
Tetragrammaton 202, 230
Thamos 80, 81, 83
Thamos, König in Ägypten
　　11, 12, 163
The Creation 165
the Eagle 254
The Garden of Cyrus 184
The Guide of the Perplexed
　　159
The Joyful Wisdom 64
The Labyrinth 190
The Magic Flute 1-7, 15, 18,
　　21, 24, 25,
　　27-28, 34-35, 40,
　　42-45, 48, 83, 85,
　　87, 89, 91, 93, 94, 96, 104,
　　119, 120, 121, 123, 127,
　　131, 158, 163, 164, 165,
　　166, 171-174, 180,
　　187, 190, 191, 196, 199,
　　200, 202, 204, 206,

211-214, 225, 230-232, 260-261
The Masters of Truth in Archaic Greece 177
The Plague 261
The three Horai 213
The Three Ladies 213
theater 31, 52, 53, 66-68, 69, 72, 82, 83, 84, 85
Thebes 111
Theogony 179
Théosophes 54
Thirty Three Degrees 200
Thor's hammer 112
Thory 148, 159
Thoth 81, 82, 84, 90, 193, 233, 236, 239
Thracians 214
Three Boys 28
Thun, Count Franz Joseph 56, 130, 135
Thun, Count Johann Joseph 56
Thun, Countess Wilhelmine 56, 135
Tiberius 256
Tiferet 207, 209
Till, Nicholas 125, 131
Tisha b'Av 107
Titurel 44, 118, 120
Titus 44, 45, 118
to mnemosynon 106
tolerance 3, 13, 46
Torah 84, 104, 105, 149, 159
torches 212
totalitarian 142
tradition 117
transpositions 26

travel 128-130, 153, 155, 159, 160
Treaty of Breslau 23
Tree of Life 208
trial 177
trial by fire 193
trial by fire and water 259
trial by water 182, 193
triumphant sun 176
Trowbridge, W.R.H. 78
tumim 106
Turk 147, 152, 155

U

Underworld 28, 39, 96, 212, 214
United States 2, 19, 154, 206
Unknown Superiors 199
Urim 100, 106
Urim and Thummim 84, 100

V

vajra 111, 112
Valhalla 45
van Swieten, Gerard 12
van Swieten, Gottfried 13, 173
Vedas 255
Vega 253, 254, 257
Venice 48, 56, 57, 61, 62, 80, 148, 159
Versailles 73, 75, 77
Vienna 2, 9, 11, 12, 29, 30, 47, 66, 69, 74, 75, 83, 86, 94, 125, 127, 130, 132, 135, 146, 148-151, 154, 196, 219, 244, 246, 247

Viennese
2, 3, 129, 145, 150
Vishnu's cosmic walk 255
Vital, Hayyim 160
Vivaldi 21
Voltaire
51, 52, 55, 67, 68, 69, 71,
89, 139-141, 224, 249,
250-251
von Baader, Franz 157
von Born, Ignaz
9, 10, 13, 14, 18, 19, 22, 30,
85-88, 94, 99, 141,
143,
166, 169, 170, 171, 196,
197, 214-216, 221,
233, 234, 244-246, 250-
251
von Dechend, Hertha 216
von Eyben, (Baron) F.L. 161
von Gemmingen-Hornberg,
Otto 135
von Hessen 133, 146
von Hund, Gotthelf 6, 199
von Kaunitz, (prince) Wenzel
12
von Retzer, Joseph 13
von Sonnenfels, Joseph
13, 82, 83, 141
von Stuck, Franz 118
Voyage en Sibérie 54
Vulcan 246

W

Wagenseil, Georg Christoph
70
Wagner, Richard
4, 25, 40, 41-45, 47,
48-49, 117-121,
122-123, 139, 193, 261
Wagner, Cosima 44
Waite, A.E. 226
Waliis-Budge, E.A. 233
Waliszewski, K. 155
Walpole, Horace 65
Wälsungen 121
War Lord Tsan 255
Warburton, William 173
warrior/lamb 188
water 183, 197, 237
Weishaupt, Adam 10, 141
Wesendonck, Mathilde 48
Wetzlar, (Baron) Raimund 151
Wieland, Martin
6, 86, 87, 88, 89, 142,
171, 245, 246, 259
Wilhelm Meister 68, 142
Wilhelmsbad 133, 200
Wilhemsbad Congress 115
Wisdom 195
witch-star 257
witchcraft 41-43, 256-257
Witt, R.E. 214, 219
Wittenberg 60
wolf 113
Wolff, Christian 55
Wolf's madness 111
Wöllner, Johann Christoph
129, 151
wordplay 26, 158, 225
Wotan 42-46, 118,
119-121, 193
Wranitzky, Paul 164
Wright, Craig 188, 190

Y

Yahve 39, 112, 121,
    165, 241
Yates, Frances 61
Young, Thomas 231
Yvon, (Abbé) Claude 53

Z

Zaide 248
zakhar 105
Zakynthos 159
Zarathustra
    37, 219, 221, 243
Zeus 115, 119,
    211-212, 215, 228
Zipoli, Domenico 21
Zohar 184, 201, 225, 226
Zoroaster 204
Zoroastrian 221
Zoroastrianism 62, 219
Zum neuen Bunde 80
Zur gekrönten Hoffnung 11
Zur neugekrönten Hoffnung
    80, 130
Zur wahren Eintracht
    9, 13, 82, 130, 170
Zur Wohltätigkeit
    126, 130, 135, 145

www.ingramcontent.com/pod-product-compliance
Lightning Source LLC
Chambersburg PA
CBHW030237030426
42336CB00009B/144